Religion, Nationalism and Foreign Policy

Critiquing Religion: Discourse, Culture, Power

Series editor: Craig Martin

Critiquing Religion: Discourse, Culture, Power publishes works that historicize both religions and modern discourses on 'religion' that treat it as a unique object of study. Using diverse methodologies and social theories, volumes in this series view religions and discourses on religion as commonplace rhetorics, authenticity narratives, or legitimating myths which function in the creation, maintenance, and contestation of social formations. Works in the series are on the cutting edge of critical scholarship, regarding 'religion' as just another cultural tool used to gerrymander social space and distribute power relations in the modern world. *Critiquing Religion: Discourse, Culture, Power* provides a unique home for reflexive, critical work in the field of religious studies.

Christian Tourist Attractions, Mythmaking and Identity Formation
Edited by Erin Roberts and Jennifer Eyl

French Populism and Discourses on Secularism
Per-Erik Nilsson

Reframing the Masters of Suspicion: Marx, Nietzsche, and Freud
Andrew Dole

*Spirituality, Corporate Culture, and American Business:
The Neoliberal Ethic and the Spirit of Global Capital*
James Dennis LoRusso

Stereotyping Religion: Critiquing Clichés
Edited by Brad Stoddard and Craig Martin

Religion, Nationalism and Foreign Policy

Discursive Construction of New Turkey's Identity

Filiz Coban Oran

BLOOMSBURY ACADEMIC
LONDON • NEW YORK • OXFORD • NEW DELHI • SYDNEY

BLOOMSBURY ACADEMIC
Bloomsbury Publishing Plc
50 Bedford Square, London, WC1B 3DP, UK
1385 Broadway, New York, NY 10018, USA
29 Earlsfort Terrace, Dublin 2, Ireland

BLOOMSBURY, BLOOMSBURY ACADEMIC and the Diana logo are trademarks of
Bloomsbury Publishing Plc

First published in Great Britain 2022
Paperback edition published 2023

Copyright © Filiz Coban Oran, 2022

Filiz Coban Oran has asserted her right under the Copyright, Designs and Patents Act, 1988, to be identified as Author of this work.

For legal purposes the Acknowledgements on pp. vi–viii constitute an extension of this copyright page.

Series design by Dani Leigh
Cover image © Yi Lu/EyeEm/Getty Images

All rights reserved. No part of this publication may be reproduced or transmitted in any form or by any means, electronic or mechanical, including photocopying, recording, or any information storage or retrieval system, without prior permission in writing from the publishers.

Bloomsbury Publishing Plc does not have any control over, or responsibility for, any third-party websites referred to or in this book. All internet addresses given in this book were correct at the time of going to press. The author and publisher regret any inconvenience caused if addresses have changed or sites have ceased to exist, but can accept no responsibility for any such changes.

A catalogue record for this book is available from the British Library.

A catalog record for this book is available from the Library of Congress.
Library of Congress Control Number: 2021947565

ISBN: HB: 978-1-3502-7088-6
PB: 978-1-3502-7092-3
ePDF: 978-1-3502-7089-3
eBook: 978-1-3502-7090-9

Series: Critiquing Religion: Discourse, Culture, Power

Typeset by Deanta Global Publishing Services, Chennai, India

To find out more about our authors and books visit www.bloomsbury.com and sign up for our newsletters

Contents

Acknowledgements	vi
Introduction	1
1 History: Religion, Turkish nationalism and foreign policy	9
2 Theory and methodology: Critical discourse analysis	49
3 Discourse analysis: Imagining the New Turkey	83
4 Conclusion	135
Bibliography	149
Index	179

Acknowledgements

Turkey has been one of the most distinctive examples in having a problematic relationship between religion, the state and society. Despite the secular character of the Republican system, since the Justice and Development Party came to power in 2002 the main reference point has become Islam in Turkish politics, which has reconstructed the nation-state identity and foreign policy discourse through a domestic power struggle. This book approaches this phenomenon critically and offers to see the New Turkey from different discourses of nationalism. By decoding the clashing narratives of the nation, it exhibits a need to subvert the dominant paradigms of Kemalism and Islamism for a more pluralist and inclusive understanding of the nation. In this context, I am grateful to the editor of Bloomsbury's series of *Critiquing Religion: Discourse, Culture, Power*, Dr Craig Martin, who welcomed my study.

This book is a product of my studies at the School of Political, Social and International Studies at the University of East Anglia. The School of Political, Social and International Studies constituted one of the most plentiful grounds for my intellectual development in exploring new insights and perspectives on studying politics. What makes me say that is undoubtedly the immense contribution that the PSI's academic members played in my overall advancement. First, I want to express my thanks to Professor Hussein Kassim, for his unique intellectual eye and contribution to my perspective on my project and for his guidance. Additionally, my greatest debt and sense of thankfulness go to Dr Sanna Inthorn, who patiently helped me resolve every single difficulty I faced during my study and, more importantly, developed my knowledge and expertise in media and politics, understanding Critical Discourse Analysis and my academic skills in general.

Furthermore, many friends and colleagues from the PSI contributed in numerous ways through many hours of discussion. I mention them with the unbearable possibility of leaving some out. However, I would like to acknowledge those who have broadened my knowledge and my perspective in the field. For their remarks and support during the doctorate coordination process and their outstanding and inspiring works in political theory, I would also like to express my gratitude to Professor Alan Finlayson and Dr Alex Brown. This study also benefited from the studies and discussions of Professor John Street in media and politics, Professor Lee Marsden in religion and International Relations and all other UEA fellows who work in the areas of Middle East studies; European studies; and media, language and communication studies. I am also thankful to UEA workers, particularly the PGR Office staff and after-midnight librarians, who made things much easier for this night owl.

Moreover, the seminars and conferences I attended in other UK universities matured my work, namely, in Birmingham, Bradford, Cambridge, Exeter and specifically contemporary Turkish studies and the ASEN conferences at the London School of Economics and Political Science. Moreover, I would like to extend my gratitude to the following international organizations and their participants: the NEPAS Project for providing me with scholarships for the research school on 'Democratization and Political Transitions in the Arab World: Actors, Challenges and Policy Options for the EU' in the University of Minho, Portugal; the ECPR Joint Sessions in Mainz, Germany for the workshop on 'Interpreting Foreign Policy'; the University of Antwerp, Belgium for organizing the UCSIA Research Summer School and funding my participation to the course on 'Religion and Nationalism'; the Bergen Summer Research School in Norway for supporting my attendance to the research entitled 'Emerging Normative Regimes'; and the University of Bologna, Italy for hosting the CEI International Summer School of Cervia and for funding my work on 'Diversity Management'.

Thanks to all the researchers and friends that I have met along the way in my quest and who have made me feel that I am at home. Like a honeybee touching colourful flowers of different gardens and aiming for a better taste, this study is a product of everyone who has made me as I am today. Lastly, the role of my family in the construction of my worldview and perspective on equality and freedom is remarkable. Thus, I am indebted to my family; without their love and support, it would not have been possible to go on. This book is dedicated to my father Akif Coban who worked hard for others, lived, and ended his life journey in such an honest and honourable way, by lighting a fire in the darkness for everyone, without any discrimination.

Filiz Coban Oran

2020

Introduction

Living in a politically polarized society has always been a challenging journey in Turkey. On your way you cannot imagine where it can hit you and make you a random victim. Luckily enough I was born after the 12 September 1980 military coup, thus I do not have any memory of this brutal period of Turkish political history. While Prime Minister Turgut Ozal was opening Turkey to the world during my childhood, my family and I moved to five different cities, including Kyrenia in Cyprus, as my father was a naval officer. The free and safe streets of my childhood welcomed me wherever we went. I remember how we enjoyed the national days of the Kemalist regime and how we were proud and passionate to repeat the National Oath in school every morning of the 1990s, in the years of rising political Islam with the electoral victory of Necmettin Erbakan and the escalating Kurdish question. In a small western city in Turkey, I was just feeling that something was getting worse. I was just twelve, the top student of my school, but my real love was reading in an unselective, exciting discovery, including Alex Haley's *Roots*, Wilbur Smith's *The Sunbird*, Fyodor Dostoevsky's *Crime and Punishment*, Orhan Pamuk's *The New Life*... One day I took the book I was reading to the school, Sule Yuksel Senler's *The Street of Peace*. I was taken to an investigation about my intention. I did not know that she was a forbidden Islamist novelist. It was unacceptable, an unforgivable mistake for Kemalists! Although the book was not more than a love story for me, our Turkish literature teacher was replaced with a new one and my grade was brought down. After that moment of injustice, the grades meant nothing to me. In the following years, the army forced out Erbakan's coalition government with a postmodern military memorandum. Nonetheless, being such a bookworm, I kept reading. I chose my own way, studied philosophy at the Hacettepe University and became a student of Professor Ioanna Kucuradi. Reading on political thinkers and ideologies – Aristotle, Nietzsche, Marx, Foucault, Baudrillard – was such an enlightenment! In the streets of Turkey, there was hope of a change as Turkey became a candidate country for European Union membership. At that time, the Islamists were in power and ironically, *The Street of Peace* was adapted to a TV series on a mainstream channel in Turkey. Soon after I figured out that working hard, being fair and impartial did not work in the New Turkey of the 2000s. The love of wisdom took me to the path of academia, however 'they' labelled me as 'she is not one of "us"', which constructed a new form of injustice. Who got power did not matter, our struggle went on against the polarization and injustice of clashing different Turkeys.

I think Gezi protests showed both that the people were emancipated from Kemalist authoritarianism and that they rejected the Islamist authoritarianism. On 29 May 2013, the largest wave of protests in Turkey's history was sparked when the Turkish police violently intervened in an environmentalist peaceful protest in Gezi Park against an urban renewal project to save one of the last green public spaces in Taksim Square, Istanbul (Bilgic and Kafkaslı 2013). This national turmoil spread to demonstrations in 77 cities, resulting in 8 deaths, more than 8,000 injuries, and approximately 5,000 people being taken into police custody. However, what may not have been expected and what made the 'Gezi spirit' unique was the huge variety of group profiles, mostly apolitical students and urban youth, including Kemalist secular nationalists, Turkish ethnic-nationalists, liberals and leftist nationalists, anti-capitalist Muslims, artists, feminists, human rights and LGBT activists, football club fans and, last but not least, Kurdish nationalists. Besides, these protests proved that new citizenship and civil society-state relationships have been emerging in Turkey. The protesters demanded participation in decisions regarding their lifestyles, common spaces and future, specifically on relationships with neighbouring countries, growing neo-liberal restructuring and destruction of cultural geography, the social memory of cities, the forests, the mountains and the rivers of Anatolia, namely, what makes them a nation (Oktem 2013). Thus, Gezi protests presented the resistance against New Turkey and its definition of the nation, which imposes socially conservative, Sunni Islamic-inspired policies in both domestic and foreign relations (Yesilada and Rubin 2013; Uzgel 2013). Despite Turkish prime minister R. Tayyip Erdogan having been elected for the third time with almost 50 per cent of the general vote in June 2011, enjoying great popular support, the massive explosion of discontent erupted towards him. He responded pejoratively to the 'other 50 per cent' of the population (Ozbudun 2014) and provoked his supporters to press for demonstrations, which sharpened political polarization in Turkey. It was 'the clash of nations' (Atay 2013) in Turkey.

Within this context, this study argues that there are different Turkeys and describes the tension involved in their attempts at both maintaining and transforming Turkey's Kemalist identity. For a better understanding of New Turkey, it is important to shed light on competing discourses about Turkish nationalism, their intermingled nature, and in particular the way the new dominant Muslim nationalism became hegemonic in Turkey due to a power struggle over the last decade. It should be kept in mind that hegemony is not necessarily imposed through coercion, but through the organization and creation of common consent for change. Hence, the object of this study is to explore the process of a power struggle over the Justice and Development Party's (Adalet ve Kalkinma Partisi (AKP)) post-Kemalist imagination of the nation that changed the image of Turkey and its place in the world.

In this context, this book presents a critical discussion on how different discourses of Turkish nation-state identity construct, interact, contrast and coexist with each other through the Turkish media by unpacking and examining the concepts of contested Turkish identity, which has great importance for mapping Turkey's place in the world of nations. To indicate the discursive diversity, this study particularly relies on a central research question – how did the Turkish media construct such discourses on Turkish national identity in dealing with domestic and foreign policy debates?

Understanding the process of discursive construction of New Turkey's identity

Since the AKP came to power in 2002, there has been an ongoing debate about the emergence of New Turkey (Yavuz 2006; McLean 2014). The first term of Erdogan's policies was the democratization period which led to success in economic progress, political neutralization of the military and Kemalist laïcité (secularism), and acknowledgement of Kurdish cultural rights and religious minorities' rights by means of instrumentalizing Europeanization. Criss Morris (2005) described this process of political, economic and cultural reforms of Erdogan's AKP as a 'quiet revolution on the edge of Europe'. The second term of the AKP from 2007 to 2011 was the period of consolidation of Muslim conservative policies in both internal and external relations by leaving the EU track. This period represents the domestic power struggle in the redefinition of Turkey's nation-state identity and the emergence of New Turkey. Significantly, it can be seen as a transition period in which two constitutional referendums (2007 and 2010) were held. Lastly, the era from 2011 to today presents Erdogan's New Turkey.

In this historical context, this book focuses on the second term of the AKP government to analyse the process of the emergence of post-Kemalist Turkish nation-state identity. In the literature of Turkish foreign policy, different notions are used to explain the role of the AKP in this change, such as Davutoglu's worldview (Altunisik 2009), the idea of pan-Islamism (Ozkan 2014), neo-Ottomanism (Sozen 2010; Fisher Onar 2009a, 2009b), new geographic imagination (Aras and Fidan 2009; Aras and Polat 2007), geopolitical vision (Yesiltas 2013), civilizational geopolitics (Bilgin and Bilgic 2011), civilizational discourse (Duran 2013), the triumph of the AKP's conservative globalization towards the domestic and international developments (Onis 2011) and the West's changing approach towards Turkey (Oguzlu and Kibaroglu 2009). Most of the studies looked at the AKP's identity with a focus on Islam or conservatism. Among others, by making use of speech act theory Fisher Onar (2011) analysed four main narratives in the AKP's discursive repertoire which helped to explain the multiple threads of AKP activism: democratization, post-Islamism, Ottomanism, and the Turkey Inc. story. Fisher Onar's constructivist approach is well suited to unpacking the contradictions in the AKP's policies and positions on a range of issues. But like other studies, her study did not cover the debates on nationalism.

If one surveys the main concepts, it is apparent that the concept of nationalism is not used to identify New Turkey's identity. The words of Islam and AKP are used together dichotomously as taken for granted, but the notion of nationalism frequently is not taken into account. However, the main power struggle in the reconstruction of Turkey's identity is based on how people diversely see a common past, present, and future of the nation-state. Nationalism is a way of seeing, interpreting and structuring the world we live in, which can be constructed or represented in several different ways by various social agents and power relations. Therefore the absence of the concept of nationalism in the analysis cloaks some discriminatory discourses in the new emerging nation-state discourse. It should be remembered that

Islamists do not avoid being nationalist; hence for analysing the construction of Turkey's new identity, the concept of national identity is accepted as the backbone of this study. Only White's (2013) *Muslim Nationalism and the New Turks* and Saracoglu (2013) defined the AKP's 'strategic depth' in foreign policy as the doctrine of nationalism. According to Saracoglu, nationalism in AKP's discourse is ignored in the literature due to the party being challenged by the official Kemalist nationalist imagination and its understanding of Turkishness. This challenge has cloaked its nationalist discourse. It is accepted that the AKP opposes nationalism; in fact, it opposes Kemalism. It is crucial to point out that the new Islamic conservative nationalism is a collective product of Turkish right-wing ideologies and traditions, which consist of a new Turkish foreign policy discourse in the present.

As we see, the academic literature mainly emphasized what the AKP brought to Turkish politics as a pivotal or hegemonic actor; however, the power struggle of nationalist discourses is largely neglected in the examination of the transformation of Turkey's identity from the Kemalist discourse to the post-Kemalist discourse. This study differs from the previous studies by going beyond these debates with a focus on the concept of nationalism and illuminating the process of the power struggle in the media for the construction of post-Kemalist nation-state discourse in Turkey.

Understanding 'the process' of the discursive construction of New Turkey's identity serves to show the historicity of nationalist discourses and their symbiotic relationships, and to highlight how Islamic conservative nationalism became dominant with the AKP government in the selected period. To sum up, this study aims to understand this process of construction of New Turkey discourse through a more fundamental question: what does it mean to be Turkish, and what is the place of this nation in the world?

By analysing Turkish media discourse in making use of the Discourse-Historical Approach (Wodak et al. 1999) it reveals how New Turkey's identity has emerged through the power struggle of contested perspectives on Turkish nation-state identity and its place in the world. It does so, first, by challenging the argument that there was a particular conception of the Turkish nation-state (Alaranta 2011; Azak 2010; Casier and Jongerden 2011; Karasipahi 2009) it empirically reveals that there are competing Turkish nationalisms which imagine different Turkeys and its place in the world. It points out that both secular and Muslim identities of Turkey are historically constructed and mutually constitutive. Moreover, it challenges the argument that suggests there is a settled preference in favour of Western alliance in Turkey based on a consensus view that Turkey's place is/should be in Europe and the West. Rather, it empirically articulates that there are competing perspectives on Turkey's foreign policy identity, and by the use of post-structuralist foreign policy analysis (Campbell 1998) it shows Turkish national identity and foreign policy discourses are reproductive and constitutive of each other. In this manner this study fundamentally argues that not only has AKP's Muslim nationalism reconstructed New Turkish foreign policy but New Turkish foreign policy discourse has also reconstructed the Turkish nation's Muslim identity and reinforced Muslim nationalism.

According to previous analyses, three main factors behind the construction of post-Kemalist nation-state identity appear: the first factor is the role of 9/11 and the post-Cold War international system; the second factor is the role of Turkey's bid for EU membership; the third factor is the role of the AKP government in changing domestic power relations. Based on this literature, this book focuses on the domestic power struggle and identifies three main domestic challenges to Turkey's Kemalist nation-state identity: the Islamist challenge, the Kurdish challenge and the foreign policy challenge. According to this identification, three case studies are selected to realize the targeted aim of studying Turkey's post-Kemalist identity. The first case study analyses the Islamist challenge of Kemalist nation-state identity, examines the domestic power struggle of the definition of Turkish nation-state identity and articulates the main antagonisms in various imaginations of being a Turk. The second case study analyses the Kurdish challenge and indicates how these antagonisms in Turkish nation-state identity determine different perspectives on the nation's self and other relations. Lastly, the third case study explores the foreign policy challenge and shows how New Turkish foreign policy discourse contributes to the domestic power struggle and reconstructs Turkey's post-Kemalist nation-state identity.

In this context, the research consists of four chapters. Chapter 1 presents the historical background of different discourses of Turkish nationalism and Turkish foreign policy. It portrays the origins of the current problems and polarizations of Turkey as different perspectives on Turkish nationalism that have different understandings of history and foreign relations based on diverse worldviews. Chapter 2 is devoted to introducing my theoretical and methodological framework. This part will review the relationships among the media, national identity and foreign policy. Specifically, it concentrates on the concept of 'discourse' in foreign policy analysis and presents the Discourse-Historical Approach in Critical Discourse Analysis for analysing discursive construction of New Turkey's identity in the media. Chapter 3, as the discourse analysis part, analyses the Turkish media discourse in three case studies to examine the power struggle in defining the post-Kemalist narrative of the nation-state. Lastly, Chapter 4 gives a general overview of the research in the context of contemporary Turkish politics.

1

History

Religion, Turkish nationalism and foreign policy

Introduction

This part of the study reveals that the discourse of Turkish nationalism has had numerous evolutions and branches from its rise in the late nineteenth century to the emergence of post-Kemalist nation-state identity in the present. At the time of the founding of the Turkish Republic, Mustafa Kemal Ataturk and his adherents set the goal of lifting Turkey to 'the level of contemporary civilization' (Lewis 2002: 292). Their images of the civilized Turkish nation-state were modern and secular, thus the way of civilization had appeared clear, distancing itself from the Islamic Ottoman past and the Eastern way of life and instead cooperating with the civilized and modern West.

In this regard, Turkey is defined as a 'torn country' by Samuel Huntington (2002: 139) in 'the clash of civilisations' in his interpretation of the world of civilizations and the remaking of the world order after the Cold War period. Turkey is torn due to its Kemalist leaders attempting to shift Turkey to another (Western) civilization, even though it has a predominantly Muslim culture. But as Huntington argued, in the post-Cold War era national, ethnic and religious identification issues continued to emerge, and Turkey's Kemalist secularist identity has been under challenge at home while its Western or European identity has been questioned more internationally. Since a response to this challenge is required, Turkey has been in the process of a redefinition of its national/state identity, which is complicated and painful, both culturally and politically. The common approach accepts that there is a cleavage between the Republican secularist bureaucratic centre and the conservative Muslim periphery (Mardin 1973) in Turkey. This study alternatively argues that the secular (European-Western) and Muslim identities of Turkey are historically constructed and mutually constitutive (Turner and Zengin-Arslan 2013) due to their power struggle; therefore, it concentrates on the diversity in existing understandings of Turkish identity, and it reveals that changing domestic power relations have changed the dominant discourse in Turkey's nation-state identity discourse and led to the emergence of a post-Kemalist discourse. Therefore, it offers a discursive approach for the understanding of New Turkey's identity and its place in the world.

This section demonstrates that the Kemalist Turkish state had not been neutral in creating Muslim secularism, which made Turkey an original example in the identity politics of International Relations studies. It is the paradox that what divides and maintains Turkish national unity is Muslim identity and its secular interpretation. Even though this paradox has highly polarized Turkey in the last decade, both sides have benefited from this struggle, as Kadioglu and Keyman (2011) defined that these are symbiotic antagonisms. This thesis therefore offers an anti-essentialist conceptualization of these identities, their differences, and mutual relations, which opens possibilities of democratic interaction, post-secular pluralism (Connolly 2000; Habermas 2008) and 'ethos of engagement' among different traditions, faiths, and ways of living them. That this engagement is becoming plural may be healing to Turkey's 'social and historical wound left open by the incompletion of the struggle of civil rights' (Finlayson 2011: 17).

To shed light on the origins of contested discourses on Turkish national identity and the emergence of Turkey's post-Kemalist nation-state identity, this chapter will provide the historical framework for analysing different elements of Turkey's identity such as Turkic, Islamic, secular, European and Western. It invokes three major factors that have urged re/construction of Turkey's identity since the end of the Cold War: the international paradigm shift, especially with 9/11 events; Turkey's bid for EU membership; and the rise of political Islam and transformation of domestic power relations with the pro-Islamist Justice and Development Party's government since 2002.

In the first decade of the 2000s, reformist AKP aligned itself with the West/EU to consolidate democracy. This attempt legitimized its actions to transform domestic power relations, significantly Turkey's self-image at the domestic and international levels. Throughout the last decade, Turkey's internal dilemmas and contradictions in identity politics have reached the top of the country's agenda in their impact on Turkey's international relations, particularly relations with the EU/West. Within this context, the object of this chapter is to present a critical discussion on the national identity and foreign policy interactions that will assist in providing a historical framework to study Turkey's post-Kemalist nation-state identity, its challenges and changing EU/West relations. To realize this goal, the chapter begins with a presentation of the historical roots of Turkish nationalism and its challenge to the Kemalist state's traditional others: non-Muslim, Islamist and Kurdish identities. Then, it seeks out the evolution of discourses of Turkish nationalism and its relations with these other identities in changing internal and international circumstances during the 1990s and 2000s.

The origins of Turkish nationalism

This section deals with the concepts of the Turkish nation while locating the perspectives on Turkish nationalism within the theories of nationalism. In Turkish nationalism studies, Nergis Canefe (2002) offers an ethno-symbolic alternative (Smith 1999; Hutchinson 2000) for studying Turkish nationalism and its popular appeal. She points out that the hybrid nature of the multi-ethnic, multi-cultural, and multi-religious Ottoman history and heritage constitutes one of the two obstacles hindering the examination of the Turkish case. Another obstacle is the political and cultural denial of the Ottoman heritage since the Republican establishment. The Kemalist tradition of secular nationalism of the Republican era is formulated against the idea of a continuum that links the Ottoman legacy and Islamic Turkish history. According to Canefe, ignorance of the Ottoman origins of the Turkish nationalist movement and an overwhelming modernist trajectory in analysing Turkish nationalism limit understanding of the Turkish case (Smith 1999: 134). This is because this Kemalist narrative has been influenced officially and popularly by the counter-narratives, their readings of history, and selection of events that differently built their imaginations of the nation. Thus, as she argues, the central problem of the construction of Turkish national identity can be identified as its dealings with its own history and hybrid character. Canefe applies a historical ethno-symbolism method to the Turkish case in looking at the myths of the Turkish people's origins, memories, traditions, and ways of life in a distinctly Muslim Turkish Anatolian society in related symbols of its ethnicity. She shows that the Kemalist narrative and myths of nation selectively highlight the history of Turkish people in Asia Minor. This specifically Kemalist reading of the political past serves for imagining a secular nation by creating distance from the Islamic character of the Ottoman era. She overcomes the clean break between the Ottoman and the Kemalist Republican narratives that hinders seeing the social, cultural, and economic determinants of emerging Young Ottoman and Young Turks movements as the birth of Turkish nationalism in late Ottoman times. Therefore, to gain a deeper understanding, the role of the national awakening, imperial legacy and power struggle in the nation-state building process are taken into account for classification of Turkish nationalism in this section.

The Ottoman Empire had a multi-religious, multi-cultural, and multi-lingual *millet* system that was organised based on religion (Inalcik 1997). In the period of the Ottomans, it was used to identify legally organized different religious communities such as Jewish millets, Armenian millets or Kurdish millets. For the sake of building a nation-state, Kemalist modernist elites of Turkey rejected the Ottoman millet system and tradition (Bozdogan and Kasaba 1997), and instead invented a new tradition associated with an imagined Turkish ethnicity that had its roots, myths and past in Central Asia (Neyzi 2002: 141). To unify the people, the nation-state would be based on the Turkish language and culture rather than on religion. Turkish was accepted as the official language of the state since it was the general language of communication of the Anatolian peoples. Thereafter, Turkish identity, history and society were redefined, systematized and centralized by the state institutions. For that matter, the words used to refer to 'nationalism' in the Turkish language are also ideologically differentiated by the users. Rather than using the term 'milliyetçilik', Kemalists prefer to use the term 'ulusculuk' (Ozkirimli 2011: 95) or 'ulusalcılık' (Bora 2003) to identify their Turkish nationalism, which has a secular modern meaning. The origins of this difference of perspectives on Turkish nationalism will be clarified in this part of the chapter to tackle the complexities of the contested debate on how Turkish identity was constructed and how it has had other branches of doctrine.

Although the words 'Turk' and 'Turkey' were mostly used to refer to the Ottomans in European literature, this usage covered not only Turkish-speaking people but also other Muslims in the empire as well (Kushner 1977: 8). On the other hand, in Ottoman writings, the word 'Turks' signified the peasants of Anatolia, Turkish-speaking Ottomans, with an insulting sense. This identification had changed by the Sultan Abdulhamid period, in the second half of the 1800s, when the term 'Turk' became widely used in Ottoman publications and even the newspapers were labelled 'Turkish newspaper' (Kushner 1977: 21). Thus, in the pre-Hamidian period the term means 'Turks as the rulers of the Ottoman Empire', and then it was used to denote a historical, linguistic and ethnic entity. It is worth noting that the ruling class and state officials had to know the Turkish language as a requirement for employment; however, Turkishness did not hold a privileged position–for instance, the state showed a definite lack of effort in spreading the Turkish language among the population and in dealing with public education. Umut Uzer (2011: 113) supports that argument by noting that Turkishness and pre-Islamic Turkish history were ignored in the Ottoman Empire due to the goal of strengthening Ottoman and Islamic solidarity.

In *The Emergence of Modern Turkey* Bernard Lewis (2002: 3) provides the literature with a much-needed general perspective for understanding the mainstream of influence that gave rise to modern Turkey: the Islamic, the Turkish, and the local (Anatolian elements such as the Hittites, the Byzantine, the Seljuk, the Rumelian, the Balkans, and Perso-Arabic influences). In the debate over the emergence of Turkish national consciousness, Lewis develops his argument from the book by P. Wittek (1952) *Le Role de Tribus dans L'empire Ottoma*' which analyses the Ottomans' descendants who are claimed as Turkish nomadic tribes, particularly the Oguz Turkish tribe of Kayi. Lewis (2002: 9) writes that at the time of Murat (1421–51), Ottoman history and literature elaborated on the Oguz legend. Significantly, a pure and simple central Asian Turkish language was used in literary schools in writing folk poetry (Kushner 1977: 3) at the end of the fifteenth century. Indeed, making Turkish the official state language in the time of the Ottomans, rather than Persian or Arabic language such as in other Turkish dynasties, such as the Seljuks and the Mamluks, did contribute to maintaining the Turkish character of the empire (Kushner 1977: 2).

According to Lewis (Kushner 1977: 9), the key here was that the sense of Turkishness was retained among Anatolian people in their folk literature, but a Turkish national consciousness bloomed in the nineteenth century as an outcome of Turcological studies, set off by Turkish emigrants from the Russian Empire. The growing interest in, and awareness of, Turkish history produced the first publications concerned with the genealogy of the Ottomans, such as Ahmet Mithat's *History of Modern Times* in 1877. According to this narrative, the state of Oguz Khan and the Turks were extensively accepted as pointing out the fathers of the Ottomans who were tribes of Central Asia (Kushner 1977: 27). In the eighteenth century, the Turks had been influenced by Islam and the language and culture of Persian and Arabic. The Turkish Seljuks brought Islam from south-west Asia to Anatolia. Moreover, the transfer of the Caliphate from Abbasid Caliphs to the Ottomans gave the Sultans a mission to expand it to the borders of Western Anatolia. They protected and spread the power of Islam against the Christian West during the six centuries. Therefore, 'Ottoman', 'Turk' or 'Muslim' had been used to identify them in European literature, and the term referred to the territories of the empire. Similarly, in the writings of Ottoman history, the country, the ruler and its army were defined with a reference to religion as 'the land of Islam', 'the Padishah of Islam' and 'the soldier of Islam' (Lewis 2002: 13).

Under the ideology of Ottomanism, all communities in the empire enjoyed their rights as long as they maintained their loyalty to the Sultan. When the empire began to collapse in the beginning of the nineteenth century, different doctrines came to be known to hold unity. During the same period, the non-Muslim public's demands upon the empire and the secularization by the Tanzimat (1839) pushed for reactionary anti-Western attitudes (Kushner 1977), while Bulgarian, Serbian and Greek nationalism and restlessness were growing like warning bells of separation. In the following decades, territorial losses made the empire overwhelmingly Muslim; therefore, the authorities and Sultan Abdulhamid emphasized Islamism and Islamic institutions of the state (Deringil 1991), particularly the symbolic power of the Caliphate among the Muslim world to strengthen the legitimacy of the regime between 1876 and 1909. It can be argued that nationalist movements among non-Muslim communities of the empire and their positions in the First World War played a role in the construction of Turkish identity as Muslim, both in the Kemalist and Islamist imaginations of the nation.

The greatest historians of the time, such as Hayrullah Efendi (1817–1876) and Ahmed Refik Pasa (1823–91) indicated the importance of the Islamic character of Ottoman history, culture, and religious affiliation to identify different groups and residents of the empire in the millet system. Equally critical was the fact that as an outcome of Ottoman modernization, the Westernized Ottoman colleges and academies emerged with a new political culture and a new class that had a vision to do politics differently (Canefe 2002: 140). Meanwhile, the Ottoman imperial system, tradition and reforms began to be questioned by the rising military-bureaucratic elite. In the 1860s the Young Ottomans movement opposed the Hamidian politics and practices with an offer of new ideological and political solutions based on Turkism. By the 1908 Young Turk Revolution, the new elite was encouraging the formation of commercial companies fostering a Turkish entrepreneurial class and created a bourgeois class among the Turks to construct a society to cope with the capitalist economy (Ahmad 1993: 45). Here it is useful to manifest how their ideas of liberalism, constitutionalism and nationalism (Poulton 1997) could reach the masses of the empire. On this point, Kushner (1977: 14–19) supplies detailed knowledge on the role of newspapers and periodicals of the Hamidian press in giving rise to debates on Turkish nationalism, Westernization, Islamism and secularism. He argues that the press certainly caused increasing awareness of separate Turkish cultures among educated elites and a desire to Westernize the country due to being aware of the scientific and technological power of Europe. The literature on Turkish nationalism supports the point on the existence of a growing body of Turkist publications in the Young Turks period (1908–1918), but there is common agreement in the literature (Hanioglu 1995, 2001; Deringil 1991; Kayali 1997) about whether the Young Turks of the CUP were Ottomanists due to their desire for the continuation of the Islamic Empire. This historical reading on the origins of Turkish nationalism as the emergence of the idea of being a part of a national community can be classified under the modernist approaches to nationalism, specifically by means of Anderson (1983) who argued that print media contributed to the rise of national consciousness and the nation as an 'imagined community' among people.

Contrary to the Ottomanists, various 'pan' movements arose, such as pan-Slavism and pan-Turkism (Uzer 2011: 114) in the period of the fall of the empire at the beginning of the twentieth century. One of the first attempts to place Turkism as an ideology distinct from Ottomanism and pan-Islamism was Yusuf Akcura's essay (1976) entitled *Three Kinds of Policy* (Uc Tarz-ı Siyaset 1904). His suggestion for 'a Turkish national policy based on the

Turkish race' was inspiring for the formulation of Turkish nationalism and ideas. Akcura claimed that Ottomanism failed to create unity in the state due to the fact there was no Ottoman nation. Pan-Islamism was challenging due to external obstacles and resistance by the Christian powers. But a Turkist policy as the third choice could provide a base of unity and loyalty within the empire among the many millions of Turks within and beyond the frontiers.

These doctrines contributed to defining the nation's linguistic, cultural and political boundaries in the wake of the First World War. It was the time of the War of Independence when Islam was used by Mustafa Kemal (1881–1938) and the Young Turks to mobilize the Muslim public (Poulton 1997: 119) against the old order and European imperialism in the Versailles system. Ozkirimli calls it 'the short-term tactical alliance of the Kemalists with Islam' (Ozkirimli and Sofos 2008: 58). In the National Pact (Misak-I Milli) that drew the boundaries of Anatolia, the religion was the only legitimized unification element in that sense. It must be noted that the press was used by Mustafa Kemal to provoke Anatolian political mobilization, to raise a freedom and independence voice against the foreign powers; specifically two newspapers, *Irade-i Milliye* and *Hakimiyet-i Milliye* played a role in spreading national awareness and turning the resistance into a national war (Kologlu 1993; Yust 1995). After a national Turkish state was established in 1923, this alliance was severed by Mustafa Kemal Ataturk and the governing elite because Islam was seen as a link with the old order and Ottomanism. As Sami Zubaida (2009: 118) notes, this break with popular religion was a deliberate part of the nationalist project designed to empower a 'progress' discourse against 'backwardness' to cope with foreign domination. In this context, it can be argued that anti-imperialism has been one of the main characteristics of Kemalist nationalism since the beginning, as a consequence of the war against European powers for Turkish nation-state building.

The construction of the official Kemalist nation-state discourse

For the governing elite, the word 'Turk' meant Turkish citizenship; it was a noun, not an adjective (Heper 2011: 50). To be a Turk, it was enough to accept the principles of Kemalism, Turkish culture and language. Nobody was excluded as long as that person was willing to be assimilated into Turkishness, similar to French nationalism (Oran 1990). Therefore, the concept of the 'nation' of the Turkish Republic had its roots in a legacy of the French Revolution, in the words of Ernest Renan 'the will to live together' (Soysal 1999: 12) rather than the ethnic or religious origins of the population. Based on this assumption, Soner Cagaptay notes (2002: 67–82) that the first definition of the Turkish nation was territorial. As declared by Ataturk, 'The people of Turkey who have established the Turkish state are called the Turkish nation', and this nation was inhabited by different ethnic groups including Turks, Kurds, Jews, Arabs, Lazes, Armenians and so on. The second definition recognized all Muslims who were in the Turkish nation in terms of the emerging Turkish history thesis. The ethno-religious definition as the third definition that accepted those who were ethnically Turkish was designated by the policy of the ruling Republican People's Party between 1935 and 1937.

Cagaptay's work demonstrates the dynamic character of Turkish nationalism in the nation-building process. Ottoman historians, Sukru Hanioglu (2011), Halil Inalcik (1998), and Serif Mardin (2006) point out continuing state and society traditions and legacies from the Imperial times to the Republican times. Like Canefe, Hanioglu (2011) refers to the pre-Republican times for identifying and classifying Turkish nationalism and its origins. Mardin (2016) diagnoses an on-going problem in the centre-periphery relations in Turkey. He notes that Turkey has a strong state tradition that always led to the top-down modernization and transformation of society. What appears differently in Inalcik's article (1998) is that he argues Ataturk's legacy, the Ottoman world state legacy with poet Fuzuli, Yunus Emre or Suleymaniye Mosque live together in every single Turk's national history and conscience. He notes that not only conservative parties but also all other political parties, and Kemalist circles too, enjoy living Ottomanist romanticism (1998: 3).

Faroz Ahmad in *The Making of Modern Turkey* (1993: 2–3), emphasizes the army's role from Ottoman times to the present in Turkish history and politics. He suggests an institutional continuity that demonstrates contested worldviews and their historical origins in modern Turkish politics. By the last quarter of the nineteenth century, some military officers had been politicized against the sultan, Abdulhamid II (1876–1909), which launched the Young Turk revolution, which continued for a decade until the defeat of the Ottoman Empire in the First World War. The Ottoman administration and the Sultan Vahdettin were not capable of resisting the Great Powers and imperialism;

therefore, the old regime agreed to sign the Treaty of Sèvres in August 1920. The Turkish nationalists and the army expected the sultan to stand up for Turkey's rights, but he was collaborating with the external powers.

That was why the army gave their loyalty to the movement led by Mustafa Kemal (1998: 8). At the very least, the army's intervention in politics continued under the Republican system which experienced three military coups in Turkish political life. Related to this, Metin Heper (2011: 51) points out that the state elites, especially the army officers, traditionally do not trust the political elite in Turkey. They attempt to change or form the way of doing politics when they see it is required because they believe that the politicians might pursue their own profits rather than the national interests. This point is significant for a better understanding of the current power relationship in Turkey. Also, looking at the political fault lines drawn during the establishment of the Republic contributes to completing other parts of the puzzle of the power and identity politics of Turkey.

For Ayse Kadioglu (2011: 45) Turkish nationalism was not an outcome of national awakening; it was a project constructed from above by the Kemalist state elites. Fuat Keyman (2011: 20) argues that nationalism dominantly affected the features of the process of making modern Turkey, and it still influences the Turkish state ideology and society in different contexts and articulations. In his analysis, the state-based transformation of traditional society into a modern nation aimed to reach the level of 'western civilisation' to save the state and secure its existence. Following a Gellnerian modernist explanation, Keyman introduces the idea that the Kemalist elite fostered a rapid industrialization and socio-economic modernization in a Weberian fashion (2011: 17) and constructed a secular and modern national identity by instrumentalization of Western reason and rationality. He makes an outstanding distinction between two state-based modernizations, from the empire to the Republican times. To compete within the European state system, the Ottoman state employed modernization, especially within the military, as the expedient to deal with the empire's decline. For instance, Sultan Mahmud II (1807–39) replaced the army of the Janissaries with the 'New Army' (Nizam-i Cedid) in 1826 to create a modern fighting force along European lines. Similarly, with modernization the Republican elite aimed to have a more secure and powerful state, but their understandings of the concept were not just martial or technological. They believed that Western advancement and its institutional political structure could be achieved by requiring regulation of state-society relations in supplementing Western cultural practices. So, this time, the state designed reforms to change every aspect of societal relations and everyday practices of individuals. In this context, Islam was identified as the main obstacle to progress, and thus secularism was seen as one of the most important reforms to enlighten people and make progress in society. In Mardin's words (2006), it was a transition from a religious community governed by a sultan to a secular nation-state. In this regard, Keyman notes (2011: 18) that 'Turkey did not rise phoenix-like out of the ashes of the Ottoman Empire.' In making modern Turkey, the Islamic identity and Kurdish identity, or the Ottoman past, were excluded as 'others' to create a nationalist identity. The Republican system was established by the Kemalist imagination and its victory against foreign invaders and the old regime supporters.

As noted, after the victory of the resistance, the Turkish Republic was proclaimed on 29 October 1923, and Mustafa Kemal became its first president. There were rivals and opponents to the new regime, from the sides that wanted to maintain monarchy and the Caliphate or seek an American mandate for Turkey. Since the beginning, Islamists would always be able to manipulate the symbols of religion as a counterforce to the Kemalists and the new regime (Ahmad 1993: 49). Moreover, the religious reaction and counter-revolution movement unleashed a Kurdish rebellion in eastern Anatolia and influenced the region in February 1925. As a result, the Law for the Maintenance of Order was passed by the National Assembly to silence the opposition. In the following two years, over 500 people were sentenced to death by the special courts known as Independence Tribunals (Ahmad 1993: 58). It can be argued that this period and how it is remembered by the Kemalists, Islamists and Kurdish people has a significant place in their images of the Turkish nation-state. After elaborating the general breaks and institutional continuities from the Ottoman past to the Republican times, in the context of Kemalist nation-state discourse and its historical challenges, the next sections elucidate the place of non-Muslim, Islamic and Kurdish identity in Turkey and Turkish identity in detail.

Non-Muslimhood in Kemalist Turkish nation-state identity

M. Kemal Ataturk's nationalism was of a pluralist kind to realize the goal of having the support of all communities in Anatolia for the newly established nation-state. Moreover, this was a 'genius' nationalism (Smith 2005: 437) in its ability to mix the organic/ethnic and the civic/territorial, even though there were almost fifty different ethnic groups in the country. In the first decades of the Turkish Republic, Turkish nationalism looked like a 'civic nationalism' based on the constitution, but in its application to practice it was ethno-religious nationalism. The state had taken actions to legalize exclusionary practices. These applications were described as 'racist' by some authors (Maksudyan 2005), while some (Aktar 2000) preferred to say it was simply a cultural homogenization process without targeting any different 'race' motif, but it was certainly discrimination of non-Muslims as an 'out' group from Muslims as a group who did belong. According to the Lausanne Treaty, only non-Muslim people were recognized as minorities. The treaty was signed in 1923 between the British Empire, France, Italy, Japan, Greece, Romania, the Serb-Croat-Slovene State, and the Grand National Assembly of Turkey after the Ankara government abolished the Peace Treaty of Sèvres of 1920 that had been agreed between the Ottoman Empire and the Allies of the First World War. Article 40 of the Treaty stated that Turkish citizens belonging to non-Muslim minorities should enjoy the same treatment and security in law and fact as other Turkish people. In particular, they should have an equal right to establish, manage, and control, at their own expense, any charitable, religious and social institutions, any schools and other establishments for instruction and education, with the right to use their language and to exercise their religion freely therein.

All citizens were defined as Turks in Article 88 of the 1924 Constitution. This looked like a civic understanding of citizenship; however, its application to social reality in the 1930s was different. It was even a 'völkisch nationalism' in Kieser's (2008: ix) words, which means an undemocratic, unequal, elitist, discriminative interpretation of identities by favouring Turkish-Sunni identity. Being a part of the Turkish nation for non-Muslim citizens included some conditions for assimilation such as internalizing the Turkish language as their mother tongue, adopting Turkish culture, and loyalty to the idea of Turkism (Bali 2006: 43) based on a willingness to live together. These provisions were still not enough; they had a strong struggle against discriminative laws in the 1930s like the Law on Settlement in 1934. These laws meant that non-Muslim citizens were differentiated from the Turkish identity.

From the perspective of the Republican elite, there were reasons for this 'de facto discrimination' (Bali 2006: 48). Non-Muslims were insider foreigners, in other words, 'strangers whose loyalty was suspect' (Bali 2006: 49). Their past was not commonly shared; for instance, they did not fight in the National War of Independence, and some of them even became allies to 'others'. Relations between the state and non-Muslim citizens became more difficult based on the attempts of writing Turkish national history and the reading of common history from different perceptions. Some historians chose to emphasize the discourse of 'We lived together for more than five centuries', while others chose to focus on just a selected part of the history, specifically the last century of the Ottoman Empire. In the 1930s Turkish nationalism was still cultural (Ozkirimli and Sofos 2008: 167), motivated and produced by a massive process of homogenization through the Turkification of names and surnames; forcing citizens to speak Turkish with 'citizen speak Turkish!' campaigns; Turkifying minority schools; dismantling their communities and non-profit organizations; and finally, nationalism took on an economic tone in the Turkification of the economy via the Capital Tax Levy in 1942 (Bali 2012; Bali 2000; Aktar 2000). Besides, the National Consumption Society was established to encourage people to buy national products and goods. Consequently, Turkish nationalism spread in various aspects of socio-economic life.

When Ataturk died in 1938, the war and the extension of German power over Europe had already brought a defensive attitude to Turkey to secure the country by following a policy of neutrality. Given this external threat and circumstances of instability, considerable inflation and economic crises emerged in Turkey. Therefore, the government decided to approve the capital tax in November 1942 for the sake of maintaining control over the national economy. The categorizing of taxation rates for taxpayers was based on their religion and nationality (Lewis 2002: 298). Non-Muslim citizens had to pay up to ten times as much within fifteen days, and people who could not pay the tax levy within a month were even deported to Askale for forced labour breaking stones for the new roads. Greek, Jewish and Armenian defaulters were subjected to punishment and were sent to Askale in early January 1943.

Bernard Lewis quotes the failure of the capital tax to achieve its economic objectives in the book by the finance director of Istanbul, Faik Okte (1951), titled *The Catastrophe of Capital Tax*. According to Okte's evaluation of the results of taxation, it caused the collapse of the price policy and benefited the black market while it had ended in an atmosphere of 'lawlessness and disorder'. More significantly, with this kind of classification of unjust and discriminatory taxes on foreign and non-Muslim citizens, the confidence of the citizens in the state and society, financial probity and religious tolerance were shattered (1951: 301). The representation of non-Muslim citizens as a threat to Turkish identity, homogeneity and socio-economic interests was not just sneaking into policies of the state, but also into everyday discourse as 'the enemy within' (Neyzi 2002: 146).

Tragically this was seen in 'the Events of September 6–7th', when the Greek minority in Istanbul became targets for racist attacks in 1955. In the outbreak of violence, the populist manipulation of national sentiments by politicians, the Turkish media, and the intelligentsia contributed to the fearful atmosphere and radicalizing and mobilizing of the discontented public (Kuyucu 2005: 375–6). Turkish press coverage of the Cyprus issue and the false news coverage that Mustafa Kemal Ataturk's house, where he had been born in 1881 in Thessaloniki, in northern Greece, had been bombed, caused great nationalist aggression in Istanbul and made non-Muslims open targets. These events documented how the politicization of a foreign policy issue by the power of the press resulted in domestic crises. More specifically, it underlined the definition of being Turk through being Muslim.

The historical origins of Kemalist-Islamist rivalry in Turkey

A deeper search in the literature shows that there are different readings on Turkish history and the evolution of secularism from the imperial times to the Republican times. Sociologist Niyazi Berkes (1964) in *The Development of Secularism in Turkey* analyses the evolution of the Ottoman-Turkish modernization and secularization from the eighteenth to the twentieth century in focusing on three originators of the ideas: Ibrahim Muteferrika, Namik Kemal and Ziya Gokalp. According to him, before Ataturk, Ziya Gokalp had already idealized a secular religion and culture for the Turks and triggered a break between the state and religion. Berkes argues that the Ottoman system was not theocratic or feudal but had an Eastern despotic character. This character inevitably and naturally had to be abandoned because of European modernization and nationalization.

As widely accepted in the literature, for the sake of being at the level of modern civilizations, the Republican system put the concept of the nation in the place of religion. Based on the concept of Turkishness instead of Islam in the establishment of the Republican system, the old order was replaced by the new one with signifiers such as the removal of the Caliphate and abolition of the fez that was the bastion of Islamic identification, and, in M. Kemal Ataturk's words, the emblem of uncivilization, ignorance and hatred of progress (Lewis 2002: 268). In other words, to be secular meant to be modern (Yavuz 1998: 11). The idea and normative-ideological state project of secularism were inherited from the Enlightenment and required constructing an anthropocentric change (Casanova 2011) in the understanding of the world through a process of maturation, emancipation, positivism and scientific reasoning.

The struggle against Islamists emerged and intensified during the single-party period (Cumhuriyet Halk Partisi, CHP) between 1923 and 1946. Hale and Ozbudun (2010: 22) call it 'assertive secularism' that bans or limits aspects of Islamic identity in the public sphere and individualizes the religion. This was not passive secularism that implies state neutrality towards religion. However, this specific tone of secularism was accepted by large segments of society, particularly among the supporters of the CHP. The fear of 'Islamic reactionism' (Azak 2010) became the fundamental characteristic of Turkish secularism. Reproduction of this fear by the political and intellectual elites spread the securitization of secularization (Bilgin 2008) to everyday life in Turkey. In this context, these listed Kemalist reforms in the regulation of political, cultural and social life served to rapidly eradicate the ties with the Islamic Ottoman legacy (Karasipahi 2009: 22):

(1) The abolition of the sultanate in 1922 by a decree of the Grand National Assembly.
(2) The abolition in 1924 of the Caliphate, which had symbolized the unity of *ummah* (the worldwide Muslim community). The origins of the Caliphate went back to the period after the death of Prophet Muhammed; Ottoman sultans had assumed the title of caliph in the sixteenth century.
(3) The abolition in 1924 of the office of Seyh'ul-Islam, the highest religious authority in the administration of the Ottoman Empire, one of whose functions had been to oversee the suitability of political decisions to Islamic law.
(4) The abolition in 1924 of the Ministry of Religious Affairs and Pious Foundations (Seriye ve Evkaf Vekaleti).

(5) The abolition in 1924 of the Seri'at courts, religious courts based on Muslim law.
(6) The abolition in 1924 of the *madrasah* (Islamic theological seminary and law school attached to a mosque), which had been important centres of religious learning in the Ottoman Empire.
(7) The interdiction of religious brotherhoods (*tarikat*) in 1925, and the ban on all their activities.
(8) The passage of a law in 1925 outlawing the fez in favour of the Western hat; the Republican regime also discouraged the veil for women although it did not outlaw it.
(9) The adoption of the Gregorian calendar in 1925, replacing the lunar Hicri and solar Rumi calendars.
(10) The adoption of the Swiss Civil Code in 1926, giving equal civil rights to men and women.
(11) The adoption of European numerals in 1928.
(12) The change from Arabic to Latin script in 1928.
(13) The deletion in 1928 of the second article of the 1924 constitution, which stated Islam to be the state religion.

Under the cloak of the multi-party system, not only was the Kemalist elites' secularist nationalism represented in politics as happened in the single-party period of the Republican Peoples Party (CHP) but also conservative versions of Turkism were integrated into Turkish politics. In the 1950s, the Democrat Party (DP) changed the tone of secularism through a discourse of rejection of the statist, elitist and military-dominated political tradition of the CHP. The DP as opposed to the 'militant secularism' in the vocabulary of religious conservatism (Kuyucu 2005: 371–2) had overwhelming popular support. Under Adnan Menderes the DP opened the Imam-Hatip schools, which were the first religious state-sponsored schools for training religious leaders. They also added an optional religion course to the curriculum of elementary schools.

The DP's successive Justice Party (Adalet Partisi, AP) represented the conservative right in the 1960s. Political Islamism benefited from the rising political and economic importance of villagers and townspeople's votes in multi-party politics (Noyon 2003: 69). Local notables and rural conservatives supported the economic aspects of modernization and social conservatism that fed political Islam on the periphery (Noyon 2003: 70). It was noteworthy that

Necmettin Erbakan was the first leader of political Islam (Kavakci-Islam 2010: 44) in the Republic, who established the National Order Party (Milli Nizam Partisi, MNP) in the late 1960s. Erbakan later led the National Salvation Party (Milli Selamet Partisi, MSP) in 1973 and the Welfare Party (Refah Partisi, RP) in 1987; however, each party was shut down by military intervention owing to religious agitation and the aim of the destruction of the existing state order. In the times of military interventions, Islamists challenged the state's dominance of religion even more. For instance, in a 1971 military coup, eighty-five students (aged between eight and twenty) were arrested due to 'studying Arabic and Islam' and wearing religious garb (Kavakci-Islam 2010: 184).

Without an understanding of the post-1980 period, the legacy of Turgut Ozal and the transition of Turkey's embedded politics to neo-liberalism in his time, there would be a lack in covering the rise of political Islam in Turkey. This also provides clues for how in the first decade of the 2000s the Justice and Development Party became the successor of conservative right parties' votes of the 1990s. Turkey's transformation of its economy to a free-market economy with the January 24th Decisions by the 1980 military coup continued with Turgut Ozal's policies of opening Turkish markets to the international market and foreign competition. The elimination of leftists and ultranationalists by the military regime and the adoption of the Turkish-Islamic Synthesis (TIS) as the state ideology of Turkish nationalism's mixture with Sunni Islam emerged as a political opportunity structure (Eligur 2010: 226) to power the Islamist social-economic movement in Turkey. The TIS was the military's solution to the political polarization of the country and the leftist communist threat (Oktem 2011) that opened the doors to organizational and mobilizational activities for the Islamist activists and entrepreneurs.

Turgut Ozal's alliance and social networks with the Islamists, particularly the Naksibendi Islamic Brotherhood, encouraged cooperation with Saudi and Kuwaiti finance and played a vital role in the establishment of the Islamist capital and wealthy business class (Eligur 2010: 227). Ozal's main goal seemed to be to promote a modern society with liberal economic rationality and the conservative values of traditional society (Kalaycioglu 2002: 46). Nilufer Gole (2000) defined Ozal's policies as 'engineering pragmatism with cultural conservatism' by making use of Ozal's academic background in engineering. The ideology of his party's Motherland Party (Anavatan Partisi: ANAP) was a combination of Islam, nationalism, economic liberalism and social democracy. Regarding this developments, Kamrava (1998) argues that the success of Islamist parties in the 1990s was based on the interplay of three factors: the nature and evolution of the Turkish political system backed financially by the country's growing Islamist business sector; the generally acknowledged failure of most political parties and politicians in the post-1980 coup era; and the organizational capabilities and populist platforms of the Islamists and their dedicated party activists which capitalized on the failures of others.

In 1993, Ozal died suddenly of a heart attack, so under the leadership of Mesut Yilmaz in the 1990s, ANAP moved towards a right-wing position committed to free-market capitalism and nationalism (Onis 2004). Suleyman Demirel assumed the position of president in June 1993, and simultaneously the next leader of Demirel's True Path Party (Dogru Yol Partisi: DYP), Tansu Ciller, rose to become Turkey's first female prime minister. This was at the end of the Cold War when the discourse of liberalism and democracy was utilized by the Islamists to articulate and expand their Islamic message of 'Just Order' (Eligur 2010: 278) to the voters, and more significantly to the socio-economically aggrieved masses, in other words, the 'excluded' voters. With the rhetoric of 'Just Order', the return of Necmettin Erbakan ended the Islamist voters' mass support of the ANAP. Erbakan and the Welfare Party (Refah Partisi: RP) had begun that gradual process since the 1991 national elections (Yesilada 2002: 67).

In 1995, for the first time in Turkish history, the RP under the leadership of Necmettin Erbakan became the leading party in the country by claiming 21 per cent of the total vote of the general election. Erbakan headed the coalition government of the DYP/RP after charges of corruption brought down the ANAP/DYP coalition in 1996. However, the Islamists could rule the coalition government for just one year. The Turkish military pushed Erbakan's party out of office on 28 February 1997, which is called a 'postmodern coup' in the literature of Turkish politics. The RP was banned on 16 January 1998, after the Constitutional Court ruled that the party's religious platform contradicted Turkey's secular constitution and 'Turkey's philosophy of life' (Hale and Ozbudun 2010: 22). This was not just a state or regime matter, but it concerned a way of living in a secular society based on the separation of religion and worldly affairs. It means the separation of social life, education, family, economics, law, manners, and dress codes from religion.

Turkish secularism was based on a Kemalist worldview and its project of modernity in the form of a legal, constitutional and institutional separation of the secular state and religion. This sounds like democratic secularism with state neutrality towards the space of religion. However, looking at the history of state regulation and management of religion demonstrates a problem of religious pluralism in Turkish society. If laicism is the separation of religion and state affairs as mostly expressed in Turkey, it requires the autonomy of religious organizations, the absence of state intervention in their organization, and independence of the state from every form of religious legitimization of its power. Legal secularity should provide civil and political equality for all Muslim, non-Muslim and non-believer citizens, along with the prohibition of discrimination.

The secular and religious distinction and its hand in juridical, institutional and everyday practices in Turkey cannot guarantee the individual religious freedom of the members of the majority and minority religions. Turkish Republican laicism forced a secular public sphere free from religion, like the means of a Habermasian concept of 'rationalisation of the life-world' (1989), but the state highly securitized secularism and politicized the majority's religion. The Kemalist state banned religious parties and symbols in the public sphere; it controlled all religions, but only financially supported Sunni-Islam (Stepan 2011: 120). According to the 2010 annual data from the Department of Religious Affairs (Diyanet İsleri), the number of mosques (81,984) was higher than the number of schools (67,000) in Turkey, while the construction of religious spaces and places of worship for minorities was illegal. The Turkish state employed 117,541 people under the Diyanet, including the clerics in the mosques. The capacity of all mosques was 25 million; however, the number of people who regularly prayed in the mosque every morning was 2 million. These numbers additionally show that Turkish secularism means a synthesis of Islam and the secular nationalism by the establishment of state control over religion and bureaucratization of Turkish Islam from the top down (Kocan and Oncu 2004: 466).

This research advocates that these contradictory policies and the historicizing and politicizing of secularism by the Kemalist state created the secular/religious binary (Hurd 2011: 176–81), which specifically has been seen in the rise of the AKP in the 2000s and its challenge to the secularist institutions of the Kemalist state. Thus, it can be argued that recent developments in

Turkish politics can be understood in terms of a projection on the Kemalist imagination of the Turkish nation-state. So, this part of the chapter is devoted to highlighting the origins of the secular/religious binary in Turkey.

The historical origins of Turkish-Kurdish rivalry in Turkey

The Kurds are one of the main Muslim indigenous people in Turkey, particularly in the southern region, but being Kurdish is not a singular identity in the region. The Kurdish population constitutes major enclaves in Turkey, Iran, Syria and Armenia; thus, it can be argued that Kurdish nationalism is a product of the interaction between local and global politics in the twentieth century (Yavuz 1998: 10). Some authors note that Kurdish political consciousness in terms of having a separate language, history and culture as an ethnic community dates back to the early 1890s (Natali 2005: 384; Ozoglu 2004: 63), with the movement of Kurdish Teali Cemiyeti (Society for the Advancement of Kurdistan). Yegen argues (2007: 119) that the Kurdish issue has constantly bothered the Turkish nationalism of the same era since the beginning of the twentieth century. However, this second largest 'territorial-linguistic community' of Turkey was provoked to assert its ethnic identity beyond resisting Turkification (Yavuz 1998).

This research accepts that the concept of the Kurdish problem is context-dependent and dynamic. It looks at the Kurdish question in the interstate paradigm of identity and power politics with a consideration of regional and transnational frames of analysis. In this context, this section shows the historical evolution of the Kurdish question in Turkey and the complexity of identifying the problem and the solutions offered through the competing perceptions. This identification of the dominant factors in the evolution of Kurdish identity in historical stages (Yavuz 2001: 2) provides its challenges to Turkish national identity formation:

- **1878–1924:** Resistance against the centralization of the Ottoman state within Naksibendi and Kadiri Islamic networks and identity differentiation.
- **1925–61:** Kurdish identity formation as 'reactionary', 'tribal', and an outcome of regional 'backwardness' to the nation-building project of Mustafa Kemal and the denial of the existence of the Kurds.

- **1962–83:** Secularization of Kurdish identity within the framework of the broader leftist movement in Turkey between the 1960s and 1970s.
- **1983–98:** The PKK-led violent insurgency, internationalization of Kurdish problem.
- **1999–2008:** The arrest of Abdullah Ocalan, the head of the PKK; Europeanization of the Kurdish problem.
- **2009–15** AKP government's Kurdish Initiative
- **2015–present** Resecuritization of Kurdish issue

In Turkey, depending on how one perceives the nature of the struggle, this recognition problem has been identified as the south-east question, the terror problem, or the Kurdish question (Argun 1999: 90). Different definitions of the Turkish nation and national identity portray the problem from different discourses through various inclusion and exclusion perceptions. In other words, it remains diverse, but what has not changed is the Kurdish problem that has emerged with continuously tragic results. Forty-thousand people died and nearly one million people from south-eastern Turkey had to emigrate from their lands. Moreover, thousands of Turkish soldiers and the militants of Kurdistan Workers' Party (PKK= Partiya Karkerên Kurdistan in Kurdish) lost their lives in the armed struggle.

According to Icduygu et al. (1999: 993), the aggressive assimilationist policies of the newly founded Turkish Republic towards other ethnicities hindered the expression of other identities and languages in Turkey. In particular, the state and nation-building deficiencies in Turkish identity caused the exclusion of Kurdish identity and the birth of the problem. On the other hand, Islamist groups claim that the main cause of the Kurdish Problem is the Republican policies of secularization that destroyed the Islamic brotherhood between peoples (Sarigil 2010). Constructing common Islamic ties in the country can end the conflict by weakening the ethnic separatism (Cizre-Sakallioglu 1998).

After the 1980 military intervention, depoliticization of the left and right movements and the promotion of the role of religion to cement the consolidation of nation and society, there was the state project that also provided an atmosphere for growing and politicizing identity politics. Although the Constitution of 1982 defined a Turk by stating, 'Everyone bound to the Turkish state through the bond of citizenship is a Turk' in a civic nationalist sense, the existence of separate Kurdish identity was not recognized. Article

89 of the 1982 Constitution stated that 'no political party may concern itself with the defence, development, or diffusion of any non-Turkish language or culture; nor may seek to create minorities within our frontiers or to destroy our national unity'.

Moreover, Article 3 of the Law 2932 on the publications in other languages declared Turkish as the 'mother tongue' of all Turkish citizens and prohibited the use and dissemination of other languages as a mother tongue, which, in reaction, turned the Kurdish language into a symbol of Kurdish nationhood (Yavuz 1999: 14). As a reaction to the TIS of the new interpretation of state policy, Kurdish ethno-nationalism intensified the ethnic struggle (Donmez 2007). On the other hand, Turkish nationalist perception of the Kurdish question, in particular the ultra-nationalist MHP's perception, was based on denial until the 1990s. For its followers, 'Kurdish-Turks' were open to the manipulation of external separatist powers, and the solution was Turkification by building the consciousness of belonging to the Turkish nation because 'Kurds are the Turks who have forgotten their Turkishness' (Bora and Can 2004).

Commonly, the Kurdish problem has been seen as an issue of regional economic development or a military security matter rather than an ethnopolitical problem (Saracoglu 2009: 240). The Kemalist state authorities claimed that their citizens of Kurdish descent enjoyed full rights as Turkish citizens (Gunter 2000: 849). The official refusal of the existence of a Kurdish problem defined it as a terror problem. In this perspective, if there was a struggle for human rights, it was a democratic demand for every citizen. Connectedly, this perception within the official discourse tended to ground the militarization of the Kurdish problem and the securitization of the Kurdish identity in the 1990s on the outcome of the Cold War bipolarity and the rising leftist discourse. Thus, when it became a national security concern (Ozcan 2011), the state discourse addressed it in a militarized and authoritarian manner.

This literature on Turkey's Kurdish question exhibits the existing diversity in understanding and naming the problem. It can be said that different definitions of the issue bring out different solutions. Yegen (2011) elaborates on the Kurdish problem using perceptions of three distinct Turkish nationalisms: mainstream, extreme right-wing, and left-wing Turkish nationalism. The mainstream version views the discontent of Kurds and their rebellion of 1925 as the resistance of pre-modern tribal social structures to the foundation of the nation-state. In other words, it was nothing, but the resistance to the logic of revolution and resistance of the past to the present. With the cessation of Kurdish revolts in the 1950s, the component of the mainstream perception had a new focus through the discourse of massive underdevelopment in southeastern Anatolia and the lack of economic integration between the region and the national market. The left-wing Turkish nationalism referred to the problem with the same vocabulary such as regional inequalities, feudal relations, and regional backwardness; however, this perception also recognized the ethnocultural aspect of the Kurdish question.

A racist version of Turkish nationalism appeared and became a political movement in the 1960s and the 1970s. Yegen (2011: 236) cites from this perspective's spectacular intellectual representative, Nihal Atsiz, who suggested that the reason behind the Kurdish unrest was foreign incitement and that they had no alternative but to leave the country as the Armenians had. One of the most noteworthy findings of Yegen is that all of the Turkish nationalisms perceived that Kurds could become Turkish; therefore, Kurds did not experience massive discrimination in citizenship practices like non-Muslim citizens did. That was because the Kurds were expected to be Turks under the umbrella of a homogenized, mono-linguistic Muslim nation. Significantly, he concludes that both the Turkish state and ordinary Turkish citizens have been revising their perception of Kurds. They used to believe the problem could be solved through re-Turkification in massive assimilation, but not anymore. Yegen concludes that building connections with non-Muslim inhabitants by saying 'Jewish Kurds' (2011: 240) or 'Armenian Kurds' indicates that Turkish nationalists perceive Kurds as a disloyal, untrustworthy people on Turkish territory.

The emergence of post-Kemalist nation-state identity

Regarding the emergence of Turkey's post-Kemalist identity, this section considers the developments brought about by the military coup of September 1980 that transformed Turkey beyond the paradigm of the 'first modernity' (Atasoy 2009: 70). First of all, the Kemalist paradigm has been faced with challenges under the neo-liberal restructuring of the Turkish economy after 1980. The consequence of neo-liberal globalization led to the emergence of an 'ideology of the excluded' (Onis 2001: 282) in demanding economic and political power from the Kemalist state. By reference to social injustices, two traditional 'others' of the state participated in the identity politics: the growing concerns of Islamic rich capitalist religious groups over political rights, and the emergence of Kurdish claims to cultural rights in the 1990s. These two groups became the main determinants of New Turkey in the 2000s.

In the 1990s, it seemed that Islamic orientation to the politics of neo-liberal social and global transformation had been more successful than the Kemalist paradigm's adaptation to globalization (Gambetti 2009). Turkish Islamic groups have participated in the institutionalization of neo-liberalism, and some of them have even moved beyond the national borders and turned into global movements by enlarging civic engagement in the economy, particularly the Naqshbandi religious order, the Nurcu community, and the Gulen community (Atasoy 2009: 108).

By the 1990s, one of the results of the Gulf War was the appearance in the news media of the tragedy of Iraqi Kurds, which caused economic and social internationalization of the Kurdish question (Yegen 2007: 135–6). The post-Cold War ideas of liberalization and globalization concerning identity, difference, culture and human rights contributed to the visibility of the discontent of the Kurdish masses and the rise of Kurdish demands. Turgut Ozal, the prime minister of Turkey between 1983 and 1999 and president from 1990 until 1993 acknowledged the Kurdish reality. He responded to the international and domestic developments of the 1991 Gulf War and the Kurdish question; in this regard, he met with the leaders of two Iraqi Kurdish factions, Mustafa Barzani and Jalal Talabani. Ozal's liberalization of the country's policy transformed the discourse of Kurdish nationalism, demanding their collective identity in a democratic context. The Kurdish parties could enter parliament, representing Kurdish demands through non-violent means, although members of the parties had close relationships with the PKK.

After the Cold War, the ideology and discourse of the PKK had a mutation that was shifting towards concepts such as 'democratic solution' and enjoying human rights within the existing borders of Turkey (Romano 2006: 124). In 1999, the capture of Abdullah Ocalan, the leader of the PKK, and becoming a candidate country for membership in the EU opened the door to constitutional liberalization in line with the EU requirements relating to the Kurdish problem in Turkey. Although Islamist groups and the RP came out against Turkey's application for membership in the European Union in the 1990s, Recep Tayyip Erdogan's newly formed party, the Justice and Development Party (Adalet ve Kalkinma Partisi: AKP), emphasized its strong support for Turkish entry into the EU in its election campaign of 2002. Although the party had Islamic roots and supporters, they changed their discourse to form an ideological moderation in domestic politics. Sayari notes (2007: 201) that Erdogan and his group were convinced that the state elites would not permit a pro-Islamist party with anti-system tendencies to stay in power even if it controlled a plurality of seats in the parliament. Discursive moderation of the party ideology strengthened the party's credibility and legitimacy with the Turkish voters, winning support from the conservative and nationalist voters. In 2002, the election was a victory for the AKP by gaining 34 per cent of the total vote. Indeed, the weakness and fragmentation of the political opposition of the 1990s have played a beneficial role in the emergence of the AKP's dominance in the post-2002 Turkish party system.

The development of Turkey in the 2000s led by the pro-Islamist AKP has affected many core problematic areas of national policies, discourses and identities in Turkey, such as the representation of Islamic groups in politics and the acknowledgement of cultural and political rights of Kurds and non-Muslim minorities. The process of Turkey's integration with the European Union empowered the ruling party AKP's legitimacy in transforming Turkish domestic and foreign policy, particularly Kemalist state structure and identity politics, such as highly sensitive issues involving religion, the military, and minorities (Toktas and Aras 2009). The EU membership process required the broadening of individual and liberal freedoms and consolidating European norms and values in Turkey. To satisfy the EU criteria, Turkey had to integrate the demands of identity politics into the national identity.

The liberal discourse on the question strengthened in academic and political debates in terms of democratization in the first decade of the 2000s. The historical steps towards recognizing certain political and cultural rights of Kurds were taken. The amendments on cultural rights with the candidacy of Turkey to join the European Union provided the instruments for the massive production and reproduction of Kurdishness in Turkey, and thus the Kurds gained a status that has a possibility of hindering their assimilation into Turkishness (Yegen 2007: 178). But, since 2006, the national disappointment regarding relations with the EU has triggered the anxiety of Turkish nationalism regarding the Kurdish question in Turkey (Tocci 2007: 141). In this context, Celik and Blum's workshop study (2007) demonstrated that the failure of the EU process would lead to a re-emergence of a more aggressive Turkish nationalism with a mixture of anti-Western and anti-imperialist sentiments (2007: 577). But an EU process that went well would create a stable political environment within Turkey (2007: 575). The EU would be a national project that both Turks and Kurds could support and would create an environment in which moderation and mutual accommodation are possible with the construction of the 'self-confidence' of both the Turkish state and the Kurdish community.

Moreover, the US occupation of Iraq changed the discourse of Kurdish nationalism by the establishment of Kurdish self-administration as a federal state in Iraq since 2003. Due to increasing sympathy with the Kurdish political authority among Kurds (Yegen 2007: 178), the scenarios of the demands of rebels for the independence of the Kurds in Turkey added a new dimension to the Kurdish problem (Saracoglu 2009: 655). That was an anxious prospect for Turkey, sourcing a fundamental change in Turkish nationalism's image of Kurds.

Indeed, there are diverse opinions on how the Kurdish national demands are being articulated within the discourse of democracy, and what is the political project of the Kurdish national movement that it seeks to build (Gunes 2009: 262). A federal type solution for Kurdish demands in Turkey is debated (Ergil 2009). Accordingly, Canefe (2008: 394) notes that Turkey's Kurds prefer to identify themselves as a part of Turkey in the European Union, instead of as citizens of a possible united Kurdistan. Contrarily, some scholars argued that taking liberal steps on the issue demonstrated that the problem is beyond human rights and democracy; whether the PKK espouses a separate Kurdish state is clear.

Furthermore, the rising tension of the reactions towards the attacks of the PKK and spreading anti-Kurdish discourse in popular media and the internet have caused the Kurds to become the 'primary other' (Arsan 2013; Yegen 2007) of the Turkish nation in daily life, with the recognition of them as separatist people. The link between the Kurds and the PKK has become more visible. The attachment between the Kurds and PKK separatism marginalized attitudes against the Kurdish people in everyday life (Saracoglu 2009: 653). In this context of regarding Turkish people's views on the issue, Mesut Yegen

(2011) argued that Turkish nationalism's perception of the Kurdish question has had an evolution from 'banditry to disloyalty'.

Besides, different perspectives of Kurdish nationalism position Turkey's Kurds differently in the power struggle. For instance, the PKK and the Peoples' Democratic Party (Halklarin Demokratik Partisi: HDP) can be seen as the manifestation of a secular and leftist version of Kurdish nationalism. Like the other type of Kurdish nationalism in Turkey, traditional elite nationalism and religious-conservative nationalism have mainly been represented under the mainstream centre-right parties concerning socio-economic reasons (Sarigil 2010). They are seen as 'loyalists' or 'pro-state' (Somer 2011: 273) in Turkish political life. Looking at this profile of Kurdish nationalism demonstrates why the AKP benefited from rising Islamic conservatism in the south-east part of the country and the weakness of opposition parties that adopted a security-orientated approach to the Kurdish conflict. Before the AKP came to power, secularist CHP had been a supporter of a democratic resolution. The sentiments against the government's conservative agenda failed their social democratic discourse. The PKK's influence on the HDP created a security dilemma for Kemalist secularists; hence they could not cooperate with Kurdish leftists to cope with the AKP's Islamic conservative political identity. Kurds preferred to ally with the Islamists in the transformation of the Kemalist nation-state identity for the consolidation of democracy in the last decade. In this manner, polarization over secularism contributed to the complexity of the Kurdish question.

The Europeanization challenge of Kemalist nation-state identity

One of the main assumptions of this study is that national identities are defined by the actor's interaction with, and relationship to, other actors in international and domestic politics. In the context of European identity, it can be argued that there is no single European identity (Checkel and Katzenstein 2009: 213); this is because the various nations of Europe have very different mean levels of European identity and very different experiences in European integration. The topic of identity in European affairs would need to be defined in terms of the various and confusing meanings of 'identity' (Cerutti and Lucarelli 2008: 3–4); thus, European identities should be understood in a broader sense in terms of pluralism, multi-culturalism and unity in diversity (Delanty and

Rumford 2005). The purpose of this section is to give an overview of the sociocultural aspects of Turkey–EU relations and to highlight the findings of some of the previous studies that were conducted to address the cultural debates on Turkey's place in Europe.

The image of the Turks in Europe has been formed and reformed for 700 years due to socio-political and cultural reasons. During the expansion period of the Ottoman Empire, particularly the fifteenth century, the time of the conquest of Istanbul by Fatih Sultan Mehmet, the image was of 'threat', 'fear', 'grand', 'enemy', 'barbaric' and 'cruel'. Muslim and Turk had no differences in the Middle Age perception of Europe, and they were considered to be the 'enemy of Christianity'. As significant historical events, the expansion of the Balkans and the occupation of Vienna had a negative impact on the minds of the Europeans (Tilly 1990: 273–6). Kula argues (2006: 307–20) that newspapers such as *Die Newen Zeitungen* printed the events, conquests, and occupations that spread the fear of Turks and created a mass fear and common perception of Turks that was dominant in the memories of Europeans during almost two centuries in Eastern Europe.

After the eighteenth century, the fall of the Ottoman Empire caused changes in the perceptions of Europeans regarding the Turks. Reformation, Enlightenment and colonialism movements transformed the social, philosophical and political relationships of Europeans with 'others' (Kula 2006). Turks had not been a 'threat' anymore in the eyes of the powerful bourgeoisie of Europe, and had been more of a mystery of the Orient (Said 1977) to discover. The spread of the movement in the works of art, music and literature that was called *Turquerie* was a main indicator in the early modern age. The Turkish culture, way of life and dressing became fashionable, especially in France, where people had their portraits done in Turkish robes and kaftans. In the diaries of travellers and merchants and the reports of envoys and consuls, the Turks were represented from both a positive and a negative perspective according to the influence of romanticism and exoticism (Soykut 2007: 203). They were 'religion-wise' the 'others' in the Middle Ages; this situation changed slightly, and they became 'culture-wise' the 'others' (Delanty 1995; Goody 2005).

The nineteenth-century visual representation of the Turks was the image of 'the sick man of Europe' that dominated the main character of the eastern question with the collapse of the Ottomans. Another important phenomenon that had a vast impact on European perceptions of the Turks was the Turkish

Independence War, which took place after the First World War, and the image of Mustafa Kemal Ataturk, 'the founding father of modern Turkey' was printed in the newspapers of many countries of the world (Colakoglu 2018).

Turkey's modernization and Westernization have been the continuous state identity policy of Turkey since the construction of an official discourse by Mustafa Kemal Ataturk in the 1920s (Ozyurek 2006). As indicated before, Turkey had taken Europe as a model of modernization (Kamali 2006) long before even the founding of the Republic. Turkish history has in some respects a striking number of parallels with that of Western Europe (Zurcher and Linden 2007: 68). The impartiality policy of Turkey during the Second World War was followed by the Western alliance foreign policy during the Cold War period. In this foreign policy context, the relations between the EC/EU and Turkey date back to 1963, the year of the signature of the association agreement. Moreover, in the 1960s Germany and the central European countries required a workforce from Turkey to repair the damage of war and strengthen their industries. The migration of Turkish guest-workers who came from rural areas with economic woes had a negative impact on hosts' perceptions of the Turks (Kaya and Kentel 2005). Although good impressions and friendships have developed between the groups, the image of migrant workers in Europe has become a stereotype of the general image of the Turk in Europe (Burcoglu 1999). Turkey's strategic significance during the Cold War encouraged its definition as 'European' (Coban 2012), but since at least the early 1970s, Europe has sought to develop a collective identity based on shared civilizational values, thus, the definition of 'European' shifted to what was described as the 'democratic tradition' of European integration (Smith and Wright 1999). Although signing the Ankara Treaty was recognition of Turkey's Europeanness, the paradigm change at the end of the Cold War caused an increase in debates on democracy, human rights and identity in international relations that triggered reinterpretation of Turkish identity in Turkey and Europe (Yilmaz 2007).

The economic, political and social factors gained importance in Europe's approach to Turkey regarding the EC, which began to put greater emphasis on standards of the candidate countries to have institutions guaranteeing democracy, human rights and the rule of law, and respecting and protecting minority rights, formulated by the Copenhagen Summit of 1993. As Verney points out (2007) Turkey's image did not correspond with the democratic European ideal in the 1990s. Turkey applied for full membership in the EC in 1987. After the Customs Union agreement was signed between Turkey and the EU in 1995, Turkey adopted a major package of constitutional change for democratic reformation and finally, the European Council granted Turkey candidacy in 1999 in Helsinki.

After the Cold War, European decision-makers started to construct their own security culture beyond the NATO security agenda. For instance, migration as a source of new insecurities has been seen as a challenge for European integration. This has had major implications for Turkey's accession to the membership. Turkey's large population and its cultural differences have been questioned after the Eastern enlargement of the EU. With the dissolution of the communist regimes of the Central and Eastern European countries, the Turkish application for full membership lost its significance for the EU with the emerging process of integration of Western and Eastern Europe. Turkey was pushed to the back of the queue as the post-Cold War Europe redefined itself (Bilgin 2009). This period made more apparent the issue of human rights in crystallizing the difference between perceptions of security in Turkey and Europe in the individual, societal and national dimensions of the term. In a nutshell, before the Cold War, Turks were the significant 'other' of Europeans over which they defined the strategic considerations of their identity. During the Cold War period, Turkey occupied the buffer state role as a barrier to the Soviet threat; thus, this perception of Turks as the others of Europe lost its significance. With the end of the Cold War era, the debate about Turkey's identity, culture and place in Europe arose once again.

Although Turkey became a candidate country for EU membership in 1999, the 9/11 attacks in 2001 changed the paradigm yet again. The aftermath of the Islamic terrorist events of 11 September 2001 and the later bombings in London and Madrid that resulted in the association of terrorism with Islam in Europe (Canan-Sokullu 2011). The events provoked mutual aggression and cultural conflicts, in other words, like 'the clash of civilisations' (Huntington 2002) that defined 'Islam' as a civilization confronting the West or Europe. The identity and security concerns of Turkey and the EU diversified in the definition of the threats in and outside the community. The EU put more focus on the military and technological dimensions of security as it is seen in border management. On the other hand, Turkey's political transformation had consequences for the redefinition of national security and the formulation of Turkish foreign policy in general. The EU accession process encouraged a change of the tools that are used in foreign policymaking (Altunisik and Martin 2011: 579). For instance, the military's power (symbolic and actual) in Turkey's political discourse has decreased (Bilgin 2011: 78). Parallel to this, Turkey put more emphasis on diplomacy in foreign policy and less emphasis on the use of force in prioritizing its economic interest. Moreover, in the shadow of the clash of civilization thesis, Turkey's conservative elites benefited from the post 9/11 atmosphere and US advocacy of moderate Islam as a state model for the Muslim world (Eligur 2010: 282).

After the trauma of 28 February 1997, in other words, Turkey's postmodern coup, the Islamists came back with new defence tactics with the discourse of democracy and utilizing European Union membership as a political opportunity and a liberal tool kit for the Islamist demands (Eligur 2010: 278). Turkish nation/state identity has been reconstructed by new emerging political elites of pro-Islamist AKP and Kurdish parties through using the EU as a legitimate power (Zucconi 2009: 25), and it has shaped what constitutes Turkish foreign policy. In the 2000s, the EU accession process provided a much-needed legitimization of the pro-Islamist AKP government, and democratic reform would also guarantee the party's political power, given the unlikelihood of the party being banned like its predecessors (Narbone and Tocci 2007: 239).

The EU conditionality triggered a process of structural change in the Turkish political system that is a response to the policies of the European Union. Changes that were closely identified with Europe have been made to direct attention to the problems of democracy as human rights and its consolidation (Keyman 2007; Ozbudun 2009). However, many of the secular elites, the military and Turkish nationalists were uncomfortable with the political reforms promoted through the Europeanization process (Muftuler-Bac 2005: 21). The harmonization packages entered into force by the AKP brought significant changes (Parker 2009: 1093) to the freedom of association, and deterrence against torture and mistreatment; and they also amended the Penal Code, the Law on State Security Courts, the Press Law, the Law on Political Parties, the Law on the Use of the Right of Petition (Gunter 2007: 117–23; Cizre 2004: 109). In addition to these, they introduced significant legal changes expanding freedom of expression, religious freedom and the right to a retrial. A state-centric, security-orientated vision of Turkey that had several serious problems (Oktem et al. 2010), such as the democratic deficit, a legitimacy crisis, human rights violations, minority rights, torture, the rule of law, and economic instability showed unexpected fundamental developments in the creation of a more rights-based citizenship regime.

Even though the years between 2001 and 2005 were very significant, from the adoption of the National Program for membership to the launch of the negotiations at the end of 2005, public survey reports found that there had been a dramatic drop in the support expressed by the Turkish public since the continued dispute over Cyprus suspended Turkey's EU negotiation talks on eight chapters in December 2006. According to the Survey of Turkey's EU Perception (published in 2007 by the International Strategic Research Organization), the rise of the 'privileged partnership' debate and sentimental issues on Cyprus engendered the fall of support of Turkish citizens for EU accession (from 75 per cent to 45 per cent) since the negotiations started in 2005. The percentage of people who think 'the EU does not treat equally towards Turkey' was 81 per cent in November 2006. In 2007, the Turkish foreign minister and chief negotiator with the EU, Ali Babacan, claimed that certain negative statements and perceptions of European officials and politicians led the Turkish people to think that they were 'not wanted' in the EU. The EU leaders' expression of a 'privileged partnership' instead of full membership in a deal with the arguments on Turkey's population, geography, and culture 'would weaken the Turkish public's trust in the EU'. Hakan Yilmaz's research project (2009), which was financed by the EU, aimed to uncover the European perceptions of Turkey, and trace the Euro-sceptic narrative. The research found that 60 per cent of the respondents agreed with the view that the EU treated Turkey with double standards.

Similarly, in September 2013 Turkish EU Affairs Minister Egemen Bagis argued that Turkey would probably never join the European Union because of prejudicial attitudes of the bloc's existing members. In this context, some factors were underlining this downward trend of Turkish people's perceptions of the EU. As an important factor, the asymmetrical relationship with the EU increased negative perceptions in Turkey (Taraktas 2008: 254). For instance, the Customs Union agreement established an asymmetrical relationship, in that Turkey had to comply with decisions but could not participate in the decision making. Also, Turkey's exclusion from the list of candidate countries in 1998 strengthened the public impression that the EU was using 'prospective accession' to exploit Turkey through the Customs Union.

Moreover, the effects of the EU on breaking Turkey's taboos have played a role in Turkish Euro-scepticism, specifically in the issues of the Cyprus policy, the Kurdish problem, civil-military relations and Armenian genocide claims. One of the significant factors has been a mutual rise in negative perceptions of the Muslim and Western world in the post 9/11 process. In addition to the anti-EU discourse, a nationalist reaction with an anti-USA and anti-globalization character began to appear in Turkish public discourse due to the growing instability and the human costs of the Iraq War. Since the crucial March 1, 2003 decision not to allow US troops through Turkish territory during the invasion of Iraq, Turkey had moved as an independent actor in foreign policy (Ozcan 2011: 74). The problematic relations with the USA have contributed to a major increase in anti-American and anti-West sentiments in Turkey (Uslu et al. 2005: 6).

In this context, European reluctance to include Turkey was not negligible. The 'privileged partnership' and 'open-ended process' debates raised by the EU leaders as well as vocal rejections by the public to Turkey's EU membership contrasted with the Kemalist idea of the 'grandeur' of the nation and produced a feeling of being undermined (Taraktas 2008: 255). Considering the historical indicators that draw a general portrait of a reluctant Europe for the inclusion of Turkey in the Union, on the other side of the coin, a deeper understanding of Turkish perspectives should also be considered in explaining both new Turkish self-identification and cultural debates in the context of Turkey's place in Europe. In this regard, as Canefe and Bora (2003: 126) suggested, the debates should go beyond the accession issue:

> Europe constitutes a key part of Turkey's relations with the outside world. However, it would be a mistake to reduce the Turkish society and the state's relations with Europe to the issue of inclusion in the European Union. Turkey has a long history of opposing, admiring, copying, denying, naming, and judging things European. In this regard, the Turkish modernization project, and its defenders, as well as its critics, have a complex relationship with the idea of Europe and what constitutes European identity. The current state of relations between European states and Turkey, revolving primarily around the issue of inclusion in the EU, thus must be examined considering this cultural background and the political debates that lie beyond the accession debate.

The changing discourse of Turkish foreign policy under the AKP government

In the second term of AKP government there was more emphasis on using soft power with dialogue, economic liberalization, and economic interdependency, which led to an increase in efforts towards engagement with other regions, especially with the Middle East due to freezing Turkey–EU relations and rising Euro-scepticism in Turkey. The main axis of Turkish foreign policy before the AKP government in the 2000s was the Turkey–United States–Israel triangle (Cagaptay 2013). In opposition to that, during the AKP's second era, Israel has became the most unfriendly country to Turkey, according to 40 per cent of the people (TESEV 2010) due to the events in Gaza in late 2008 and early 2009, the Davos incident between Prime Minister Recep Tayyip Erdogan and Israeli President Shimon Peres, and the flotilla episode with Israel's military intervention on the flagship Mavi Marmara in March 2010. The United States was also seen as the second most unfriendly country to Turkey by 33 per cent of the people of Turkey, followed by Greece and France. On the other hand, the countries considered most friendly towards Turkey were Iran (13 per cent), Azerbaijan (10 per cent), the United States (10 per cent), and Pakistan (9 per cent). Consequently, it seems that EU membership and alliance with the West lost its attraction in Turkey while interest in the affairs of the East and Muslim countries was rising. Turkey has improved its relations with its regional neighbours and involvement in the Middle East in increasing economic and political relations with the Muslim countries.

Turkey's improving relations with Iran and its vote against the resolution of the UN Security Council about the Iranian nuclear programme caused questioning of whether it was shifting its axis, moving away from its traditional Western orientation to the East or the Islamic world. Since 2008, indicators of Islamization of international relations increased (Criss 2010: 53). In July 2008 during the African summit, Ankara hosted Sudan's president, Omar al-Bashir, who is responsible for the massacre of 200,000 non-Arab Africans. Moreover, the deterioration of Turkish–Israeli relations after the Gaza War (2008–2009) created a scandal at the Davos World Economic Forum on 2 March 2009. Turkish prime minister Erdogan in anger shouted insults at Israel's President Shimon Peres in the meeting. The AKP government's relationship with Hamas also strengthened the view that Turkey has been diverging from a Western orientation in its Middle East policies. The AKP's emphasis on Turkey's geopolitical position and its cultural and historical connections to be a regional and global power have changed the axis of its relations with regional powers. But internal and international dynamics create new challenges to follow a democratic project, as was seen in the Kurdish issue.

The Minister of Foreign Affairs Ahmet Davutoglu's (2009–14) 'Strategic Depth' approach (Davutoglu 2006), was blended with five new principles: the balance between security and freedom; zero problems with neighbours; multi-dimensional and multi-track policies; a new diplomatic discourse based on firm flexibility; and rhythmic diplomacy. Based on a new geographic imagination (Aras and Fidan 2009) and civilizational geopolitical vision (Bilgin and Bilgic 2011), the AKP's conservative ideology repositioned and reconstructed Turkey's political terrain in foreign policy in terms of creating a new sense of a macro-identity among populations that share the Ottoman Islamic heritage and targeting zero problems with Turkey's neighbours. In the new geographic imagination, Turkey is located outside Western civilization and it is imagined as the leader of its civilization, which changes the definitions of 'us' and 'others' (Bilgin and Bilgic 2011: 173). The logic of this transformation is a worldview that is constructed based on a selective reading of Ottoman administrative practices in the issues of religious, cultural and ethnic identity. In this regard, it offers re-articulation of Turkish nation-state identity from a post-Kemalist perspective which imagines a New Turkey.

The literature review on New Turkey's identity

Is the New Turkey Western and Muslim? Or Middle Eastern and secular? There are multiple answers to these questions based on which knowledge is referred to in history and politics. Looking at the final years of the Ottoman Empire and its failure in political and economic systems, the West was seen as a source of insecurity but also the inspiration for establishing a new system (Bilgin 2011: 74). Thus, Turkey's identity and security policies came to run in parallel with Europe and the West. Although the military and economic Westernization process of Turkey dates back to the times of the Ottoman Empire, which was a way of improving security at home and abroad, it has been recognized as a fundamental principle of the Republic since 1923. The difference between the two periods (Fokas 2008: 88) is the twin aims of Westernization and Europeanization of Turkey linked with the secularist programme of its founder and first president M. Kemal Ataturk (1881–1938). As Thomas W. Smith noted in 'Between Allah and Ataturk: Liberal Islam in Turkey' (2005: 308), Turkey became the only secular, democratic, pro-Western country in the Islamic world. During the Cold War, Turkey maintained Westernization in the Kemalist line and had distant relations with the Arab and Islamic world. Security reasons, such as the Soviet threat, also pushed Turkey further to the West. NATO membership and Turkey's Western-orientated policies contributed to the country's Western identity (Bozdaglioglu 2003).

With the end of the Cold War, Turkey searched for a new identity in international relations. Although Turkey became a candidate country of the EU in 1999, the 9/11 Islamic terrorist attacks in New York diversified the definition of the threats in and outside Europe. The EU has put more focus on the military and technological dimensions of security as has been seen in border management. The growth of identity-based conflicts and 'securitised' culture (Waever 2000) through the 'war on terror' has repositioned Turkey and redefined its importance for the West. While Turkey historically and strategically emphasized its Western identity over its Eastern identity, the main references changed from being Western and secular to being Muslim and democratic. In other words, Turkey's 'moderate' Islamic character became 'marketable' (Tank 2006: 470) as a model for the other Muslim countries. This phenomenon brought forth a new agenda for Europe in dealing with Turkey's position within the framework of 'the clash of civilisations' (Huntington 2002) and its implications for the country's EU accession. In the context of the relationship between democracy and Islam in the post 9/11 era, Turkey's Muslim population and Western values changed the currency of the idea that it is a bridge between the East and the West, Christianity, and Islam (Somer 2007). However, Kemalist secularist circles began to express their anxieties about the idea that Turkey was represented as a model of Muslim rather than secular democracy (Yavuz 2009: 245). Concerning this process, Binnaz Toprak (2009) published an outstanding empirical study that proved the fear in secularist circles of the increasing social and political pressure of religious lifestyles upon secular lifestyles.

In this context, rather than the Muslim–secular dichotomy, with a focus on the concept of 'national identity', this study sheds light on the 'process' of the emergence of New Turkey's identity through a power struggle of different nationalist discourses and reveals Turkish national identity and foreign policy discourses to be reproductive and constitutive of each other. Hereby, it exposes how Turkey discursively constructs its own identity; thus, it differs from the following publications analysed Turkish foreign policy.

In his book *Strategic Depth*, the main architect of the New Turkish foreign policy, Foreign Minister Ahmet Davutoglu argued (2006) that the Kemalist Republican elite neglected the Ottoman past and cultural ties in the Middle East and caused Turkey's alienation from its historical and religious ties with the Arab/Islamic world. Given this perspective, some previous decision-makers, such as the president Turgut Ozal (1989–93) had defined his approach as neo-Ottomanism and the coalition government's foreign minister Ismail Cem (1997–2002) represented Turkey as 'straddling civilizational divides' (Bilgin and Bilgic 2011: 173) between the West and the Islamic world. He aimed to develop cultural and economic relations with its neighbours; however, Turkey's relationship with its neighbours inevitably focused on security and military relations at his time; Turkey had an 'active', but hard/confrontational policy in the 1990s (Hale 2012; Oran 2011; Bilgin 2005), mostly tied to the Kurdish issue (Altunisik and Martin 2011: 570). Unlike during the 1990s, Turkey developed a deeper relationship with the Arab/Islamic world in the 2000s. In particular, the problematic relationship with the EU, growing security interests in the post 9/11 process, and the rational approach towards the West have encouraged new strategic thinking in Turkish foreign policy. According to Davutoglu's discourse, Turkey could not wait forever at the EU door (Murinson 2006: 952) and needed to form its 'axis' to develop a re-engagement with the Middle East, the Balkans, the Caucasus, and even with Africa. The representatives of the AKP claimed that the Middle East was not an alternative to Europe and that Turkey has had active diplomacy in the region to bring stability to Europe (Rumelili 2011: 241). They argued that the traditional Kemalist foreign policy of Turkey had a focus on the importance of military security and balance of power that was based on securitization and threat definition. This perspective hindered improving relationships with the region. In the last decade, the military's power (symbolic and actual) in Turkey's political discourse has decreased (Bilgin 2011: 78). Parallel to this, Turkey put more emphasis on diplomacy in foreign policy and less emphasis on the use of force in prioritizing its economic interest. The cost-benefit calculations and adoption of a pragmatic approach in relationships with the EU and the US caused a 'shift of axis' from the transatlantic to Eurasia, and Turkey's pivotal role as a benign regional power (Onis and Yilmaz 2009) emerged a Middle-Easternization (Oguzlu 2008) tendency in Turkish foreign policy. Growing disagreements over Iraq, Iran, Syria and Kurds have determined mutual relationships, especially with the US, and increased speculations about Turkey's foreign policy choices.

The Iraq War and Turkey's 'no' vote for the deployment of US troops on 1 March 2003 had provided an example of Turkey's shifting identity (Tank 2006: 469). Regarding Tank's point, Oguzlu and Kibaroglu (2009: 577–8) claimed that the West's approach towards Turkey led Turkish decision-makers to adopt different policies. In the post-Cold War era, Turkey's membership in NATO had no longer guaranteed its place in the Western international community. That means, not just that Turkey repositioned itself, but the West's new perspective located it in the Greater Middle East rather than in Europe. In Cagaptay's (2013) analysis, Turkey's revisionist new position neither challenges the Western order nor changes its axis from the West, it has broader international cooperation in the world within deeply embedded economic and political bonds with the Western world. These bonds rest on more than shared strategic alignment (2013: 803). Turkey's political tradition and success in foreign policy, democracy, secularism and women's emancipation have been consolidated within the Western order.

The notion of geographic imagination is employed by Aras and Fidan (2009) to analyse new official Turkish political rhetoric. They argue that renewed geographic imagination and activism in foreign policy launched intensive security, trade, energy and cooperation relations in the Eurasian region. Fidan (2010: 109) argued that Turkey reconstructed its foreign policy in parallel to the post-Cold War developments. However, it failed due to a lack of confidence. AKP's new political elite changed this tendency and Turkey has had self-confidence for the democratic reform process and reformulation of foreign relations. Like Fidan, Sozen (2010: 106–8) used the concept of 'self-confidence' in explanation of the paradigm shift in Turkish foreign policy by the revival of Ottomanism in national and international policies of Turkey. Instead of a Kemalist positivist-modernist narrative which is built on the rejection of Ottoman heritage, Turkey's relations with Arabs, Muslims and Kurds moved to a resurgence and normalization track in the revival period. Neo-Ottoman orientation brought Turkey closer to the Islamic world. In Yesiltas's analysis

(2013), a liberal-orientated geopolitical practice and a conservative Islamist vision represented the main rupture from the old Kemalist geopolitical vision in Turkish foreign policy. Ozkan (2014: 134) referred to Ahmet Davutoglu's writings of the 1980s and 1990s and reminded that Davutoglu believed the Western model democracy was not adequate for the Islamic world. The lack of religious values turned the West into dangerous mechanical supremacy; thus, the political regimes of the Middle East would derive their legitimacy from Islam. He explained it as the logic behind why Davutoglu supported An-Nahda in Tunisia and the Muslim Brotherhood in Egypt and Syria with a pan-Islamist vision but ignored the influence of Arab nationalism, sectarianism, secularism and socialism in the region (2014: 136).

Significantly, Bilgin and Bilgic (2011) investigated how concepts of civilizational geopolitics have created a 'new geographic imagination' under the AKP. They highlighted what is different about Davutoglu and AKP's approach to the New Turkey. In the new geographic imagination, Turkey is located outside Western civilization and it is imagined as the leader of its civilization, which changes the definitions of 'us' and 'others' (2011: 173).

Conclusion

Self-imagination of a nation is about how a nation reflects on its identity in the presence of others; in other words, self-image is always constructed vis-à-vis another. In this context, throughout this part, it is demonstrated that Turkey's self-image is often constructed vis-à-vis the West or Europe. Kemalists imagined Turkey as a secular, modern, Western and a Turkic country with a specific focus on Republican times. The Republican elites' perception of the Turkish 'self' as European with a civilizing mission caused Turkey's inclusion in different Western institutions like NATO and the EC provided necessary institutional grounds for the statist elite to restructure domestic politics. This part defined three main challenges of Turkey's Kemalist nation-state identity which played a role in the emergence of the new Turkey: the post-Cold War international paradigm shift, Europeanization process, and the domestic power struggle over the reconstruction of Turkey's identity.

Since 2007, under the leadership of Recep Tayyip Erdogan, the reformist Islamists have identified a reimagined Ottoman imperial project and searched for a non-territorially defined identity more effective in conditioning and shaping the state's policies and the society's perception of 'self'. For a comprehensive understanding of this normative change in Turkish politics, this study contributes to the existing literature by analysing the power struggle in the revision of Turkish national identity and Turkish foreign policy. In this manner, this study argues that there are different Turkeys with different imaginations of the nation and its place in the world. In comparing the different discourses of Turkish nationalism via the case studies in the national and international context, it shows Turkish identity as a negotiated concept and deconstructs long-lasting polarizations in definitions of Turkish national identity, particularly essentialist, naturalized concepts of the nation that predominantly hinder the solutions to live together. Also, the questions of how the 'us/other' relations emerge through these discourses and how various ideological positions are formed, are useful to shed light on Turkey's place in the world and its international relations.

2

Theory and methodology
Critical discourse analysis

Introduction

This chapter argues that the discipline of International Relations can benefit from interdisciplinary studies to analyse the role of new actors in world politics. To analyse the case of contemporary Turkey's identity, it appeals to nationalism and media studies. In this context, the chapter employs these studies through a comparative discourse analysis in the Turkish press to reveal how the Turks define themselves and view their place in the world. In the debate on how nations have emerged, three main classical theoretical approaches address the nature of the nation and nationalism: the primordialist, the ethno-symbolist and the modernist (Ozkirimli 2000). The primordialists (Shafer 1955) consider that nationality is a natural part of human beings and predetermined in the same way as being a member of a family. For the ethno-symbolists (Smith 2000, 2001), nations come from pre-existing ethnic ties and the features of political and social landscapes that rely on a legacy of myths, symbols, values and memories of the past. Benedict Anderson (1983), John Breuilly (1994), Ernest Gellner (1983) and Eric J. Hobsbawm (1991) represent the modernists and explain that nations are the products of the direct or indirect consequences of political movements and the rise of the modern state.

Rather than using these pioneering approaches, new approaches to nationalism transcend the classical debate by proposing interdisciplinary analyses in such areas as globalization studies, post-colonial theories, feminism, postmodernism and discourse analysis (Ozkirimli 2000: 198). These fields of study place nationhood in the daily reproduction of specific ways of life, ways of viewing and interpreting the world. This distinction in approaches to nationalism is useful to elucidate different perspectives on Turkish nationalism and how Turkishness is defined through these diverse perspectives. For instance, the Kemalist perspective can be accepted as a modernist approach, while the ethno-nationalist perspective can be considered as a primordialist approach. However, to demonstrate competing perspectives and the struggle to redefine the Turkish nation-state identity during the last decade, this study approaches nationalism from a discursive perspective. The discourse-analytic approach connects the nation and state by indicating national unity as a discursive construct (Calhoun 1994). According to this approach, the nationalist way of thinking, feeling, evaluating and speaking makes people understand and define themselves as a nation.

In this context, the leading role of Turkish media is considered in interpreting, constructing and representing different ideologies of nationalism across the country. A deeper understanding of the struggle between competing versions of the definition of 'Turkish', Turkish foreign policy vision, even different answers to the question of where Turkey's place should be in the world of politics is suggested to be had by applying the Discourse-Historical Approach (DHA) (Wodak et al. 1999) to the coverage of different Turkish newspapers. In this context, this chapter presents a detailed theoretical and methodological background for the study. More specifically, to explore different discursive constructions of Turkish nation-state identity in the media, as related to Turkey and EU/West relations, this chapter presents a framework of the concepts of the media, national identity, discourse analysis and their interactions. It leads to a theoretical and methodological understanding of how the concepts of the Turkish nation and domestic power struggle over its definition, as they are constructed in the media, and how the media construct and negotiate concepts of the nation in their coverage of foreign policy.

The media and politics: imagined communities and banal nationalism

From this study's perspective, the roles of media in expressing, reproducing and spreading ideologies and values to wider social and international structures or supporting/confronting them constitute a crucial relationship between society and the media (Richardson 2007: 114). These roles make the media ideological instruments that produce meanings and naturalize power relations; thus, they become the means to realize domination. Thus, the role of media discourse is crucial in the expression of ideas regarding how people think about themselves and others and how they live in a particular way. In the literature, the media's power in politics is discussed widely, particularly in terms of construction and distribution of the images of political actors and building a global civil society, public sphere, and political activism (De Jong et al. 2005). Essentially, local, national and international news agencies circulate information and images between countries and form relationships between people from the local level to the international level (Boyd-Barrett and Rantanen 2001: 127). According to Nye (2004), increased information flows through the media have caused the loss of the government's traditional control over information concerning politics. The speed in moving information has created a system in which power over information is much more widely distributed, which leads to decentralization and less official control of government agendas (2004 : 53). In that spirit, the media are not just the means of reproduction of power relations, but also pluralizing forces that work against the government's ability to influence and control.

Moreover, the media are powerful channels for the 'soft power' (Nye 2004) of states in setting the political agenda in politics, distributing the foreign policy discourse and convincing people to improve cultural, political and economic cooperation among nations. Thus, in twenty-first-century world politics, the new communication and mass media are increasing the importance of soft power, specifically its ability to achieve desired outcomes in international affairs through attraction rather than coercion. These developments encouraged the strengthening of non-state-centric discourses and the entry of media studies into the discipline of International Relations (Golding and Harris 1997). In Taylor's (1997: 58–9) summary of the historical development of the media and international political relationships, the television station CNN is presented as being a direct channel of diplomacy among politicians, the public and the rest of the world:

> Much has already been written by historians about that increasing role, from the Anglo-German press 'wars' in the build-up to the First World War to the role of newspapers, the cinema and radio in the program of

'moral rearmament' before the Second World War. A growing amount of literature also now exists about how the media came to be deployed as a psychological weapon, at home and abroad, first between 1939 and 1945 and then subsequently during the Cold War. Today, however, if a statesman wants to make a public statement or send a message across the world, he has the option of doing so on CNN rather than through traditional diplomatic channels.

As Taylor noted, government departments, individual officials and ministers use mass media as direct channels to societies to explain the policy to their nation and overseas publics in order to advance or conceal policy opinions. It can be said that the media enable the evaluation of international society by distributing information that builds bridges between groups and individuals around the world. This makes the media an integral part of international relations. Connectedly, Livingston (1997) defined different approaches to the concept of the 'CNN effect' in international politics. Moreover, to encompass the use of new media as tools in every aspect of global affairs, ranging from democratization to terrorism, Seib (2008) used the concept of the 'Al Jazeera effect' and took the media influences a significant step further.

Robinson (2004: 31) suggests that the media play four roles in the policy–media interaction: a supportive media, an uncritical role for official policy; non-influential and non-supporter of any side of the debate; critical media, having limited influence to change policy; and side taker media, effective in policy outcomes. News coverage can be useful for justifying state actions by shaping what people think. For instance, after the events of 9/11 and the declaration of a 'war on terror', the war against Iraq in 2003 was defined as a war of liberation by the White House in the United States and the government produced a media campaign to support that policy. The media were a considerable ally in provoking the war and sustaining public support for it. The media helped the state to legitimate its power. With those points as guidance, the news media have an important job in defining issues, primarily to help the public understand the newest array of priorities and alliances. It can be argued that the media may use its power to shape public opinion and influence politicians (Cohen 1965). In the literature of media and politics, some studies point out the role of the media in political economy (Herman and Chomsky 2002), political communication (Semetko and Scrammell 2012), the state's propaganda (Jenks 2006; Taylor 1999), provoking war (Beck and Downing

2003), humanitarian crisis (Goving 2004; Shaw 1996), justifying policies (Seib 2006: 22), legitimating the system (Gans 2003: 74), consolidation of democracy (Schudson 1999), mobilizing people and political activism (Cottle and Lester 2011; Taki and Coretti 2013), changing the state-citizen relationship (Street 2011: 262–4), agenda-setting (McCombs 2014; Boydstun 2013; Protess and McCombs 1991) and some examine how the media effect on decision making and policymaking (Holsti 1992; Gilboa 2002; Cusinamo-Love 2003; Wolfsfeld 2004; Miller 2007).

Instead of these various media influences on politics, this chapter limits its scope and focuses on the media's role in identity politics, namely their function in the re/construction of national identity discourse. It confirms that the media have an important role in mapping a nation-state's place in politics and the world of nations. The media have contributed significantly to the social construction of images of the nation and its place in the world. As a tangible illustration, in the case of the US print media's influence on its international relations, Van Dijk (1995) demonstrates the description of the positive in-group and negative out-group in US foreign policy based on the discourse of the *New York Times*. In his analysis, in the American prestige press, Israelis represent the 'we' group in a favourable light, and the Hamas leaders, Muammar Gaddafi and Saddam Hussein typically represent enemies, and 'them'.

As widely acknowledged in the literature (McNair 1998: 6), the media as an ideological communicative vehicle do not just transmit the facts to audiences but also the contested assumptions, attitudes, beliefs, values and worldviews of society. Thus, the media are agents of socialization and powerful sources of social meaning. Put all together, they reproduce the social norms and ideologies in the social construction of reality for audiences (Devereux 2009: 15). In shaping people's understanding of social reality, the media constitute a primary source for the definition of an image of social identities concerning culture (McQuail 2000: 4). Despite these facts, the role of the media was ignored in most of the writings on nationalism and identities (Madianou 2002: 28). Early studies in this area did not directly address the relationship between communication and nationalism. Karl. W. Deutsch's (1953) *Nationalism and Social Communication: An Inquiry into the Foundations of Nationality* is accepted as the most prominent study in the area. Later, Elizabeth L. Eisenstadt's (1979) *The Printing Press as an Agent of Change: Communications and Cultural Transformations in Early-Modern Europe*, Ernest Gellner's (1983) *Nations and Nationalism* and Benedict Anderson's (1983) *Imagined Communities: Reflections on the Origin and Spread of Nationalism* point out the role of the print technology and their contribution to the emergence of nationalism: 'The convergence of capitalism and print technology on the fatal diversity of human language created the possibility of a new form of imagined community, which in its basic morphology set the stage for the modern nation' (Anderson 1983: 46).

For Anderson, the print media, in particular, the newspapers and novels standardized the language, played a role of creating a sense of belonging to the same community for the readers and considering themselves as parts of this imagined community. Newspapers remind readers that they are members of a particular nation and belong to a homeland through the nationalist thinking reflected in the content of the newspaper text. In routinely repeating habits of language in using small words (Billig 1995: 93) such as 'we', 'our' and 'us', the daily ritual of reading a newspaper reproduces and distributes the national discourse and creates different 'imaginations' (Anderson 1983) of the nation. Micheal Billig (1995: 97) points out that 'banal nationalism' as people's daily nationalism is established by social arrangements that appear 'natural' or unnoticed. The nation is reminded, indicated and 'flagged' (1995: 6) in the daily lives of citizens. Newspapers play a particularly important role in building the daily national discourse and production of nationalism by nationalizing the news with their various messages and stereotypes. Here, it must be noted that this study is not interested in the relationship between audiences and media such as the questions of how audiences interpret and appropriate media messages and how media texts have any nationalist effects. With consideration of massive literature on the issue (Morley 1992; Morley and Brunsdon 1999; Livingston 1990; Ruddock 2000; Murray and Schoder 2003; Gillespie 2005; Nightingale 2011; Sullivan 2012) it can be argued that the media represent ideological dilemmas, controversies and debates as people engage in sense-making and debate with different ideological and cultural positions.

Regarding this point, Billig (2009) argued that people use the rhetorical tools of 'common sense' for thinking and sense-making. The stress here is that information-processing is a public activity. That means individuals are not simply passive receivers of information and messages of the media, thus the media audience is not homogeneous. By underlining the link between argumentation and thinking in his psychological perspective, Billig (2009: 348) explained that his study on the unconscious aspects of nationalism is based on a psychology of the unnoticed, which presents the daily world as belonging to the world of nation-states. In this context, on one hand, this study accepts the diversity of perspectives both in the media and in the public; on the other hand, it limits its interest in how the concept of Turkish identity is negotiated in the media. That is to say, it does not analyse how the media affect the public. As is noted in *Reading Media Theory: Thinkers, Approaches, Contexts* (Barlow and Mills 2009: 288), the media tell the person in the mass who he/she is, they gave him/her identity; they even say what she/he wants to be, how to get that way, how to feel she/he is that way. The media bring the reader, listener, viewer into the sight of larger, higher reference groups – real or imagined – which are looking glasses for his self-image.

Sabina Mihelj makes a critical revision of Benedict Anderson's *Imagined Communities* in her *Media Nations* (2011) as an appropriate starting point to develop an alternative approach to nationalism and the media with an emphasis on their link with power and politics. Mihelj comments on the reasons for the worldwide appeal and popularity of Anderson's theory. First, the idea of nations as imagined communities had its 'iconoclastic potential' (2011: 12) in post-1989 Europe due to rising anti-nationalist sentiments after the Cold War. This process urged thinking alternative, post-national, global or cosmopolitan forms of collective imagination and belonging. Anderson's book was used for critical reflections about nationalist claims, rejecting the nationalist appeal and inspiring the option of a universalistic identification or the option of not belonging (2011: 13).

The second reason for the iconoclastic potential of *Imagined Communities* was what it offered among the modernist theories of nation and nationalism. Rather than seeing that nationalisms were reflections of fundamental realities in the modern world such as industrialization, decolonization or revolution, Anderson's theory examined the cultural aspects of nationalism and different forms of national imagining over a variety of historical contexts (2011: 14). However, Mihelj argued that the link between national imagination and its genesis and distribution by the power of print capitalism in particular social and economic contexts was neglected and unexplored (2011: 15). *Media Nations* challenges this trend in exploring how nationalism structures the world we live in and becomes embedded in institutionalized categories, routines and expressions in our everyday lives. In this context, drawing on the theory of alternative modernities, comparative media research, and historical research on national belonging, Mihelj looks at multiple political projects of modernity and their multiple configurations of nationhood and mass communication. Her case studies show that the media transmit competing conceptions of histories and nationhood, while general themes of nationalism seem virtually universal and taken for granted.

In addition, Mihelj shows that Billig's theory can be applied to non-Western and non-democratic nation-states and their banal reproduction of national symbols. It can be done at different levels such as national, sub-national, supranational, and non-national. Therefore, she offers a discursive approach to nationalism which allows for explaining multiple attachments to collectivities, complex and hybrid webs of cultural and social formations in the international context, and beyond existing boundaries of the nation-state system. This approach enables the unpacking of various social, political and economic mechanisms shaping national imagination and operating through the micro-level and macro-level relationship of power, structures and state policies.

As this chapter argues, Mihelj points out that nationalism is much more than a political doctrine, movement or sentiment (2011: 17). In this discursive approach, nationalism is a way of seeing, interpreting and structuring the world we live in, which can be constructed or represented in several different ways by various social agents, structures and power relations. This means that just as the social world is fundamentally divided and structured according to power relations and perspective differences, there are different national imaginations and nationalist visions of the world. To be accepted and institutionalized, these nationalist perspectives would compete to act as a representative of the nation and serve the nation's interests. Thus, there would be a struggle for achieving legitimacy (2011: 19). This introduces a new analysis of which social norms, values and memories are fundamental to the nation in interpretation and justification of being a nation and in the definition of ongoing struggle both within and between ideological groups to dominate others. Related to this question, Michael Skey (2011: 10) explores which interpretations and categorizations of nations are taken for granted by particular groups and how they are accepted as 'common sense'. Each group may seek to stabilize the benefits that community membership accrues (2011: 29) and privilege their own definition of what the nation is physically, culturally and historically (2011: 12). The dominant group defines and regulates conditions of belonging within the nation-state. For securing a sense of self, community, and place, a power struggle would happen between them. They struggle to maintain a knowable and manageable sense of identity and community in response to the social and political transformations due to the fear of uncertainty. They aim to be dominant to reduce uncertainty and provide an ongoing secure sense of place in a threatening world.

Nations construct their narratives from past experiences to the present and with a will to live together in the future; their existences are happening, changing, developing or vanishing among the traces of history. This is why the nation cannot be treated as a stable entity to observe its characteristics. Both continuity and change should be accounted for in the process of reproduction of meanings of nationhood. Intending to conceptualize ongoing struggles of perpetuating or challenging nationalist discourses, Skey (2011) offers to use the concept of 'sedimentation' (Skey 2011: 12) which enables us to see that a bifurcation of perspectives on national identity entails bifurcation of interests in both domestic and foreign policy.

National identity and foreign policy

Various definitions of nation and explanations of the rise of nationalism have been offered in the literature on nationalism (Hutchinson and Smith 1995; Ozkirimli 2000); however, the concepts that define the 'nation' revolve theoretically around two approaches and arguments linked to them: the political nation by the will of a state's citizens and the nation that is linguistically and ethnically defined by culture. According to the Habermasian definition of the concept (1989), national identification is based on constitutionally equal citizenship and patriotism that take place in the framework of universalistic principles and political culture, regardless of any differences in race, religion, gender, language or ethnicity. This type of civic nationalism can be evaluated in terms of Ernest Renan's concept of nation that is based on the will of individuals to live together. In a culturalist perspective, Anthony D. Smith's (2009) definition of a nation is a 'named human population sharing a historic territory, common myths and historical memories, a mass public culture, a common economy, and common legal rights and duties for all members'. In the sense of cultural or ethnic nationalism, what gives unity to the nation is inherited by birth and blood (Ozkirimli 2005: 23).

Although the distinction between civic and ethnic nationalism is useful for description, the terms cannot capture the complexities that inhere in the culturalisation of politics and the politicization of culture. This classification leads to a normative project of dividing nationalisms into two camps, one is the civic-good nationalism of the West, and the other is the ethnic-bad nationalism of the Rest (Ozkirimli 2005: 24). However, all nationalisms combine both the cultural and the political together and all nationalist discourses have common dimensions: the spatial, the temporal, the symbolic and the everyday (Ozkirimli 2005: 179). Ozkirimli reminds us (Ozkirimli 2005: 25) of Roger Brubaker's (1998) categorisation of nationalism as the 'state-framed' versus the 'counter-state'. To what extent these are exclusive is equivocal, thus seeing nationalism as a form of 'discourse' can work for capturing what is common in all nationalisms, how different nationalisms challenge, overlap and intersect with each other. It means that nationalism is not just a collective political identity of modern society, but also a particular way of seeing and thinking about the world through a nationalist discourse.

The reality is that we live in a world of nations and all fundamental rights and other social and economic rights are defined, regulated and institutionalized by this system. Even though a person would argue she/he is a world citizen without a nationality it does not allow her/him to cross borders and travel the world without identification of a place and a nation. The logic of national thinking makes sense of action in the contemporary world, frames language, habits, doing things, organizing social, political and legal frameworks. This system locates the nation physically, legally and socially within the world of nations. Hence, it can be argued that the nation-state identity in international politics is constructed in interaction with both domestic and international 'others' rather than simply in one or the other. Locating the nation as a distinct group involves locating other nations, which provides categorization and identification of 'in-group' and 'out-group' members (Billig 1995: 66). This establishes a unity based on imagination, recognition and definition of 'us' and 'them' by promoting a sense of belonging together in a common present, past and future. In other words, national identities are situated within the historical narratives that construct the 'imagined communities' (Anderson 1983) in a narrative (Wodak et al. 1999) that shares the past through the present and expected future.

As noted, this chapter attempts to analyse Turkey's identity discourse considering national and international factors, with a specific focus on the nationalist ideologies, values, beliefs and perceptions in the media. This idea considers the importance of the national context in the determination of foreign policy positions of all relevant actors and the reasons why a policy works and changes in a particular way at a given time. In this context, Rosenau (1980) proposes to include individual, governmental, societal and systemic factors as the sets of independent and explanatory variables in his study. The existing literature presents a framework that identifies the domestic factors in foreign policymaking about conditional parameters that depend on the geographic, political and social context of cases. As the framework for domestic sources of foreign policy and mapping of a model for the analysis of foreign policy discourse, Clarke (1996: 22–37) defines six sets of variables. These are the constitutional 'power map' of the state political culture, beliefs, psychological processes of the key political leaders and officials in decision making, group dynamics of policymaking, and the information-processing characteristics of any system. Within the new approaches of foreign policy analysis, the impact of domestic factors on foreign policy is explained by three main approaches (Alden and Aran 2011: 47–55). One primarily says that foreign policy is sourced by the structural forms of the state, such as the institutions and regime. The second focuses on the economic system and interests of some elite groups and, last, the pluralist approach perceives foreign policy as a product of sub-state and non-state actors, societal interest groups, state decision-makers, public opinion and the media. These contributions may work in multi-level analysis, but this study focuses on the media to address the domestic power struggle over the definition of Turkey's identity, which enables us to understand New Turkey's post-Kemalist identity through combating national imaginations, shifting perceptions and priorities in domestic and foreign policy.

In the literature of International Relations (IR), even the realists argue that the national identity and culture make a difference among nations, as Hans Morgenthau (1993) noted in *Politics among Nations*. However, there is no agreement on how identity matters should be studied within the constructivist and rationalist frameworks in the literature of IR theory. In the classical realist tradition of international political analysis, which has been the dominant approach to explaining interstate relations in the literature, foreign policy should be made by politicians, attuned to the national interest and free of the influence of extraneous domestic factors such as national identity (Mermin 1999: 147). Waltz's *Theory of International Politics* (1979), as a key contribution to realist International Relations theory, assumes that the international system is a material structure consisting of military and economic resources rather than ideas and norms. Under this realist fundamental assumption, neo-realism (Mearsheimer 2001) does not allow us to theorize the construction and reconstruction of state/national identity. Neo-liberalism (Keohane and Nye 1997) also does not offer an explanatory theory of how nation-state identity is constructed, since its focus is on political economy, environmental issues and human rights. Within the contemporary mainstream approaches of International Relations, both these approaches fail to consider the role of political culture, norms, identities, domestic interests and non-state actors in foreign policy decision making.

As a critical reaction to these mainstream theories, social constructivism is concerned with normative structure (Barnett 2008: 168) and ideas. By analysing the effects that political identities, norms and culture have on national interests and policies in specific historical contexts, the social constructivist approach (Katzenstein 1996; Lapid and Kratochwil 1997; Went 1999; McSweeney 1999; Wilmer 2002) has demonstrated the importance of the social dimensions of international relations. Constructivist scholars argue the identities shape perceptions and determine intentions for the states' policies. As a source of interests and preferences, national identity has considerable influence on political decision making, because it shapes a vision that is a possible, legitimate outcome (Saideman 2002: 177). Hill and Wallace's (1996: 8) statement also supports the assumption of the study based on the crucial linkage of national identity and a nation's place in the world: effective foreign policy rests upon a shared sense of national identity, of a nation-state's 'place in the world', its friends and enemies, intersects and aspirations. These underlying assumptions are embedding in national history and myth, changing slowly over time as political leaders reinterpret them and external and internal developments reshape them.

The discursive approach in foreign policy analysis

In the most essential Foucauldian meaning in spoken or written language use (Fairclough 1995: 131), 'discourse' frames the objects of knowledge, beliefs and values and simultaneously constitutes social identities, social relations and systems of knowledge and belief. Thus, it sustains or changes social relationships in society and among societies (Mayr 2008). Different discourses reflect different perspectives on the world, regulating and determining individual and collective actions that shape society (Fairclough 2003). Discourse constitutes what people know, how people know, what they speak about, and what they silence about themselves and others. It governs how to think and write about the nation (Fairclough 2001) under the influence of power relations and interest order. In this context, the discursive constructive vision of the nation as an imagined community (Anderson 1983) is useful in identifying strategies used in the definition of self and other relations. Hence, discourse analysis works well in examining how discursive practices convey meaning to nationalist discourses through both contestation and communicative action.

There is a plurality of theoretical approaches and methods within discourse analysis. Four theoretical approaches and methods of discourse analysis can be delineated (Carta and Morin 2014): interpretive constructivism; discursive institutionalism; post-structuralism; and Critical Discourse Analysis (CDA). In the versatility of discourse analysis, interpretive constructivist authors such as Kubálková (2001) use the most ideational approach which focuses on the concept of cooperation. As the second theoretical approach of discourse analysis, Vivien Schmidt's discursive institutionalism (2008) explores discursive interaction and the representation of ideas within a given institutional context. According to this approach, institutions influence agents and are being influenced by agents (2008: 134).

Post-structuralist studies, as the third approach of discourse analysis, emphasize the concept of the power. For instance, Ole Waever (2001) offers a discursive view of an identity that is more unstable, where identity explanations are measured with material factors such as economics, energy or military power. This can tackle the shifts in national identity and foreign policy and elucidate why the same nation-state identity can lead to very different policies. Post-structuralist discourse analysis offers a mechanism and a systematic account of internal responses to international impulses. It applies to both official and non-official texts (Waever 2001: 26), but predominantly to public texts that stretch the concept of 'political', involving dominant discourse, its opposition, and resistance. It creates a structure, or frame, which can link different elements of decision making, such as bureaucratic politics and institutions, domestic pressure and interest groups, and perceptions of individuals in the general policy line. According to this perspective, national identity is a source of power and different imaginations of identity produce different policy outcomes. A change in national imagination denotes shifting perceptions on the 'self' and 'other' identities and policy priorities, that is, the perceptions about who we are and who our friends, rivals and enemies are. This framework also supplies a way to examine how national interests are formed and articulated within a wider political debate. This is also a tool for understanding how official discourse is reproduced, represented, legitimized or resisted by the larger public. This 'multi-layered structure of discourse' (Diez 2001: 14) enables us to observe continuity and changes in the construction of nation-state identity. Therefore, it provides a good indication of power relations and how national identity discourse might change. To sum up, the discursive approach to national identity clarifies the mechanisms of norms and ideologies in their production, transformation, and how they exercise their power and influence in a historical context.

As another example of a post-structuralist study, in *Writing Security*, David Campbell (1998) analysed the construction of US identity during the Cold War through foreign policy discourse. According to Campbell, US foreign policy discourse during the Cold War had productive influences on state identity. He argued that the Soviet threat in the discourses and practices of security during the period was an identity-constitutive tool for the United States. In the field of security studies, the Copenhagen School (Buzan et al. 1998; Neumann 1999) has done works on particular acts of securitisation, determined by speech-acts; but Ole Weaver and some of his colleagues (Diez 2001; Hansen and Waever 2001) are more interested in how a certain vision and meaning of Europe relates to the concepts of nation and state. As a pioneering study, Ole Waever (1990) demonstrated in *Three Competing Europes: German, French, Russian* that different organizing principles, different 'European' values and different boundaries to the West and East of these three 'Europes' constitute the contrast between their approaches to European cooperation and integration. In this regard, Henrik Larsen (1997) elaborated domestic political discourses on Europe in France and Britain and their impact on foreign policy. William Wallace (1998: 681) pointed out that Larsen's study failed by not addressing how British and French discourses were constructed and reconstructed through the active process of political debate on Europe. That means it requires a clear understanding of the processes of the struggle and interaction between actors and their competing discourses.

As the last theoretical approach of discourse analysis, Critical Discourse Analysis (CDA) can be used to deal with this shortcoming, which enables the exploration of the versatility of discursive constructions of the nation, produced by various agents and in various historical and political contexts, their competing concepts of the nation in flux and dialogue with other forms of identity (Inthorn 2007). CDA goes beyond the other three approaches; like others it seeks to understand and explain the social world and politics, but it also aims to criticize and change society. Discourses are seen as tools that reproduce the social relations and domination of one group over another. It has the clearest commitment to practical ways of linguistic analysis of texts.

Thus, Larsen (2014) showed in his latest study that post-structuralist studies can work with linguistic methodological tools of CDA. Both approaches are interested in the analysis of the historical and political context of discourse and its critical stand on taken-for-granted knowledge (Aydin-Duzgit 2014); however, CDA does more with its goal of emancipatory critique which covers the comparison of different representations of the discursive and non-discursive aspects of social reality. How language is used by people, how meaning is created in context, how language use represents the exercise of socio-political power and control in abuse, dominance, and inequality are particular interests of CDA (Richardson 2007: 115). Making these ideological effects of particular ways of using language more visible, CDA has a political stance on the side of dominated, disadvantaged and oppressed groups (Wodak 2001: 188) and against dominating groups and inequality. By taking an explicit position CDA provides an essential motivation for analysis for understanding and exposing the bias of what has been naturalized in everyday experience and actions. In this context, the questions arise as to how some groups of people are labelled and categorized; how some forms of emphasizing negative sameness and negative common features of generalization are used to represent contrasting identities, which are expressed by discursive practices. Understanding the manner in which social relations and issues of power are reproduced through various forms of representation gives clues about where to start for a change and transformation concerning equality, emancipation (Forchtner 2011), democracy, and pluralism. In this context, this research sees nationalism as an ideology, as patterns of belief, practice, assumptions, habit, and representation are reproduced daily. Specifically, Ruth Wodak's DHA of CDA (1999; 2011a; 2012) is suitable for use in research that explores nationalist discourses in their own historical and linguistic production context. It defines the linguistic constructive strategies of national identities which allow understanding the changing and competing meanings of the identities through the discursive changes.

The Discourse-Historical Approach in Critical Discourse Analysis

Language structures our thinking, reflects and produces meaning and arguably defines all social phenomena (Finlayson 1999: 47– 8). Thus, different worldviews operate within a certain framework of language habits. In a nutshell, different discourses constitute meanings about social relations and different forms of life. Secularist or Islamist, Europeanist, or Eurasianist, all perspectives are internal to a variety of ways of thinking and living in the world. Concerning this assumption, this research looks at how different discourses in the Turkish media represent the way people think about their nation and identity. Also, it maps the distinctions of challenging discourses and the way such distinctions may be mechanisms of the reconstruction of identity politics in both Turkey's domestic and international relations.

With the previous points in mind, this study argues that discourse analysis is the most appropriate method for identity questions in the politics that concentrate on self/other relations, often engaged in contrasting narratives of identities as 'others' being the opposite of 'us'. This research's investigation has a distinctive motivation that sees varying contested, converse or complementary ways of conceptualization, recognition and configuration in Turkey's identity construction as attuned to the complexity of in-group and out-group definitions. Determining how these groups involve, exclude, engage and connect and how their identities are embodied and expressed in the media discourse are the most urgent tasks for this research.

Different narratives of nationalisms are different constructs of the nation and different evaluations and mappings of it (Wodak et al. 1999). Based on this complex approach to nationalism, this thesis argues that Turkish national identity is discursively constructed and that a fundamental conflict has existed between the competing nationalist discourses in Turkish society (Canefe 2008: 394) over the definition of what Turkish identity should be and how to place Turkey in the world. Changing and separate definitions of 'Turkishness' shed light on the struggle between the domestic actors and ideologies and illuminate competing views of the world that form different perceptions about Turkey's regional and world role.

Seeing the nation as a discursive construct moves it into the context of the concept of narrative. People narrate different understandings of their social world, themselves, and collective experiences (De Fina et al. 2006: 17). Narrative recapitulates past events with temporal and logical order. That is to say, the construction of a collective self-image concerning collective national identity is formed through the narrations of common past, present and future. Narratives, therefore, are about the birth of the nation, its past events, developments, where it came from to its present situation, and where it is going to go in the future. This perspective understands national identity discourse in a social and historical and context-dependent setting.

The collective memory of the nation is based on a selective reading and construction of history (Inthorn 2007: 10). Different memories of the past inform the way to think about the nation and its identity. Thus, a change in the dominant understanding of history can transform dominant concepts of national identity. It matters due to a specific nationalist discourse and its institutionalism and legalization by the state legitimize hierarchy and formulate a particular domination that directly constitutes power relations among actors. A dominant group (and its discourse) imposes its self-image on a wider population and builds its hegemony over other groups, namely, different ethnic or religious groups and disadvantaged groups.

In summary, like other identities, nationality is a narration that people use to talk about themselves and the position of others. A narration of an 'identity' is a specific way of telling, related to how collective experience is expressed, discussed and negotiated in members of a specific community. This sets them aside from other communities. Searching through these different narrations of the collective experience allows us to see various contradictory experiences and perceptions; more specifically different constructions of a so-called single identity in a certain time. Thus, the perception of national identity in a narrative configuration (Wodak et al. 1999: 14) enables us to see its continuity, discontinuity, diversity and dynamism. Therefore, for a better understanding of domestic power struggles for hegemony and reconstruction of Turkish nation-state identity, nationalism must be placed in the context of competing ideologies and their historical integration and exclusion dynamics in Turkey.

Ruth Wodak et al. (1999) developed the Discourse-Historical Approach in Critical Discourse Analysis and dealt with diverse understandings of nationhood in the case of Austria by analysing different discursive constructions of Austrian identity. On the nation's political present and future in the narrative of Austrian national identity, they analysed commemorative speeches and policy addresses of Austrian political representatives of the European Union and Europe. For instance, the analysis of Chancellor Franz Vranitzky's (1986– 1997) speech (Wodak et al. 1999: 100) exemplified how a political discourse on a foreign policy issue (European Union membership) simultaneously constructed the national identity (Austrian) discourse. In Vranitzky's discourse, the EU member, Austria, was positively portrayed by using a strategy of perpetuation to demand continuity of the status quo which imagines the Austrian community as an internationally respected, social and stable nation-state. According to Wodak, this positive self-representation alleviated the fears regarding Austria's membership in the EU. As seen in the example, this approach helps to show various discursive constructs of a specific national identity that are given different shapes according to context, public and language. This leads to a comparison of different discourses on the same topic and how they interconnect and challenge each other. This approach is suitable for use in research that explores the diversity of discourse on one national matter.

Because of these, Wodak's constructive strategies and Discourse-Historical Approach are adopted as a valid tool of observation of the continuity, shifts and diversity in the discursive construction of Turkish national and international identity. Significantly, specific characteristics of the Turkish case requires the consideration of three aspects of 'critique' (Wodak et al. 1999: 8– 9), to uncover contradictions and dilemmas in different discourses of Turkish nationalism ('text or discourse immanent critique'), exhibiting the functions of discursive practices in aiming manipulation, persuasion or resistance ('socio-diagnostic critique'). Furthermore, DHA enables us to cope with the main problem of Turkish national identity, which shows how it deals with its hybrid character and its past. It is used in criticizing the present way of dealing with Turkish history ('retrospective critique'), at revising an actual 'picture' or 'narrative' of the collective past as a new, responsible way of dealing with its consequences and effects. DHA was employed to integrate information about historical sources of diverse perspectives on the Turkish nation-state with their social and political backgrounds and diversity. This interdisciplinary, problem-orientated approach (Wodak 2001: 69) has powerful and efficient features for the methodology:

- DHA includes **systematically available background knowledge** of the context and the case in the analysis and interpretation of the text (Wodak and Mayer 2005: 188).
- DHA sees discourse with their **historicity** (Krzyzanowski and Wodak 2009: 31) related to their struggle in continuity, change and transformation. This focus makes it a more suitable approach by CDA to understand a historical and political process through its specific temporal and spatial conditions. Using DHA contributes to indicate how diverse local, national or regional discourses exist and their contradiction to different forms of change and transformation.
- Linguistic realizations on all levels of language in their specific context in which they were made address the origins of power relations, specifically the problems of inequality and discrimination; thus, **the context-dependent** discursive analysis provides the secret key to decoding the presentation strategies employed in production and reproduction of these kinds of stereotypic and unequal socio-political relations.
- DHA enables one to see **pluri-perspectivity** related to various positions and voices in a certain socio-political field.

Among important contributions to the existing empirical works in the literature, Clary-Lemon (2010) used the DHA in analysing oral-history interviews with 15 members of the Irish Association of Manitoba to explore how national and subgroup identities such as immigrants are discursively constructed in the context of assimilation and dissimilation. Within the Romanian context, Tileaga (2005) examined the notions of ethnicity, racism and ideology to provide a critical investigation of the taken-for-granted forms of prejudice and discrimination about ethnic minorities. In order to challenge existing stereotypes, Prentice (2010) studied social attitudes towards Scottish independence by analysing historical debates on British and Scottish identities through structured survey methodology. In terms of national identity and religion, a CDA of discourses of 'national piety' has been carried out by Hjelm (2014). Hjelm's work challenged the privileged position and hegemony of the folk church in Finland by deconstructing the discourses that reproduced the status quo of religious inequality and national identity.

Some studies utilized the corpus techniques in CDA such as the corpus linguistic method, namely automated semantic tagging (Baker and McEnery 2005; Baker et al. 2008). Besides these studies, a significant amount of research has been undertaken on discourses of identity in the newsprint media from a variety of geographical contexts (Flowerdew et al. 2002; Achugar 2004; Burroughs 2015). Li (2009) compared discourses of two daily newspapers in the US (*The New York Times*) and China (*China Daily*) in two selected events to find out which particular discursive strategies were employed to construct national identities. Dekavalla (2010) analysed the discursive construction of national identity in Scottish and English/UK newspapers. With a focus on the UK's two general elections after Scottish devolution with a specific focus on the 2001 and 2005 campaigns, she compared an Anglo-British perspective and Scottish perspective in the coverage of the issues.

However, the case of Turkish national identity has not been studied yet. Some studies have examined discourses of Turkey's bid for EU membership in the newsprint media in the UK, Greece, Slovenia, Germany, France and Spain (Aksoy, 2009; Koenig et al., 2006; Negrine, 2008b; Negrine et al., 2008; Schneeberger, 2009; Tekin, 2008, 2010; Aydin-Duzgit 2011; Buckingham 2013). Tekin's study (2008) pointed out the French media's negative portrayal of Turkey's candidature; moreover, it showed that the discourse that constructs Turkey's EU membership also constructs a collective European identity. Connectedly, Buckingham's findings (2013) indicated that despite the official support, the media narrative in the most respected newspaper of Spain, *El Pais* depicted Turkey as Europe's cultural other with references to Turkey's democratic deficits, historical cultural differences, and the place of religion in Turkey's society. This study aims to both build upon these works benefiting from CDA, with a specific focus on Wodak's DHA, and to address a gap in the literature by examining how Turkey constructs its own national identity in Turkish newsprint media discourse.

Analysing discursive construction of Turkish identity in the media

The DHA as a methodology in Critical Discourse Analysis can demonstrate how the media discourses create meanings about the national identity of Turkey that serve to justify people's positions and interests of *themselves* and to criticize *others* in relationship to each other. In turn, the crucial question is 'Which media discourse?'. In consideration of Gencel Bek's study (2004) titled *News Reporting in Turkish Television and Tabloidisation*, Akkor Gul's (2011: 34) study on the structure of private television broadcasting in the 2000s and Akser and Baybars-Hawks's (2012) arguments about the media autocracy in Turkey, it seems that the goal of this study cannot be achieved by analysing television discourse. Big business in the television sector dramatically drives self-censorship for reasons of saving their economic interests in other sectors such as education, construction and telecommunication' and failing to develop a presence independent of the state (Christensen 2007; Sozeri and Guney 2011). Therefore, the big media patrons lack the ability and will to function properly as the 'fourth estate' that challenges the state's interests and policies. Turkey has witnessed new ownership and control relations in the economic polictics of the media for the last decade (Aydin 2015). Beside the neo-liberalization of political Islam, the neo-liberal media have become conservative under the AKP government (Cam and Sanlier-Yuksel 2015: 67).

In fact, in the history of media and political relations in Turkey, the subject of political pressure on the media has in most cases been the armed forces, the elected government, and the judiciary. The Turkish state's control of the media discourse has become a part of its construction of a particular citizenship and civil society-state relationship. The law and regulations draw the borders of the media discourse, based on the state's conception of the ideal citizen, which hinders the media's function in promoting deliberative, oppositional and pluralist voices in society. Nevertheless, there were Turkish style of journalism in Turkey that must be considered to assess how and why the goal of 'my study was realizable in the period of this study'. Newspapers were very helpful in identifying various discourses based on different ideologies and in understanding the struggle of power and strategies of the logic of equivalence and difference within identity constructions. The characteristic peculiar to Turkish newspapers was that they have very courageous columnists who run the risk of opposing and getting sent to jail as Noam Chomsky expressed in an interview in January 2012. According to 2012 data from the International Press Institute, more than 700 journalists were on trial in Turkey in cases brought based on several provisions of the Press Law, the Penal Code and the Anti-Terror Law. The International Committee to Protect Journalists report (2013) pointed out that Turkey has been the world's leading jailer of journalists; for instance, 232 journalists were behind bars in 2012 and 59 journalists lost their job just during the Gezi Park protests in 2013.

Moreover, CDA requires minding whose discourse is represented in the Turkish media. Turkish national dailies are not purely opinion newspapers of regular writers and journalists; they rank citizens' discourses that have different backgrounds such as students, political activists, poets, soldiers or doctors. *Radikal* newspaper has been chosen due to the fact it uses public discourses to speak out on socio-political matters where the editorial articles tend to remain silent. *Cumhuriyet* newspaper also devotes its second page to this purpose.

As was noted before, in a theoretical context, two prepositions underlie the framework of this research. The first central assumption is that the media's role in identity construction demonstrates the daily construction of nationalism and its discourse-historical production (Wodak et al. 1999). In this context, analysing newspaper discourses is useful for understanding ideological relations in society and how the relations and structures of power are embedded in everyday language. The second assumption of this study is that identities are dynamic; thus, there can be different, unstable discursive constructions of national identities depending on the different contexts. In other words, since nationalism can shift with different ideologies and contexts, there is no single national identity. This means that diverse concepts of national identity can coexist (Wodak et al. 1999).

Two propositions are built on the 'imagined communities' concept of Benedict Anderson (1983) and 'banal nationalism' of Michel Billig (1995). According to these propositions, belonging to a nation means imagining the 'we' opposing the 'other' in terms of domestic and external relations. The imaginations of the nation map its place in the world and define its conception of insiders and outsiders, allies and enemies. Departing from these points, this study argues that the media, particularly the press, are one of the main sources of nationalist beliefs; therefore, the influential forms of institutionalized nationalism reside in the media discourse, which may produce a sense of belonging to a nation but also the stereotypes and prejudices in everyday lives towards other nations. Analysis of media discourse is a useful resource for studying ideological and identity relations in domestic and external relations to develop an understanding and awareness of how self and other relations are embedded in everyday language (Bell and Garret 1998). Therefore, in this research, the leading role of Turkish media is considered in representing different ideologies of nationalism (Kadioglu and Keyman 2011) as well as interpreting and constructing power relations in the Turkish political sphere.

As noted before, interpretation of contradictory memories of the past embodies different meanings and perspectives on the present, national days, rituals and other matters; thus what people know or how people look at the history determine today's struggles to secure the nation's future in terms of how they want to live it, their ways of life and perspectives of the world (Inthorn 2007). That means there would be competing narratives (Wodak et al. 1999) that are used to justify their own national imaginations and interests. In this conceptual context, this thesis reveals that the main problem for Turkish nationalism is dealing with its hybrid character and history (Canefe 2002), in other words, different narrations of nationhood. In a paradox, the attempt to create a 'democratic society' has reiterated the past traumas of traditional 'others' of Turkey that were, until then, locked in the pages of the past. In terms of religious and ethnic identities, different versions of the national narrative have been spoken in dealing with the 'common past'. Reinterpretation of the past has also urged a rethink about citizenship and the situation of minorities in Turkey. The demands for equal, civic, democratic and constitutional citizenship pushed authorities to do something in legislation. Although many of the secular elites and the military were uncomfortable with the political reforms promoted through EU conditionality (Tocci 2005), the harmonization packages which were brought into force by the AKP, brought significant changes (Keyman 2007; Ozbudun 2009; Parker 2009) to the minority rights, religious freedom and right to life and retrial.

This process prompts and embodies the limits of domination, exclusion and inclusion in the concept of the nation and citizenship. More importantly, it determines the struggle over economic, political and symbolic resources and who owns and controls national, cultural, material, even natural capital. With this emphasis on and interest in differences, discourse analysis makes it possible to have a more dynamic framework for studying the clash of different worldviews and identities, which can acknowledge the wider socio-political relations and structural changes. Thus, this study applies the DHA to map out a range of Turkish national identities, their power struggle in the reconstruction of New Turkey's identity, and their perspectives on Europe and the West in general.

As noted, the collective memory of the nation is based on a selective remembering and forgetting of past events. In the aftermath of the collapse of the Ottoman Empire and the National Independence War, Mustafa Kemal Ataturk and his friends established the Turkish Republic in 1923. Despite the fact that the country's population was overwhelmingly Muslim, the Kemalist revolution embraced a secular identity to build a modern nation like the European states in the West. In addition, the military and the legal system were structured to protect this Kemalist secular identity.

However, three main factors have triggered a reconstruction process of Turkey's identity since the end of the Cold War: the paradigm shift in the international relations with 9/11 events and its influence on Turkey's international identity; Turkey's Europeanization efforts; and a fundamental change in Turkey's domestic power relations with the rise of the Justice and Development Party. In November 2002, the AKP with Islamist roots won more than a third of the vote and formed a single-party majority government in the Turkish Grand National Assembly. Although almost half of the general vote was left unrepresented due to a 10 per cent national threshold, gaining almost two-thirds of the seats and the legislative apparatus, the AKP changed the internal power relations and struggle for hegemony in Turkey. The AKP's historical success in Turkish politics doubled when it managed to increase its vote to 46.5 per cent in the 2007 general election despite the economy playing the biggest role in determining voter preferences (Kalaycioglu 2010: 29), followed by religiosity and other cultural factors that help determine party identification. Islam and Kurds as traditional others of Kemalist nation-state identity had power in Ankara against a secular military-civil bureaucracy (Casier and Jongerden 2011). This was the beginning of a silent counter-revolution that transformed Turkey's identity and reconstructed the post-

Kemalist nation-state identification. This study argues that this struggle more than the centre-periphery cleavage (Mardin 1973) is a clash of different Turkeys. In this regard, the empirical part of the research sets out to answer these questions: how do these different Turkeys engage, converse and struggle with each other in defining Turkish national identity? What impact, if any, did the governmental transition in November 2002 have on Turkey's identity in terms of domestic and international relations?

Instead of the Kemalist Republican secular construction, the AKP's Islamic conservative nationalism has been transforming Turkish nation-state identity at the level of state institutions and public culture (White 2013), which also indicates there is an on-going struggle between different definitions of national tradition. The logic of post-Kemalist transformation is a worldview based on a selective reading of the Ottoman and Turkish history of religious, cultural and ethnic identity. Newly emerging Islamist ideology is repositioning and reconstructing Turkey's political terrain in foreign policy in terms of creating a new macro-identity among populations that share the Ottoman Islamic heritage (Davutoglu 2001).

In the case of Turkey, the argument of the research is twofold based on the political and historical context of the last decade. The first part of the argument is that Turkish Kemalist nation-state identity has been redefined by the new Muslim conservative political elite and Kurdish identity by using the post 9/11 international politics, European integration process (Zucconi 2009: 25) and its democracy discourse. Remarkably, the EU adaptation process became one of anchor to and guarantor of the very legitimacy and policies of Erdogan's party. The second is that Turkish foreign affairs minister Ahmet Davutoglu's effect in Turkish foreign policy directly targeted the Kemalist worldview. Identifying a reimagined Ottoman imperial project (Fisher Onar 2012: 63) became more effective in conditioning and shaping the state's policies and the society's Islamic perception of 'self' (Saracoglu 2013). In a nutshell, both the developments in domestic and international politics enhanced the AKP government's power of construction of Turkey's post-Kemalist nation-state identity.

To follow the post-Kemalist transformation of Turkish nation-state identity and its challenges, four contested main discourses of Turkish nationalism (Ozkirimli 2011) can be observed in Turkish media: Kemalist nationalism; Islamist nationalism; ethnic nationalism; and liberal nationalism. In the three selected case studies, different ideological perspectives on the Turkish nation will be compared to show how and why they struggle to resist or maintain the post-Kemalist reconstruction of Turkey's identity. Primarily, the media discourse contributes to our understanding of the ways in which Turkish national identity and its place in the world is imagined, discussed and embodied through the daily practice of reading a newspaper. It illustrates different everyday forms of Turkish nationhood in their continuity and change. It also aims to have a better articulation of how discourses are stabilized or challenged through daily routines and discussion patterns, in particular daily forms of taken-for-granted language and practice. It gives substantial clues about how people make sense of their nationality and how it reflects their imagination of the nation's collective past, present and future.

Consequently, the aim of this research is not just identifying multiple discourses of Turkish nationalism and their struggle to shape new Turkish nation-state identity, but also to reach a deeper reading historical and political production, negotiation and evolution of these competing identities in the nation's narrative. It explores the privileged and disadvantaged status of particular groups within the Turkish national setting and identifies which discourses and their repetition in everyday processes contribute to realization of the ongoing construction of the post-Kemalist sense of Turkishness as the new national self. Specifically, it focuses on how Islamists justify their new status and benefits, how secularists challenge their dominant position, and how other nationalist discourses contribute to this power struggle in the redefinition of Turkey's identity. Finally, the case studies are examined in a particular historical framework, allowing a comparative element to transform self/other relations in a systematic analysis of the national and international context. Seeing the symbiotic nature of antagonisms in Turkish nationalism, the results also impact considerably on contemporary attempts to cultivate a Turkish nation-state identity in the process of writing a new constitution for a post-secular and pluralist understanding.

In the national media, the linguistic processes and strategies in the creation, negotiation and establishment of identities construct how people and nations define who they are (De Fina et al. 2006: 18) and how they map their nation in the world of nations. In line with these assumptions, this study attempts to analyse Turkey's identity discourse in the national media considering national and international factors, with a specific focus on the domestic actors' ideologies, values, beliefs and perceptions. With these points as guidance, this dissertation examines how the meanings of a particular national identity and nationalism are constructed in newspaper discourse, which serves to justify the positions and interests of particular groups in their relationships with each other and the West. Thus, CDA is used as the method for media research to find such linkages among changing power relations and empowering ideological discourses in Turkey.

In consideration of these points, this approach is used in three case studies in this research as a pertinent tool to observe the shifting and on-going discursive constructions of the Secularist-Islamist binary as represented in the Turkish media in the first decade of the 2000s. The first case study demonstrates the multiple articulations of Turkishness in complex constellations of competition and interaction of definitions. In the second case study, the media discourse illustrates debates over Turkish national identity and its particular challenge with the Kurdish issue. The third case study examines how the discursive construction of Turkish nation-state identity in the media can be projected on the 'West' by understanding the debate on the axis shift in Turkish foreign policy. In the last case study, the linguistic analysis investigates how foreign policy discourse works as an identity-making tool that erects boundaries and specifies what constitutes the self, its allies and enemies and their changing meanings in the construction of post-Kemalist nation-state identity.

Related to the data collection, the selection procedures are developed in parallel to the main research question which seeks to highlight the diversity and dynamism of Turkish national identity discourse. Therefore, four daily newspapers – Muslim conservative *Zaman*, the best seller *Hurriyet*, Kemalist *Cumhuriyet* and liberal-leftist *Radikal* – are chosen for surveying and comparing different discourses of Turkish nationalism in the Turkish press. The websites of the newspapers permit an archive search; in particular, *Cumhuriyet* lets us access the electronic copies as they were printed from the 1920s to 2000s; but the other three newspapers' online archives are not like the printed versions. Therefore, after attaining a general portrait of the discourses in each newspaper and each year by online keyword search, in Ankara National Library is visited for working on the printed versions of the newspaper on the selected dates.

Because the data collected from Turkish daily newspapers are all in Turkish, the example statements of discourses should be translated into English. Language and translation surely matter for the analysis of the issues of bilingualism. However, avoiding the semantic shifts and transformation to keep the meaning in two languages is still possible in certain respects. Translated texts are double-checked by native bilingual translation expert. Second, the sources of original texts of the data will be added in the references section of the research. Significantly, the methodology of research, DHA, provides very detailed historical background information for the social contexts and the cases. With this given knowledge we can try to overcome the difficulty of studying in two different worlds of meaning, thus it can be argued that bilingualism will not affect the research's discourse analysis in the terms of meaning or content.

The newspapers' language use in referring to the social actors and the events, their background, context, or consequences tends to be based on ideological choices that depend on interests, concern and positions. What is reported and how it is reported can change or maintain the understanding of the narratives in a dynamic process. As stated, narratives are about reporting past events that impose certain meanings of world and stereotypical ways of thinking to serve the interests of power (Gillespie and Toynbee 2006: 114–15). In this context, news reporting and opinion articles on the events that appear in the selected newspapers,provide essential clues in uncovering ideological fault lines and the power struggle in the Turkish political sphere.

The keyword search also shows whose names appeared on a topic, and how many times. The columnists are chosen based on their intensity of salience in the newspaper. The columnists who intensively commented on the daily political agenda and openly identified their ideological views are considered for the discourse analysis. Most of them have written in their newspapers every week during the last decade and the articles of columnists are easily accessible online. Every single search on the selected topic frequently addresses regular writers.

To sum up, the specific dates of the events, the keywords with the key themes and the key writers are taken into account in sampling for the analysis. Bearing in mind the different ideological standpoints within the interpretivist qualitative research, generalization from the sample to the whole nation is not intended. However, on the assumption that repeated discourse in each newspaper would be representative of ideological argumentations in particular perspectives and privileging certain viewpoints, the systematicity in 'purposive sampling' (Bertrand and Hughes 2004: 199) is searched to establish a profile for distinguishing the perspectives of the main discourses of Turkish national identity.

Three stages of Discourse-Historical Approach

For the analysis of Turkish national identity discourse in the press, the discourse-historical analysis consists of the following three stages: (1) to establish the main themes of a specific discourse; (2) to investigate the discursive strategies used; and (3) to examine the linguistic means and realizations of the discursive strategies (Reisigl and Wodak 2001: 93). This guide, using these stages, is used to conduct the analyses of the data. Therefore, a description of the key themes of the discourses in three case studies of the research is a useful departure point. This will be followed by an outline of the discursive strategies used in the investigation of Turkish nationalisms as ideologies and the discursive construction of national identities. The last stage demonstrates how to search for the linguistic means and realisations of discursive strategies in order to observe how particular themes can be argued to contribute to the re-construction of Turkish nation-state identity.

The first stage: establishing the main themes of Turkey's identity: As stated before, the main context of the empirical research is intra-national and international (Wodak et al. 1999: 30) giving various discursive constructions of Turkishness in Turkish media. All aspects and complexity of Turkish identity cannot be covered in this study, and this is beyond the scope of it. Rather, this study indicates how the distinguished discourses can be said to contribute to the establishment of post-Kemalist Turkish national identity. Specific themes should be defined. After reviewing the case of Turkey, it can be seen that the Kemalist construction of secularist Turkish nation-state identity has been challenged by Islamic and Kurdish identities in the last decade, both at the national and international level, particularly whether 'to be' or 'not to be' a Western country. In order to examine different discursive constructions of Turkish nation-state identity in the national and international context, three themes are laid out in three selected case studies: being Muslim, being Kurdish, and being Western. The first case study focuses on the secular and Muslim character of the nation; thus, it analyses the largest Republican meetings against presidential elections in April and general election in July 2007. For the second theme of the study, the reconstruction of post-Kemalist nation-state identity through the transformation of Turkey's discourse on the Kurdish problem, the discussions of Kurdish Opening in the media discourse are taken into consideration. For the last theme, the West and Turkey's Western identity discourse are searched by sampling from discussions on the 'axis shift' of Turkish foreign policy in 2010.

Using both manual and digital search for key words reveals how elaborately and associatively these themes are presented in the coverage of Turkey's identity. To tackle the large body of these articles, these selected themes qualify and limit the 'sampling frame' (Bertrand and Hughes 2004: 67).

The second stage: investigation of the discursive strategies: After designing the research, defining the themes, and managing the data, the question then arises of how to analyse and evaluate the data, which requires finding discursive strategies. According to the content of each case study, the discursive strategies in the constitutive process of national identity are investigated to demonstrate how these themes contribute to particular power relationships and/or ideological standpoints. Strategies can work as constructive, destructive, perpetuatory, or transformatory (Wodak et al. 1999: 33–42) to achieve certain political, psychological, or other kinds of objectives in the national narrative. This research mainly seeks to search *constructive strategies* that attempt to construct and establish New Turkey's post-Kemalist national identity. In order to show the challenges of this identity along with the domestic power struggle, it reveals *strategies of perpetuation* which aim for continuity of Kemalist national identity; and *strategies of transformation* which aim to transform Kemalist national identity and its components into the post-Kemalist identity. The discursive strategies will be searched in:

(1) The linguistic construction of a common political past for an Islamic Ottoman or Republican-Secular charter of the national self.
(2) The linguistic construction of a common political present and future in the representation of the AKP's presidential candidate Abdullah Gul.
(3) The linguistic construction of a common present and future in the context of Turkey's Kurdish question.
(4) The linguistic construction of being Western in the context of religion and secularism.
(5) The linguistic construction of the issue of 'axis shift' in Turkish foreign policy's Western orientation.

The third stage: examination of the linguistic means and realizations of the discursive strategies: In the first case, constructive strategies are chosen for the observation of the sense of belonging together in the common past and future with a feeling of unity and uniqueness that defines insiders and outsiders (us/them) of the Turkish nation. In this context, the first case study attempts to identify how Turkish newspapers constructed national identity in the last decade, within the debates of presidential elections. The analysis concerns the secularist and non-secularist identity contradiction and is appropriated for an indication of the 'us' versus 'them' rhetoric in the religious theme of Turkish national identity.

Concerning Turkey's secular/Islamic identity, on one hand, the case of the presidential elections in 2007 would show how perpetuatory strategies are applied by Kemalist discourse actors to maintain the Republicanist state/nation tradition; on the other hand, how transformatory strategies work to change the secular component of Turkish national identity into another identity in Islamic discourse or liberal discourse. After the definition of the content and strategies of the first case study, the last dimension of the analysis looks at the linguistic means in the discursive construction of Turkish national identity. To find out the linguistic realization of narratives of common past, present, and future, the analysis should focus primarily on lexical units such as personal references, spatial references and temporal references (Wodak et al. 1999: 35). Discursive strategies of nomination in referring to people, events, or objects, distinguish the different collective representations via anthroponymy, personal deixis, synecdoche, metonymy and metaphors. Linguistic representation of social actors and events indicates sameness and difference between people in connection with constructive discursive strategies. For instance, particular ways of representation of AKP's presidential candidate Abdullah Gul or President Ahmet Necdet Sezer as a symbolic name for Republican secularism demonstrate a clear difference. Therefore, inclusive or exclusive, activated or passive, personal or impersonal and specific or generic reference to the events, people and places is closely associated with the newspaper's standpoint that empowers the voices of certain actors and silences others (Li 2009: 94).

In the analysis of the first case study, the use of personal pronouns such as 'we' and 'they' to address the self/other relations, are important in understanding who are included in the definition of the Turkish nation and who are excluded. In the observation of indicating ways of representing different perspectives of the nation and world in Turkish political discourse in the last decade, the media coverage of the presidential elections in 2007 gives fruitful material for the data analysis of the power struggle on re/construction of national identity discourse. For this analysis, the data is selected from the year of 2007 with a specific focus on the daily coverage of particular events: the nomination of Abdullah Gul as the AKP's candidate, the reactionary Kemalist mass demonstrations in Istanbul, Ankara and Izmir in April, the general election in July and the election of Abdullah Gul in August. Even the critical landmarks in this process are selected to narrow down the empirical source material of the case; the selection of the articles is further narrowed down qualitatively based on the joint appearance of the words 'Turkishness', 'Islam' and 'laicism' (*laiklik* is a more appropriate word instead of secularism in the case of Turkey).

The second case study deals with changing the perception of Kurdish identity in both the opposition and supporting argumentations through the representation of the Kurdish Initiative and nationalist conceptions constructed in the national press. Therefore, the focus of the linguistic analysis of these themes is both constructive and deconstructive in the constitutive process of national identity in the context of the Kurdish Initiative. This also shows to what extent Kurds are included and excluded in the different narratives of the nation. In dealing with social inequality and racism (Reisigl and Wodak 2001), the problem of prejudices and discrimination in Turkish national identity discourse will be located in the power struggle of competing self-definitions of the Turkish nation.

The last case study searching for Turkey's foreign policy identity, particularly its Western identity, focuses on the axis shift debate. This debate thematically serves to analyse the vision of Turkish foreign policy from a social constructivist and identity perspective. That means this study's interest is limited to how the Turkish press represents and constructs the self/other relationships in the means of Western identity. Therefore, the security and military dimensions of the issues are not covered in the selection of the data. Specifically, the third case reveals how the West is linguistically represented in the media and how these representations discursively construct post-Kemalist Turkish national identity and contribute to the domestic power struggle and the debate on Turkish foreign policy's axis shift.

The methodological critics and limitations

One of the main questions in the critic of Critical Discourse Analysis is about what motivates the selection of a fragment for the analysis (Molina 2009). Widdowson (2004: 63) argues that the pretext in CDA forms determines the selection of features for special attention in the discursive action. He identifies it as 'interpretative partiality' that causes pretextual positioned reading based on the purpose of analysis. To what extent does what is unaccounted for in the analysis matter to particular textual features that come into play in interpretation? Is CDA imposing selective attention, as Widdowson perceived? He claims that readers follow analysts' samplings, leading to confirm their findings by imposing interpretation (2004: 166). Surely, the textual analysis depends on the relationship between the text, context, and pretext (2004: 166). Thus, different contexts and pretexts might give rise to diverse interpretations and analyses.

What Widdowson (2004: 169) is suggesting, then, is that CDA might be more critical about its practices in consideration of different readings of the text, different social-cultural backgrounds and ideological positions of readers to understand the text (2004: 170). These assumptions are perceived as irrelevant if one looks at how the method of CDA is improving. Here it is thought that CDA is critical regarding not seeing the findings as conclusive or definite, which invites researchers to make an inspiring re-evaluation of the data. For interpretations, giving a general account of the historical context of the focus period does not necessarily drive a correlation or a certain analysis of discourses. On one hand, pretext given demonstrates the sources of specific language usage; on the other hand, tracing the discourse can drive new insights into reading social practices and historical processes. By following the principle of triangulation of the DHA (Weiss and Wodak 2003: 22), rather than simply focusing on the linguistic dimension, this research incorporates historical, sociological and international dimensions of the construction of Turkey's identity in three different case studies. Therefore, it is nourished and advanced from multi-case discourse analysis and multi-disciplinary work, including politics, history, sociology, nationalism and media studies. DHA enables us to show how the media narrative realizes representational and actional meanings of discourse in different intertextual relations in particular content, and constructs specific understandings of Turkey's Kemalist and post-Kemalist identities and positions.

Moreover, the concept of 'intertextuality' (Chilton 2013: 53) allows identification of the linkage of all texts to other texts through reference to the same themes and actors in the narration of the nation. This includes the reappearance of a text's topic or main argument in another text in different ways and for various purposes, including political purposes that reshape power structures. In this manner, intertextuality enables us to observe the shifts and stabilities in the discursive construction of national identity (Leeuwen and Wodak 1999). In this regard, coverage of the events in media discourse contributes to the continuous transmission of meaning over time. The themes of national identity appear in the media texts again and again through references to the meanings of the themes derived from its context and recontextualized or repeated utterances producing the same meaning of the events in different historical circumstances. Therefore, the DHA is chosen for this research to demonstrate the dynamic and hybrid character of Turkey's identity. Widdowson also notes that unstabilized and unfixed methodology in using a synthesis of different theories produces institutional and pedagogic disadvantages. But we can see this point as a powerful aspect of this methodology in its break with usual traditional procedures in doing social sciences, leaving the tendency to fit studies unequivocally into one box of a paradigm or a school. This has been already argued in *The Future of International Relations* (Neumann and Waever 1997) in saying 'No more masters!' with the attempt to trace unboxable persons in the discipline of IR and presenting comprehensively some authors who are difficult to be labelled. Moreover, CDA does not offer systematicity in doing analysis, but it brings a new epistemic order based on a moral stance. Working against unquestioned inequality and the status quo in social relations as a mission, not drawing concrete lines for working encourages improving the limits of open ways in analysing without stabilizing or normalizing 'given' principles, which is also parallel with its socio-political stance. Additionally, this moral position works in a parallel way of doing social science.

3

Discourse analysis

Imagining the New Turkey

Introduction

According to the Ankara University European Union Research and Application Center's academic survey (2010) on Turkish public perceptions on Turkey's identity, a clear diversity appears in the answers. Of the survey participants, 28.9 per cent defined Turkey as a European country, 22.6 per cent said Turkey is a Turkic country, 15.5 per cent viewed it an Islamic country, 11.4 per cent said Middle Eastern, 8.7 per cent noted Mediterranean and 8.6 per cent defined it as an Asian country. Moreover, this quantitative study of ATAUM showed the diversity of perceptions on Turkey's foreign policy identity; 37.5 per cent of the participants identified the United States as Turkey's enemy, 10.9 per cent Armenia and 10.6 per cent Israel. The country most likely to befriend Turkey was Azerbaijan with 29.9 per cent, None with 16.7 per cent and KKTC (Northern Cyprus Turkish Republic) with 15.6 per cent. Here, it was clear that Turks abroad were defined as friends of Turkey.

In this context, from a qualitative perspective by making use of Discourse-Historical Approach in Critical Discourse Analysis, this project contributes to the debate with a further understanding of why and where these different perceptions exist and come from, and how they relate to and challenge each other. Thus, this chapter aims to explore the emergence of the post-Kemalist narrative of Turkey and its challenges through analysing different discourses of Turkish identity in terms of religion, ethnicity and foreign policy. To articulate the construction of post-Kemalist Turkish nation-state identity in Turkish media discourse, this chapter analyses three cases of the national tension during Turkey's presidential election in 2007; the Kurdish Initiative in 2009; and the axis shift of Turkish foreign policy in 2010.

The Islamist challenge: the case of Turkey's presidential elections in 2007

As one of the main principles and components of Turkey's Kemalist nation-state identity, secularism is seen as fundamental for the conditions of democracy and modernity in Turkey. This case empirically shows that 'religion' is a major constitutive content of post-Kemalist nation-state identity and it has played a crucial role in the domestic struggle in redefinition of Turkey's international identity. In this context, Secularist-Islamist nationalist polarization will be analysed in the case of the presidential election of Turkey in 2007. It can be argued that every election resulted with the victory of the AKP used to legitimatize the power of government in questioning Kemalist tradition and reconstructing the post-Kemalist nation-state identity on a non-securitization of Islamic identity. Arguing that it is representative of the majority of Turkey, the AKP has managed to change some 'national habits' which have never been touched by any other previous governments – topics such as abandoning the celebration of the Commemoration of Ataturk, Youth and Sports Day in the stadiums on 19 May (which is the symbol of the start of the National Independence War), or giving more importance to the commemoration of Sultan Abdulhamid rather than Ataturk in the parliamentary agenda. Moreover, using democracy discourse for emancipation of religious 'freedoms' in order to live in an Islamic way in every aspect of social life, and using governmental support, brought about a deep polarization in the terms of secularism debates in the 2000s in Turkey. Stressing secularism and defence of Republican values raised a sharp contradiction of Islamist–Kemalist understandings of the nation in 2007.

With the influences of this circumstance and tension, a nationwide political crisis was provoked by secularists and the army when Turkey's Foreign Minister Abdullah Gul was nominated as presidential candidate by the ruling the AKP in April 2007. As a response, an e-memorandum on the website of the military was published to warn that it would intervene if secularism was put at risk. The main opposition party, the CHP, brought the issue of the presidential election to the Turkish Constitutional Court, arguing that the first round of voting in parliament was invalid on procedural grounds. This caused serious unrest among the AKP followers. Society was fragmented into camps. Kemalist secularist masses with the discourse of protecting the Republican state system organized mass demonstrations against the AKP's hidden agenda to islamize Turkey (Hojelid 2010: 468). In opposition to that, the AKP and Islamists complained about the non-pluralist and illiberal form of secularism and state– society relationship that discriminated against religious people and inhibited religious freedom (Hojelid 2010: 476). The gap between the incumbents and the CHP has continued to widen (Ciddi 2008: 438) before the election of July 2007 which affected the results. The Republican People's Party came in second with 20.8 per cent of the vote, trailing behind the AKP's 46.5 per cent which represented a slight increase in the vote share of the CHP from 2002 (19.4 per cent) and a large increase for the AKP (34.4 per cent in 2002). It shows that political polarizations in Turkey are used for maximizing the political profit from the turmoil by sharpening political party affiliation. What is missing and forgotten in this political calculation is that it is not a win-win game. The politicization of identities jeopardises mutual respect and confidence among people. Both the ways of dealing with assertive secularist practices and religious pressure on people are threatening and ominous, whereas the main point is guaranteeing pluralism in society. This chapter demonstrates how Turkish media represents this power struggle between secularist and Islamist circles through this selected historical political process in order to see how they imagine Turkey and the Turkish nation in terms of religion and secularism.

On understanding the nation and nation-state identity: which Turkey?

The events in 2007 showed that the secularization project of the Kemalist elites reached to the level of the broad masses and had a strong influence on Turkish society in terms of modernization. According to Merve Kavakci-Islam (2010: 41), the Kemalist reforms as 'forced modernisation' caused a fragmentation of society in Turkey into two camps: one modern Turkey and the other Turks who lived, thought, and dressed differently. In the case of dressing, her volume on 'headscarf politics in Turkey' discovers the linkage between politics, a woman's body and clothing. She argues that the Kemalists' strict anti-veil politics created 'a war waged by women against women' (2010: 42). Kemalist women perceive the black veil as embarrassing for a modern image of Turkey in the eyes of other nations (2010: 44), which is seen humiliating or undermining the way of life of the 'other Turkey'. It is also evidence of how the top-down invention of a tradition expanded to the masses and was internalized by Kemalist circles. If one accepts that women are the main reproducers of the nation biologically, culturally and symbolically (Yuval-Davis 1993), the importance of divided perceptions on 'womanhood' in Turkey can be well understood.

Alev Cinar's *Modernity, Islam, and Secularism in Turkey: Bodies, Places, and Time* (2005) provides an even deeper account of Turkey's revolutionary break from the Ottoman Islamic way of living with a specific focus on the concepts of 'clothing the national body' and the appearance of women in public places. Through the regulation of clothing, the categorizing of gender, class, status, and religion, a public-private distinction was operating through different interventions upon the body. Clothing is one of the most effective signs for recognition and differentiation (2005: 55) which determines these identity categories, most crucially the national identity. States and nations are represented by their people in the body of man and woman. Thus, as is noted by Cinar, the body is metaphorically employed not only as a symbol of the nation and its boundaries, but also as a material space where the boundaries of the public and the private are drawn toward the construction of the national public subject.

In other words, the politics of body serves to form a sense of belonging to a nation. In the case of Turkey, unveiling the female body during the formative years of the Republic constituted the public realm as a secular domain. This gendering intervention was legitimated with the rhetoric of liberation of the body/nation (2005: 62) from the Islamic covering, closing or hiding culture. The state encouraged the visibility of women representatives in various jobs such as pilots, lawyers and politicians, wearing elegant European dresses in the public sphere and in the media as national signifiers of Western-orientated secular modernity. In this way, the Turkish woman had a distinctive body, face and voice. This emancipation of the female body generated a new order of power relations and made the secularists' elite circles advantaged groups in the centre. The state elites' particular interpretation of modernity sneaked into the state's citizenship regime (Donmez and Enneli 1332011: 1) as an inclusion/

exclusion mechanism for managing society. Beyond the constitutional discourse, it functioned to gain privileged positions for secularist Kemalist identities and pushed others, namely conservative Islamic identities, into a secondary position. This point elucidates the origins of the power struggle in Turkey's last decade. Imagining Turkey as secular or Islamic is not just a matter of state regime, but also a matter of lifestyle that determines how the Turks want to live.

In the last decade, the argument about AKP's islamization of the country and state institutions is mostly promoted by pro-secularist *Cumhuriyet*'s news reports, with numerous examples of negative connotations of political continuation driven by the ruling party. For instance, a report titled 'the headscarf ban is not operational' noted that 'Hacer Yildirim, who is working as a teacher in the Narli town of Lacin, a sub-province of Corum, enters the classroom wearing a headscarf since the AKP came into power' (*Cumhuriyet*, 27 October 2005). These kinds of news items were used for verifying their argumentation of what had been changed by the AKP. In another example, the ban on alcohol was regarded as an attack on 'the secular and democratic Republic, fundamental rights and freedoms'. It was reported that the ban on alcohol in Lake Mogan and Goksu Park in Ankara met with a strong reaction. Moreover, it was identified in negative connotations by using the words of 'a disgrace for the capital' (*Cumhuriyet*, 20 October 2005). Similarly, in a report titled 'Waiting for God for Help', the argumentative scheme which was used as a strategy of transformation indicated a change in the AKP period: 'Are we in the modern times? The municipalities of AKP who are busy with the alcohol ban disregarding human health… Diarrhoea continues in Malatya… The situation is clear… Applicants to the hospital have reached eight thousand. The number of infected people has reached to forty thousand…' (*Cumhuriyet*, 3 December 2005).

In this quotation, the adverbial expression of 'the modern times' in the question is employed for establishing an oppositional discourse to the government's local policies, which argues AKP is not doing the necessities of modern life, instead it is taking society to pre-modern times. The argument is supported by illustrations of AKP's policy on alcohol, ignorance of the public's health and raising an epidemic in Malatya. A common activity in negative predication is to compare and to contrast the positive traits with the negative traits. The pro-secular media discourse exhibits a resistance against the transformation driven by the pro-

Islamist AKP. With the metaphor of 'TRT, AKP's farm' (*Cumhuriyet*, 8 June 2006), it was claimed that TRT, the state-owned television and radio institution, turned into the media organ of the AKP with their programmes propagandizing the sharia. The 'farm' in the lexical structure of the description of TRT addresses a relationship between the word and some aspects of the material world (Fowler 1991: 81), where the AKP does what it wants as it owns this state institution.

In the debate on Islam and modernism, in *Hurriyet* (24 August 2007) Ozdemir Ince writes an article entitled: 'Headscarf and Semiology' which claims that using Islamic symbols in the public space such as in academia or in a hospital does not indicate the interdependence of modern public and private life in a society, but shows the 'fragmented individual' and Islamic society: 'The headscarf of a woman who uses the computer and microscope, who works as a doctor or a CEO, does not represent a modern and secular individual or society but signifies a fragmented individual and a totalitarian Islamic community which uses technology.'

Given that content, the last passage also serves to see how some ideological groups perceive the relationship between Islam and modernism in terms of science and secularism. Frequently visible in the articles are the signs that belief in religion and modernity cannot operate together. In this discriminatory and orientalistic approach, the scientific and religious identity of a woman represents a totalitarian Islamic nation. This Kemalist discourse constructs an antagonism between secular/modern society and Islamic/totalitarian society. This perspective can be accepted as a Kemalist positivist approach as well. Moreover, Ince (*Hurriyet*, 26 August 2007) underlines the objections to stressing the Muslimhood of the population: 'Nobody is even aware that sentences beginning with "a country in which 99 per cent of the population is Muslim as in Turkey" are a violation to secularism and killing secularism.' In this anthropomorphic presentation of secularism, it is clear that Islam is seen as a direct 'threat' to the Republican-secular system by Kemalists. In April 2007, this topos of threat was widely used in the pro-secular discourse of the newspaper *Cumhuriyet*. Its columnist Erdal Atabek described this threat as Turkey's transformation and separation: 'Turkey is being transformed to two separate countries: "Secular, independent Republic of Ataturk" and "religion axial moderate Islamic republic". Secular, independent Republic of Ataturk is clearly in danger. It is now clear that Turkey is aware of the danger' (*Cumhuriyet*, 23 April 2007).

Atabek warns against heteronomy in using the words 'two separate countries' in a comparison. Positive self-presentation is a remarkable strategy in making a selective use of lexical and adjectives such as 'independent' character of the 'founding generation' (Wodak et. al. 1999: 41) and M. Kemal Ataturk's Republic. In addition, there is a negative connotation of political continuation in state– religion relations. The warning against the loss of national autonomy and secularism is emphasized with the topos of danger, which demonstrates a resistance to the Islamic transformation of the state to a moderate Islamic Republic. In this example, 'Turkey' appears as a metonym: first it implies the country, then in the last sentence it refers to the nation or the people. Moreover, 'Republic of Ataturk' is a synecdoche of the state, 'Turkey'. These examples of language use show that the meanings of the state and the nation overlap in the discourses. Thus, the pro-secular circles interpret the recent changes in the state discourse as a threat to their identities and nation. Ersin Kalaycioglu (*Radikal*, 14 April 2007) explains how this threat is perceived by some circles, particularly by 'young officers of the army': 'These people do not only consider their lifestyle under threat, but that their lives are also under threat. They are afraid that those without headscarves will be attacked with acid and hanged as in Iran.' The point made by the example of Iran is highly important to see how some groups have internalized the secular system and ways of life in Turkey, therefore the pro-secularist discontent is more than a resistance to a regime change, it is a deeply rooted fear of death. In this context, Turkish President Ahmet Necdet Sezer (*Radikal*, 14 April 2007) stated that the political regime had never been in more danger since the foundation of the Republic and added:

> However, there are three important facts that these circles need to be aware of: First bringing the theocratic state – whether it is moderate or radical – and democracy is an approaching violation to history and science. Second, it is inevitable that the moderate Islam will quickly turn into radical Islam. Third, the Republic of Turkey made her choice of regime 84 years ago with the foundation of the Republic. This regime is an enlightened and modern regime bound to the principles and revolutions of Ataturk and the nationalism of Ataturk based on a secular, democratic and social state of law.

In this speech of President Ahmet Necdet Sezer, three aspects of 'critique' (Wodak et al. 1999: 8–9) can be examined in the search of specific characteristics of the Turkish case. *'Text immanent critique'* uncovers contradictions in different discourses of Turkish nationalism, namely Kemalist nationalism and Islamist nationalism. '*Socio-diagnostic critique*' explores the functions of discursive practices in advocating persuasion or resistance. The emphasis on positive characteristics of the secular regime such as being *enlightened, modern and democratic* intends to maintain Kemalist nation-state identity and resist an Islamic transformation. Furthermore, '*retrospective critique*' reveals how a narrative of the collective past plays a role in the ways of dealing with its consequences and effects. The stress on 'Turkey made her choice of regime 84 years ago' and Ataturk nationalism based on 'a secular, democratic and social state of law' illustrates the current way of dealing with Turkish history and the pro-secular perspective on present problems.

Radikal also gave place to opinions on the side of the government. Abdullah Gul commented on the concerns of the President: 'I am not fully aware of what Mr. President said but the Turkish people do not believe that. On the contrary, it is not only Turkey but also foreigners trust Turkey today.' *Zaman*'s (14 April 2007) report took the line of supporting Gul's statement that noted Turkish people did not agree with Sezer's ideas on the regime. According to *Zaman*, President Sezer's statement given one month before the end of his term had been met with strong reactions. Sezer claimed that the regime was in danger, but he could not put forward tangible evidence. 'Most of the people' did not share Sezer's views. This statement serves to support the AKP government's claim that they represent the majority of the Turkish people. They claim that Turkey was governed by a Kemalist elitist minority who were not aware of the Turkish people's demands and sentiments. Hence, the AKP government and the new elite in-state bureaucracy aim to change the old image of Turkey and offer to do things in their own way.

Although there was rising tension on the side of Kemalist circles against Islamization, the members of the AKP opted to use the concept of conservatism. Consistently and insistently, they said that they were not Islamists but conservative democrats. Therefore, liberal and some leftist circles were supporting the changes driven by the government. On the other side, the opposition around the CHP produced the discourse that Islam was coming. Using the terms 'threat' and 'anti-revolution' caused politicization of Islamic identity and its holders, including those who never intended or even thought about opposing the state's regime and secularism. While describing the turban as an ideological weapon of political Islam, the masses with any kind of ordinary headscarf were pushed towards the polarization discourse that took Turkey to an early general election decision driven by the presidential election crisis.

Being the president of Turkish Republic: who should represent the Turkish nation?

President Ahmet Necdet Sezer stated that 'The political regime has never been in more danger since the foundation of the Republic.' Opposing that, the president of the Turkish Great National Assembly, Bulent Arinc (*Hurriyet*, 14 January 2007) harshly reacted: 'We will elect a religious president' and 'It is not the regime that is in danger but the power of the status quoists that is in danger. This is a bitter and relentless claim.' In this expression, there is a presupposition claiming the Republican system created the status quo of its advantaged and disadvantaged groups in the construction of power relations. Arinc's sentences represent the views of Islamists who think the Kemalist nation-state system requires a change in existing power relations. The AKP transforms the nature of central administration and bureaucracy by bringing the voices of the religious masses to Ankara. *Zaman* (22 April 2007) illustrated this resistance to change in the context of President Sezer's use of his veto power against the government. Emine Dolmaci claimed that Sezer's definition of the president was 'a shield to state, a barrier to action'. She compared Sezer with Kenan Evren who was the president of Turkey at the time of the 1980 military coup: 'Sezer who has vetoed fifty-nine laws during his four years with the AKP government, double the amount achieved during the coup when President Kenan Evren vetoed twenty-six laws.' Comparing the negative aspect of the past with Sezer's present acts also portrays the opinions of people who think the opposition parties are preventing AKP's attempt to consolidate democracy.

What kind of president should represent Turkey? Author Ayla Kutlu answered this question for *Cumhuriyet* (30 January 2007). She expressed her belief that the first six articles of the Constitution defining 'the form of the state, the characteristics of the Republic, unity of the state, official language, flag, national anthem and capital and irrevocable provisions, fundamental objectives and duties of the state, sovereignty' simultaneously defined the beliefs, philosophical thought system and protective notion of the president of the Republic of Turkey. Kutlu noted regarding the concerns about the spouse of a president who is wearing a headscarf as a role model to women: 'The spouse of the President should at least have a modern identity.' This expression demonstrates the Kemalist understanding of modernity and its links with the nation's secularist identity; therefore, the wife of the president, as the female face of Turkey, should have a modern appearance.

Cuneyt Ulsever (*Hurriyet*, 26 August 07) transcended the symbolic power of the headscarf and its usage in the public arena with a specific focus on how social policies could influence other ways of life and how Islamic dress might be politicized and used for putting pressure on the sameness of some citizens and the differentiation of others:

> While social policies determine how to behave, dress and eat, they also determine how we think, whether we are aware of it or not. The dominant lifestyle gradually affects the 'other'. For example, a lady who basically covers her head with a headscarf may begin to use a turban just because of the interrogative looks she receives. The National Vision, which thinks that it is seizing control of the state by electing Abdullah Gul as President, may further increase the social imposition in this term.

Ulsever's text is useful to connect the nationalist discourse and power. If a certain discourse becomes dominant, it has the power of control people's ways of thinking and behaving. As noted in previous chapters, nationalism is a way of seeing, thinking and structuring the world we live in, thus it is much more than a political doctrine (Mihelj 2011: 17). The social world is fundamentally divided and structured along power relations and perspective differences. There are different national imaginations and nationalist visions of the world and for achieving legitimacy these perspectives would compete to act as a representative of the nation. Each group may privilege their own perspective of what the nation is physically, culturally and historically (Skey 2011: 12). By the example of the headscarf issue, Ulsever expressed the anxiety of the secularist circles and their struggle to secure a sense of self and maintain a knowable and manageable sense of identity and community in response to the social and political transformations due to the risk of Islamic imposition.

The Republican demonstrations in the Turkish media

This section articulates that there are different interpretations of Turkish nationhood and nation-state identity. In the discourse analysis of the Turkish print press, how in-group and out-group presentations are constructed by using the words of 'we' and 'you' show different identifications in Turkish society. In addition, the analysis of mood structure (Reisigl and Wodak 2001: 83) of the comments serves to understand the struggle for power between the pro-secularists and Islamists during the Republican meetings in 2007. Moreover, the examples highlight the interference of concepts of 'nation' and 'state' in the Turkish case. For instance, *Cumhuriyet* (14 April 2007) underlined the significance of the secular Republican regime and the Islamist 'danger' towards to the 'Republic of Turkey': 'The Republic of Turkey, for the first time in its history, is in such great danger. Hundreds of thousands of people meet in Ankara Tandogan Square to manifest that the Republic is not without ownership. We are aware of the danger.'

This expression implies that the pro-secularist community imagines 'we' as the guardians of the Republican system and rhetorically its owners. In this context, during the spring of 2007 *Cumhuriyet* newspaper called people to the squares of the country for the demonstrations against the AKP government and its 'Islamic' policies. Mustafa Balbay (*Cumhuriyet*, 30 April 2007) stressed the co-responsibility of everyone in Anatolia to protect the modernity of the country, secular regime of the state and the unity of the nation:

> We are in a time in which Ataturk's statement 'If the issue is country, the rest are details' fits perfectly. At this point, it is not about the left-right, the military-civil, but just Turkey. Everybody willing to preserve the national unity, secular structure and modernity of Turkey should take part. In this context, the left-right political circles, the NGOs originated in Anatolia, the professional chambers, the military, civilians, everybody has a duty. Tandogan-Caglayan is the manifestation of this responsibility.

In contrast to the pro-secularist *Cumhuriyet*'s discourse, Vahap Coskun (*Zaman*, 14 April 2007a) used a different rhetorical perspective towards the Republican demonstrations, in noting 'Please admit that you are having difficulty in absorbing democracy.' He added that there was rising tension in society about the presidency being in such a central position in the system, made by others who consider themselves to be 'the real owners of the state and the landlord of the people'..

According to *Radikal*'s coverage, the participants at the meetings, most of whom were coming from other cities, chanted the slogans: 'We are not pro-coup; we are revolutionist', 'We do not want an Imam in Cankaya', 'Cankaya is secular and will remain so'. The crowd objected to Prime Minister Tayyip Erdogan's ascension to the presidency and targeted the United States: 'Damn American imperialism!' *Radikal* reported that Ataturkist Ideas Organisation vice Director Nur Serter said: 'Turkey says "stop" to those who treat the democracy as a tool and who seek alliance with the peshmarga camps. We are nationalist, Kemalist and patriots. We are the enlightened future of Turkey, the real children of the country and follow in the footsteps of our Ataturk.' This speech reflects the mentality of Kemalist nationalism. Kemalists' definition of 'we' is an example of positive self-presentation, which is seen in the lexical units such as 'enlightened future' and 'real children of the country'. The hidden meaning in Serter's speech is that participants of these meetings think that democracy is not the real destination for the government, but is a vehicle to arrive at the other intended destination. In this text, combination of propositions supplies a typical narrative of Kemalist nationalists who argue that the AKP has an agenda of Islamization for Turkey. This instance implicitly constructs sameness within the group and cannot avoid the usage of 'we' meaning 'the Turks' but only 'Kemalist one'. The statements are used as an important device to express the views that Kemalists do not want a person with an Islamist past in Cankaya, where the house of Ataturk and Republican system is symbolized. This discourse aims to promote a certain, secular image of Turkey: here, Kemalist self-identification as 'the real children of the country', the expression of Islamist critic on Kemalist mentality.

By referencing Nur Serter in lexemes with semantic components constructing difference and exclusion, *Zaman* (14 April 2007b) establishes a different narrative on the meetings associated with non-Muslimhood and anti-headscarf discourse. It is claimed that Serter was the member of the sect who believed they encountered the spirit of Jesus. This argumentation employs a trivialization strategy that has the function of othering Serter and degrading the Republican protests. *Zaman* reminded that Nur Serter established persuasion chambers in the university against the headscarf protests when she was the vice rector of Istanbul University. For a short note about the headscarf protests, the headscarf was banned in 1987 in Turkish universities. When the Turkish Army compelled the Islamist Erbakan government to implement the ban without exception in 1997, some professors and teachers tried to persuade female university students in 'persuasion rooms' to take their headscarves off. This caused the spread of headscarf demonstrations in the country (Celik Wiltse 2008; Barras 2009; Guven 2010; Guveli 2011; Akboga 2014). Reminding readers of Serter's role in the headscarf protests and labelling her with a membership of a sect, constructed a discourse of 'they are not like us' and built an opponent discourse against the secularist protesters. What people know or how people look at the experiences and struggles in the past is based on a selective reading of history (Inthorn 2007), but this determines present struggles to secure their future as how they want to live it with their ways of life and perspectives of world. What is forgotten here is that people who call themselves secularist in Turkey are also the members of Muslim majority in Turkey. What divides Muslims are the ways they want to live their life and beliefs.

Zaman (14 April 2007b) used massive negative associations and connotations to describe the participants of the pro-secularist meetings: 'Ataturkist Ideas Organisation members are uncomfortable at being called pro-coup.' Linking the AIO with the military coup was also supported by a visual means of realization, a photograph showing one of the banners in the meeting read: 'The laws of the military intervention shall be in effect.' *Zaman* argued that the leftist, revolutionist groups – according to Islamists these are non-religious groups – organized the demonstrations: 'The only right-wing to attend the meeting was Yasar Okuyan.' This example corresponded with a trivialization strategy in presentation of the meetings. More noteworthy was that the modality of *Zaman* appears in a first page report by just giving a small detail from the meeting of thousands of people in Tandogan. Without noting why this event was organized or what its agenda was, and its content, demonstrations were directly connected with the AIO with other negative other representations: 'Tuncay Ozkan's provocation angered even the AIO. Ozkan's speech, even if he was not in the programme, caused chaos.' With limited knowledge and making personal references to the leftist, revolutionist or pro-coup masses, this coverage allowed different readings of the events and what was actually going on in the country. In this context, *Radikal*'s (15 April 2007) interpretation of the meetings was entitled 'important warning for Erdogan' by giving details of the aims and discourses of the participants.

As is seen in these examples, Islamist and Kemalist discourses construct, deconstruct and re-form each other. Beyond the Islamist-Secularist polarization, Baskın Oran (*Radikal*, 20 May 2007) noted that the other participants in the meetings defended the third way in the discourse of 'neither the patten (medieval shoe) nor the army boots'. According to his observation, one of the most important slogans of the Republican meetings was anti-imperialism. What were common and easy to observe in these meetings were the direct and indirect forms of marginalization of non-Muslims and the West:

> They aim to establish the Pontus, they will turn Fener into Vatican, and they divide us by using missionaries, Armenians demand land, transsexuals are everywhere, etc. More direct ones are: The EU will divide Turkey. One of most common banners is: 'Neither the USA nor the EU'... Of course, there are those in the meetings who say, 'neither the patten (medieval shoe) nor the army boots'. But the majority of those say: 'If we are losing secularism, our Army will be our crown.'

The Turkish media coverage of the results of the 2007 national elections

The AKP achieved a rare success of having 46.5 per cent of the vote in the general elections of 2007 held during the tension of the discussion about the presidency and the memorandum. *Radikal*'s (23 July 2007a) comment on the results was 'the memorandum of the people'. It was supported by a quotation from Erdogan's speech: 'Upon the question "Did Mr. Gul's ineligibility affect the result?" Erdogan replied: "Of course. People reacted both to the Constitutional Court and the barriers on the way of Mr. Gul."'

Mahfi Egilmez (*Radikal*, 23 July 2007c) demonstrated the main reason for the AKP's success was the economic performance following the economic crisis: the decrease in inflation, sustainable growth, decrease in budget deficit, decrease in debt burden and tolerable current deficit rate and direct foreign investment in Turkey all contributed greatly to AKP. In opposition, Emre Kongar (*Cumhuriyet*, 30 July 2007) argued that it was surprising that the AKP could not get more votes; only reaching 46.5 per cent due to the AKP using both religion and money as election tactics and also the fact that it had these powers behind it : 'international capital, national capital, the USA, the EU, international media, national media, central bureaucracy, municipalities, religious communities, some of the minorities, Northern Iraq

Kurd Administration, Iraq's Kurdish origin Head of State, Greece, Cyprus Greek Administration.'

In addition, *Cumhuriyet* (24 July 2007b) reported that AKP had increased its votes mostly in Eastern and South-eastern regions. AKP received 60 per cent of the votes in the region and this was mainly because AKP resisted the Army's operations in Northern Iraq before the elections and thereby gained the support of the people. Another reason was that the community leaders of the region – where the religious communities are quite strong – steered their followers towards AKP which meant that illiterate voters could not be organized to vote for the independent deputies of the Democratic Turkey Party (DTP). This information argues that the general increase in AKP's votes was based on the Kurdish people's support in Eastern and South-eastern regions of Turkey. It was a fact that the alliance of Kurdish and Islamists for reconstruction of the Kemalist nation-state identity has been a crucial factor in reconfiguration of power relations during the last decade.

In order to challenge the Kemalist state legacy, there was populist support for the AKP. Some liberal and leftist writers also joined this camp for the consolidation of democracy in Turkey. Hadi Uluengin (*Hurriyet*, 24 July 2007) wrote that it was a civil victory against the militarist, secularist and old Kemalist paradigm. The newest paradigm was born on July 22. Mehmet Barlas (*Hurriyet*, 28 July 2007) supported this argument in noting the elections of 2007 changed the power relations in Turkey. The centre, the power and the cities were shared by both urban and rural populations. Cengiz Candar (*Hurriyet*, 24 July 2007) declared that the election result was a glory of democracy. He added that this made him happy to be a part of this country and nation. Bekir Coskun (*Hurriyet*, 24 July 2007) interpreted the AKP's success and its overwhelming victory as the acknowledgment of Turkey's changing face, which he described as the transformation of a secular republic into a moderate Islam through these elections. The high level of votes meant that the support for the AKP enabled it to realize its image of Turkey.

From a bigger picture of the results, Haluk Sahin (*Radikal*, 23 July 2007d) noted three discourses of Turkey associated with the election results. This demonstrates that different priorities constitute different messages and solutions as to what comes first for Turkey, namely, Islam, democracy, secular Republican system, equal constitutional citizenship or pluralism. It refers to the political polarization in Turkey and constructs intra-national difference, in other words, internal sub-national differentiation between Turkish people:

> I have thought that this election would have three messages before we started to get the results: if the AKP reaches a majority more than 40 per cent 'Do not touch my democracy', if the total votes of the CHP and the MHP reach to 40 per cent 'Do not play with my Republic'…And of course depending on the votes of the independent deputies: 'We are here as well!'.

Conclusions

This case study showed that the national media not only symbolize and represent the nation but also construct it by speaking for and to the nation. The media coverage of the events from 2007 demonstrated the national tension and power struggle for maintaining Turkey's Kemalist nation-state identity and challenging post-Kemalist discourse. The newspaper texts regarding politically and culturally important events, namely the Republican Protests for examination of Turkey's post-Kemalist identity were chosen, and the data was tested based on the content, strategies used in the discursive construction of national identity and the linguistic means employed. The ideological stance of the newspapers was a determinant in the national imaginings they represented. Therefore, the presentation of the actors, the political past and present in the texts were primarily between the strategies of perpetuation and of transformation depending on the ideological, political affiliation of the newspapers.

The study confirmed that there are competing narratives of the Turkish nation. The power struggle was fundamental among the secularist and Islamist versions of the Turkish imagination of the nation. During the struggle, the AKP's post-Kemalist official discourse of national identity was challenged by the discourse of Kemalist and ethno-nationalist people. In addition, the discourse of otherness of non-Muslims was dominant in the newspapers, which revealed its impact on popular discourses and its power in all Turkish nationalist ideologies while Muslim identity appeared as the main component of Turkish national character. The examples confirm that being Muslim constructs a unity in Turkish people, but the ways of living it divide them. In this context, the nation-state's foundation and formation of secularism are problematic components which diversely appear in the competing narratives of the nation's history.

What is very much alive in the Kemalist imagination of the Turkish nation are the memories of the Independence War and Republican legacy of Mustafa Kemal Ataturk. In the present, its ideologists are constructing a new independence war discourse with a strategy directed against the AKP and its transformation in Turkey's Kemalist domestic and foreign policies. It points out that the negative aspects of the present must be confronted in a continued fight for a change aimed at the AKP; therefore, Kemalists organized Republican demonstrations and called Turkish people to a rise up. Common to all Kemalist discourse is their belief that the Republican system and their secular life is under Islamist threat. In *Cumhuriyet*, certain political continuities are portrayed in a negative way that presents the achievements of the Republican system as being in danger. In the selected texts, the fear is interwoven that Turkey could again become a 'dark' country by the supposed proof that reaction has always been there, today more than ever, and, of course, it is strongest within an international alliance of internal and external enemies of the Republican system. The main strategy in the Kemalist *Cumhuriyet* newspaper underlines the threat against the secular system and the aim of maintaining the Kemalist narrative of the nation.

This perpetuation strategy, which has been used several times, is the strategy also used by the columnists of the *Hurriyet* newspaper in the simultaneous emphasis on secularism. On the other hand, Islamists use the strategy of transformation and express a perception that sees these opponent movements as the resistance to change and democracy. Therefore, *Zaman* writers stress that Kemalist opponents seek for the status quo that perpetuates their privileged positions against the 'Muslim majority'. Islamists claim that there has been a downward Kemalist pressure on their way of life since the early years of the Republican system. On the whole, it can be said that the strategy of self-victimhood and the 'we are the victims' thesis are common in both sides, referring to 'others' as being very one-sided. On one side, Kemalists blame others for having threatened the secular and modern character of the nation in expressing a concern about a possible loss of significance of Kemalist Republican structure; on the other, Islamists blame others for having controlled their expression of Islamic ways of living and raise concerns that Kemalist nationalism ended the multi-cultural legacy of the Ottoman Empire; thus, the Republican state fed racism and racist actions towards others.

It can be said that the analysed texts from Dogan Media Group's *Radikal* and *Hurriyet* show that these newspapers covered oscillating news reports during the the Republican demonstrations in 2007. Where it occurs in the texts, it frequently not only serves the purpose of self-representation but is also part of an aim of promoting national identification and an emphasis on the difference between secularists, Islamists and liberal interpretations of Turkish nation-state identity. It can be easily identified through the analysis that there is a common problem. A critical feature of these different discourses of Turkish nationalism is their failure to promote an alternative language for living together without the exclusion of any other different lifestyle or worldview. They harshly compete for hegemony. Once they have the chance to get power, they use this power to oppress others. Beyond the main clash for reconstruction of Turkish nation-state identity, the most disadvantaged group seems to be the non-Muslims whose future and identification depends on the highly polarized and politically divided Muslim majority. It can be said that New Turkey's identity constructs a post-secular, privileged, modern Muslim identity, builds a xenophobic relationship with non-Muslims and seeks a pragmatic relationship with the 'Christian' West. Thus, post-Kemalism as the new dominant nationalist discourse fails to challenge the shortcomings of Kemalist nation-state identity and citizenship formation. Nevertheless, top-down neo-conservative social engineering reproduces and sharpens the domestic antagonisms between different discourses of nationalism in Turkey.

The Kurdish challenge: the case of Kurdish Initiative

Specifically, Turkey's Kurdish question provides numerous instances associated with Turkey's tension in the preservation and redefinition of national identity in the last decades. Keeping this point in mind, this case study is devoted to seeing how the Turkish media address the links between the AKP's Kurdish Initiative surrounded by this tension. This section reveals the ethnic side of the post-Kemalist Turkish nation-state identity construction in analysing how Turkish media represent the Kurdish question in dealing with the domestic power struggle on redefinition of Turkish nation-state identity and its relations with the Kurds.

As noted in previous chapters, the Kemalist state has not recognized Kurds as a distinct group when nominating all Muslim communities of the Turkish Republic as the Turks. It would be interpreted as the Kurds having equal positions such as the majority, the Sunni Muslim Turks. This requires recognizing their cultural rights and sharing power equally. Kemalist discourse in the media supports this state argument, thus in coverage of the problem they mostly call them 'Kurdish originated citizens' which means they are Turks. Instead of calling them 'Turks', *Turkiyeli* (from Turkey) accepts the distinct identities of Muslim and non-Muslim communities of Turkey. It signals the distinction between being a part of a people and being a part of the state/land. Using the pronoun 'we' and identifying all as 'Turkiyeli' has a solidarity-enhancing function (Wodak et al. 1999: 100).

The Kurdish question in the Turkish media discourse

In terms of narrating the national history of Turkey, particular historical events and facts are portrayed through certain linguistic means. These linguistic realizations identify exactly how Turkey imagines itself as a nation. Inevitably, a nation's origin and foundation are mostly addressed (Wodak et al. 1999: 83) in these narratives. Regarding this point, Islamist, liberal and leftist discourses refer to the established time of the Turkish nation-state to indicate the historical and political roots of the Kurdish problem, specifically the denial of Kurdish cultural rights in the nation-building process of the Republic. In both the Islamist and Liberal discourses, there is a common factor which determines the ways in which the origin of Kurdish Question is referred to and which actors and institutions received attention from these explanations. Islamist *Zaman*'s columnist Mumtazer Turkone and liberal *Taraf*'s author Ayhan Aktar, focus on the exclusion of Kurdishness in the discursive construction of the common political past of the nation. Turkone adopts the topos of 'fear' to demonstrate the causal relations in the evolution of the Kurdish problem and their exclusion in the nation-building process. He reminds us that Turkey was built like a Simurgh mixing the ashes of the empire and underlines the way to get rid of the fear of losing was to create a nation who would live within the state. He argues that the ones who attempted to create the nation with this fear were unfair to the Kurds:

> They ignored their native languages and identities because they thought that these would make them 'another nation' and tried to destroy them. Today, we are looking for the consent of a nation consisting of the honourable and equal individuals, and the state in which the Kurdish will live with their native language and identities based on this consent. Now we are in a moment that means fate can tip the scales for hope. Perhaps, we will change the history continuing for 210 years, in 2010… This year will be the starting date of a civilised life in which the armed tyranny will end, this beautiful country will get rid of the gangs forever, and everyone will be on his own way, self-and-future-assuredly. (*Zaman*, 1 January 2010, p. 7)

In the article, Turkone reminds us of the collective past of the nation and how the fear of intervention and the loss of the homeland motivated the Independence War against external others. This even reflected the first words of the Turkish national anthem as 'Do not fear', which calls on the sovereignty and flag of the nation to be defended until the last man dies in the homeland. Then he notes how this fear turned to create 'internal others' in the construction of the Turkish nation-state. The lexical units in the text, particularly the personal pronouns, give clues in blaming 'other' strategy. He uses a negative connotation, a metaphor of the 'armed tyranny' to present 'them', the foundation elites of the Republic, namely the Kemalists. On the other hand, a 'we-group' is formed in the argumentation of 'we will change the history continuing for 210 years, in 2010'. By the strategy of transformation, a necessary discontinuation is referred to in the representation of the common present and future with the will of a civilized life for everyone. Significantly, this example confirms how Muslim conservatives and Kurds became successful in creating common consent for challenging the 'Kemalist army-state' and the construction of post-Kemalist nation-state identity.

In the first chapter of this book, the citizenship status of minorities in Turkey is given to provide background information for a variety of possible nominations for minority identification. It is also noted that Muslim communities, including Kurdish people, are not considered as minorities in Turkey. If one looks at the empirical studies, the majority of Kurdish people (75 per cent) identified themselves as the citizens of Turkish Republic and viewed themselves (65 per cent) as a part of the large Turkish nation (Yilmaz 2014). These identifications are followed by religious Muslimhood with 34 per cent and ethnic identity with 8 per cent. Turkish as a common language has been a significant factor in contributing to the national feeling and construction of a common culture and identity in Turkey. This idea makes some Turkish nationalists critical against the argumentation of supporting the linguistic distinction of Kurdish language and culture. Certainly, language is the most important element of Kurdish ethnic identity. Therefore, the debates on the Kurdish problem constantly involve the discussion on the right of education in their native language.

In this context, just like Turkone, Ayhan Aktar mentions how the foundation elites of Turkey imagined a 'unique' nation and he criticizes the Kemalist Turkism, its ethnic interpretation of citizenship and exclusion of other languages due to their fear of heteronomy and collapse of the state. He employs a sarcastic language use with idioms like 'turning over in their graves' and punctuation marks such as an exclamation (!) in order to strengthen his power of critique. Through this discursive representation of the past, he emphasizes the difference between before and now that contributes to the change of status quos and reconstructs the common pluralist national identity with recognition of other ethnic differences:

> I guess, the people who have the Turkism ideology within the founding of the Republic are nowadays turning over in their graves. They have mainly had the dream of a nation consisting of a people who are involved in the Turkish ethnic identity or a people who are ready for going up in smoke in the consciousness of Turkism. According to them, it is out of the question for other ethnic groups 'speaking languages other than Turkish' to be in the Turkish nation. The formula of 'one language=one nation' was true for pure-blooded Kemalists. Speaking another language among people would cause the foundation of a nation in the state and separatism, 'maazallah' (God forbid). (*Taraf*, 8 June 2009)

For an illustration of why liberals supported Islamists in the construction of a post-Kemalist state citizenship and identity politics, Ahmet Altan's following remarks in *Taraf* shed a light on this process. He addresses the main problems in recognition of freedom in Turkey through the references to Kurdishness, Aleviness, Muslimhood and individuality:

> We are in the same fight since the founding of the Republic. There are four major topics. The religion problem is symbolized by the headscarf. The Kurdish problem is symbolized by the mother tongue. The Alevi problem is symbolized by the compulsory subject. The individualization problem is

symbolized by the military service issue. The source of all these problems is based on the same place and the same reason. Sunni pious says to the state: 'Accept my existence' while saying 'Accept the headscarf of my child'. Alevi says to the state 'Accept my existence' while saying 'accept the djemevi as a place of worship and don't forcibly teach my child Sunnism'. Young people say to the state 'Accept that I'm an individual, I have a life' while saying 'Don't impress me, don't intervene with the course of my life'. The state gives all of them the same answer: 'I do not accept; you do not exist'. (*Taraf*, 23 October 2010)

In Altan's presentation, the personal pronoun 'we' is used in the meaning of people or public in Turkey. The topos of 'we are in the same boat' positions people of Turkey against the Kemalist state. He adopts an anthropomorphic usage for referring to the position of the state as the 'other' that is responsible for the problems and power struggle in the country. By noting the problematic issues created by the state system, such as seeing all of the people as a potential 'criminal and enemy', he (*Taraf*, 8 January 2011) contends that 'It's time to establish a new republic by burying this one.' The strategy of dissimilation in argumentation directly demonstrates the will of reconstruction of Turkish nation-state identity in the 'new republic'. He presents it as everybody's demand for the change which supposes a state for people's life, not people's life for the state: 'The public started to say, "what kind of regime, brother."'

As the examples point out, liberals and Islamists share a consensus on the opposition to the Kemalist system's imagination of a Turkish nation-state and the army's position within it. According to these perspectives, the largest common denominator of the Kurdish political movement was 'hostility to the state' due to the Turkish state prohibiting their language, torturing them, murdering people being almost the only reasons for a harsh Kurdish rebellion (*Zaman*, 31 July 2011). However, the components of the Kurdish issue have been changing. It was argued that the power against PKK was not armed authorities or military-state anymore, therefore the weapons and terrorist acts could not be effective in the face of legitimate power. With this argumentation, *Zaman* contributed to construct the AKP's discourse of New Turkey. On Kurdish rights, Islamists build their arguments on the emergence of a new paradigm and destruction of the old Republican one in the context of Kurdish problem:

The Republic tried to 'create' a nation in which the Republic thought that the state would be safe in the use of all of its possibilities. The Kurdish language was banned. The Kurdish identity was denied. Here is the reached point: This paradigm completely broke down. Today, this policy thought to portray the state as one piece, is the most serious threat against the existence of the state. We need a new paradigm. (*Zaman*, 28 October 2011)

In the passage, it is argued that the old Kemalist paradigm has been changing and the perspective of enemy-state is replaced by the AKP, which has gained the votes of half of the general population and 40 per cent of the South-east region where the Kurds mostly live in. If one looks at the numbers of the Kurdish seats in Ankara (more than 100 in 550), this is a valid argument. As the main aim of this book, for a better understanding of the 'process' of the power struggle of redefinition of Turkey's identity, it is crucial to reveal how the Islamist version of Turkish nationalism looks at the Kurdish problem. Moreover, it must be underlined that this study reveals the essentialist understanding of Turkish national identity in the search for different discourses of Turkish nation-state identity. It accepts different levels of identifications and belongings to the nation; thus, it does not exclude Kurdish or Armenian voices in Turkish media.

Regarding the last point, in the next article, the leftist BDP's Kurdish Deputy Aysel Tugluk (*Radikal*, 18 September 2011) presents a disagreement on the AKP's role in the solution of the problematic relationship between the Kurds and the state:

They met on a new state strategy as: 'We will solve the problem based on a liberal state and individual rights' with the approach of 'There is not a Kurdish problem; there are the problems of my Kurdish brothers'... The Kemalist elites and traditionalist conservatives, who are the different faces of the same administrative device, played the role of the state on the Kurdish issue on every occasion. Nowadays, this is the issue... the actual effective actor and the projection in determining the work style and political perspective should have included the Imrali and the peace works and negotiations. That the meaning of it has never been achieved shouldn't be drawn. I mean that it should be the main axis.

Here, such as the previous examples, Tugluk emphasizes 'the role of the state' in the Kurdish problem of Turkey. However, she rejects both Kemalist army-state and neo-conservative liberal state. She expresses a different solution which can be provided by the Kurds through negotiating with the PKK and its leader Abdullah Ocalan. The metonymy of Imrali is employed when referring to Ocalan, though it is the name of the place where he is a prisoner. In fact, there are sharp differences in perspectives on Ocalan in Turkey. The emphasis on 'Imrali' symbolizes the Kurdish fight for 'freedom'; it explains why it is noted that it should be the main axis for the solution. This discursively constructs a kind of heteronomization and autonomization in Turkey's national identification. In addition, it shows differences in the Kurds' imagination of Turkey's common political present and future as Hasan Yilmaz's (2014) empirical study showed the diversity of Kurdish identifications and belongings to the Turkish nation.

Like Tugluk, another deputy of the Kurdish party, Sirri Sureyya Onder, wrote for the leftist *Radikal*. In the following quotation, Onder used the strategy of justification and relativization (Wodak et al. 1999: 36) in order to emphasize the difference and heteronomy of Kurds in Turkey. Specifically, he highlighted the difference between the Kurds. He narrated this difference and different imaginations of the homeland by making use of a question in Kurdish 'Tu ji kîjan welatê yi?' which means 'Which village are you from?':

> The witnesses of the speaking of two Kurds who met in their province know that the question is: 'Tu ji kîjan welatê yi?' This question means: 'Where are you from?' or 'What is your country?' But both of them are actually from Urfa or Viranşehir, Siverek, Diyarbakır, Kahta… I mean they are both from the same town and city, but it is their village or lineage that determines them and makes them known. And this lineage or village is a kind of DNA chain, they are so important. It detects their movements, shames, prides, honours and all the social behaviours… Each of them has their own 'homeland' habits, language, timbre, flavour, colour. Of course, this is different from the concepts of 'homeland, country, and state' that you know. Yes, there is no flag, no school, no mosque and no police station in this homeland. Let's just say that there are water wells, sheep, kids wearing rubber shoes, women with colourful dresses, kohl-full eyes, cherry caftans, and men with shalwar-keffiyeh. (*Radikal*, 25 January 2010)

The linguistic construction of 'national body' (Wodak et al. 1999: 30) in this text distinguishes Kurds' 'natural space' and culture from each other at the subnational level with a reference to their localities. Hyperbole is used in stressing the different and colourful culture of the Kurds. The presentation of the Kurdish homeland without the state and the state institutions demonstrates the gap between Turkish state and Kurdish people in this example. This imagination of a stateless land of the Kurds is problematical in terms of institutionalization of nationhood and everyday production of Turkish national identity in the means of the construction of 'collective national consciousness' (Wodak et al. 1999: 84) in their homeland. Especially, it identifies the lack of feeling of belonging to a Turkish nation-state. In this regard, what they do not have in their village is the constituent of what is common between them. It can be seen as a 'recognition' matter in the mutual relationship between the Kurdish society and Turkish nation-state.

To point out his perspective on the Kurdish question and solution, S.S. Onder wrote (*Radikal*, 8 November 2010): 'Today, the AKP government and liberals, by their nature, do not work apart from creating obstacles for peace… The solution can only be found with the common wisdom of the Kurds and socialists.' The use of linguistic expressions manifested that a democratic or a liberal solution is clearly repudiated by the BDP members. They distance themselves from this kind of liberation or emancipation. Their discourse implies that they fight for a socialist solution. In the terms of discursive construction of a common future in relation to the problem, he makes a division between a 'we-group' including the Kurds and socialists and a 'they-group' including the AKP and liberals.

On this issue, the liberal and left perspectives offer a redefinition of constitutional citizenship for guaranteeing the group and cultural rights to build the unity of the nation. The Islamist perspective's suggestion for the road map of the Kurdish solution is based on religiosity in the region, which means establishing an ideological umbrella of Islamic political identity as an alternative to Kurdish nationalism. Since then, 'conservative democratic' discourse has highlighted its Islamic shade more and more in the internal and external policies of Turkey after every national election victory of the AKP.

As noted before, Prime Minister Erdogan stated in his 2005 Diyarbakir declaration that the Kurdish problem in this country was a reality. In 2008, Erdogan argued that they solved the Kurdish problem by the consolidation of democracy, but the PKK problem did not end. The government named and described the problem through a security perspective. In this process, it was not just the government that changed its discourse on the Kurdish question, but also liberals and leftists reviewed their perspectives on the problem. They became more critical on both sides of the issue. In order to set up a basis in which peace could be achieved, the AKP launched a 'Kurdish Initiative' in 2009 (Larrabee 2013). This can be accepted as a milestone in the evolution of the issue. In the next section, the Turkish media's Kurdish Initiative coverage is analysed in order to see how dynamically national identity has been referred to and how the process and meanings have been readdressed.

The AKP's Kurdish Initiative in the Turkish media

Although the main theme of this chapter limits the analysis of the Kurdish question in the ethno-political dimension from a rights-based perspective, it should be noted that the Kurdish question's security dimension has inevitably influenced the power struggle and contributes to the complexity of the problem. In fact, the PKK side of the problem is frequently covered by the Turkish media in respect of the attacks, military operations and the funerals of martyrs. Esra Arsan's work (2013) points out that a revenge discourse and 'we versus them' discourse is common in the coverage of the funerals. She argues that while the Turkish media heroize the deaths for the Turkish side, they dehumanize for the Kurdish side. In her examples from Turkish newspapers, it can be argued that there is both a dehumanization and misidentification tendency in the coverage of the PKK and its members. In the news report of martyr funerals, they do not use the word 'Kurdish' out of hesitation of linking the PKK problem with the Kurdish problem. However, when the AKP government launched the Kurdish Initiative, the media could not avoid presenting this connection.

As a part of disarmament of the Kurdish Initiative, 34 PKK members entered through the Khabur border gate in October 2009. In the news coverage of events, linguistic representation of the actors in using the concept of 'terrorist' or 'people' made a difference in the eyes and images of public in their identification of PKK members. Prime Minister Erdogan said (*Radikal*, 22 October 2009): 'We set out with good faith. We are saying that mothers do not cry anymore. Look, thirty-four people returned to Turkey, and they were released within the framework of our laws. Hopefully, we are looking forward to many more. I'm looking forward to returning all our people to the mountains, leaving their weapons behind' On the other hand, *Hurriyet* reported (22 October 2009) that in his press conference, CHP Leader Deniz Baykal criticized the return of the terrorists to Turkey and said: 'The terrorists have become heroes.' The pictures created a tension in Turkish society because they were 'showing off' as if this process was the PKK's victory.

Linguistic representation of a 'democracy initiative' or 'national unity projection' in the Turkish media was crucial for disarmament and peacebuilding. In this respect, Cengiz Candar (*Radikal*, 23 October 2009) warned 'Do not be blind' to peacebuilding. Murat Belge (*Taraf*, 24 October 2009) underlined that 'there are no victory or defeat in peace'. But ethno-nationalist MHP leader (*Cumhuriyet*, 18 August 2011) called for the government to abandon 'the so-called demolition project'. Due to a massive opposition to the process, Turkey again went back to the strangulation of Kurdish problems by retreating government from the democratic negotiations and intensifying attacks of the PKK in 2010. The data analysis in the following section gives a detailed account of the different discourses on the AKP's Kurdish Initiative in the Turkish media. It demonstrates that since 2006 the matter of EU membership has lost importance on the political agenda of Turkey, the external 'other' in Turkey's Kurdish question has been replaced, going from 'the EU' to 'global forces', in other words, the USA or the West (Europe and the USA).

The AKP's Kurdish Initiative in the pro-secular discourse

The data from the study of *Cumhuriyet* and *Hurriyet* newspapers demonstrates that Euro-scepticism, anti-globalization and anti-Westernization are closely connected with the reaction to the changing dynamics in the necessary reconstruction process in Turkey. However, in the context of the AKP's Kurdish Initiative in 2009, opposition to transformation is expressed with an emphasis on 'globalization' in both discourses. As can be seen below in Bahceli's statements, external sources of the PKK problem are shown as aiming to bring about the downfall of Turkey. Moreover, the AKP is pictured as being an ally with the global forces (*Hurriyet*, 22 June 2010): 'Chairman of MHP Devlet Bahceli said that: "The AKP is a global political vendor. PKK is a global armed vendor. Both vendors have undertaken the tender of destroying our country from the same centre, but by using different channels by the global negotiation method and have already gone to work on this". Similarly, a Kemalist writer, Suheyl Batum nominates the Kurdish Initiative as the Barzani Initiative:

> We always say, 'a minority group' drove out Turkey's nail day by day...
> Moreover with 'the support of international status quo' this 'minority group'

went totally wild. All they wanted was to govern Turkey which could not govern itself, by taking advantage of this deficiency and this was supported by foreign policy, Armenian policy, Cyprus policy and the desire to seize the judiciary. There was also 'Barzani Initiative', written by the new bosses whom they tried to palm off as South East or Kurdish Initiative… The thing which was good for global capital was considered good for them as well. International scale bosses are still trying to write the 'scenario'. Their 'puppets' that are in Turkey are playing. (*Cumhuriyet*, 23 July 2010)

This passage portrays the leftist tone of Kemalist nationalism which describes the current political situation in Turkey as being highly dependent on the external powers. Warning of a threatened national interest in foreign policy issues and blaming 'government' tacitly for collaborating with the international bosses can be interpreted in reading the power struggle in Turkey. He adopts the strategy of blaming others using the idiom 'driving out Turkey's nail', meaning an attempt to collapse Turkey. To trivialize 'government' he calls it 'a minority group' in an effort to identify those who are responsible in the present situation. He employs the allegory of puppets in order to argue the AKP and its foreign policy serve the interests of 'new bosses' of 'global capitalism'. Based on a similar argument, in a previous excerpt, it is shown that Dursun Atilgan (*Cumhuriyet*, 13 October 2005) addressed Islamists as the 'betrayal side'. Kemalists complain that 'they' who are in power get their powers from global capitalism to maximize their interests. This also reflects their fears of globalization of the Kurdish issue. In the following example, Deniz Som (*Cumhuriyet*, 17 January 2008) enlightens the changing domestic and external power relations in the terms of references to the 'strategic partner', the 'martyrs' and the 'murderers':

> The principles of the full independence and the national sovereignty of Kemal Ataturk are already buried, and the funeral prayer of secularism is performed! Also, when 'the strategic partner' ends the trouble of terrorism, welcome to Moderate Islamic Republic of Turkey!… Turkey is sold, destroyed, burned and made Arab. While martyrs are described as head and the murderers are described as dear, he is a Prime Minister who says these things.

In this text, Som warns against the loss of national sovereignty and the independence principles of M. Kemal Ataturk. He pays particular attention to the laicism principle and the way it is personified. He makes his argumentation with the topos of funeral prayer which points to laicism being murdered. Punctuation marks and bold characterization of Kemal Ataturk signal the seriousness of the current situation. The fear of losing national sovereignty and independence of Kemalist principles is expressed. Ironically, 'Moderate Islamic Republic of Turkey' is welcomed by Som. He refers to 'the government' through the metonymy of the 'strategic partner' which marks AKP's relationship with the United States and implicitly addresses its alliance in the Great Middle East Project. What is noteworthy is his warning against Arabization of the nation. This can be read as a discontent about the religiosity in Turkey, in other words, Islamization of the nation. As mentioned in previous chapters, for the Kemalists, not Arabization but Europeanization of Turkish identity is frequently perceived as a positive component in terms of modernization. He also notes that the Prime Minister describes 'the murderers' as 'dear'. Here, in a hidden meaning, he refers to the PKK's leader Ocalan and expresses his disturbance by calling him as 'Dear Ocalan'. It should be reminded that the PKK members are identified as 'baby killers' in the Turkish media. Moreover, the nomination of 'martyrs' as 'head' is criticized, which can be interpreted as complaining about the trivialization strategy in reducing it to quantization for the function of alleviating the importance of the Turkish army's losses. Through the strategy of discontinuation, he emphasizes the difference between the times of 'before' AKP government and 'then'. In a nutshell, the topos of changed circumstances and 'threat' indicate the resistance to the post-Kemalist transformation by a strategy of perpetuation.

The Kemalists also see the Kurdish problem as a matter of national sovereignty. In the following example, through an emphasis on Turkey's 'unilateral dependence on the EU' and the 'global dependence', it is argued that global dynamics are shaping country's domestic power relations, and the Kurdish Initiative is illustrating this dependency:

> It is an interesting paradox that a wide range of people who are troubled by the Islamist policies are now in a position supporting unilateral dependence on the EU. It is an implicit result of the global dependence on a situation which they have brought to a choice position between the Middle East dependence (mandate) and Western dependence (mandate)... While the right and the extreme right are strengthening in Europe and the USA, the new policies for Turkey and the region are making the internal dynamics of the country more dependent. For example, Southeast (or Kurdish) initiative

is completely carried out by global dynamics. In fact, it has become a global problem for Turkey's geography, not an internal problem of Turkey. (*Cumhuriyet*, 22 November 2010)

In a tacit discourse, this text contends Turkey should keep its unique identity and policy without any influence from the external forces. Turkey's external relations are portrayed with the negative connotation of 'mandate'. In the text, neither the Middle East dependence nor Western dependence is recommended in Turkey's foreign relations. This is an explicit warning of a threatened national sovereignty. However, it identifies the globalization of internal issues, in the terms of internationalization of Kurdish problem in the region. The text names it 'south-east' which signifies the regional difference and identification and uses a parenthesis for naming 'Kurdish'. This shows that Kemalist reluctance to define the problem as 'Kurdish' has been changing. It was the official Kemalist discourse which has put forward the social and economic underdevelopment of the region as the origins of the problem and to justify Kemalist state's identity politics.

Opposing the Kemalist and ethno-nationalist circles, the liberals, leftists and Islamists were eager to have a consensus on the achievements in the Kurdish issue. This claim was validated by these groups' 'Yes' decision on the referendum for the new constitution in 2010 as Fuat Keyman wrote in *Radikal*:

> The decision of 'yes' by 58 per cent and 'no' by 42 per cent is the appearance of the demand of the public on the solutions of social problems in the political area and the consent of public shown in this direction as a result of referendum. With this result, the society of Turkey 'called for citizenship' for (a) a New Constitution and (b) the solution of the Kurdish problem and request the solutions of this problem from the political parties in the 'political area'. The decision of 58 per cent 'yes' is a citizenship call for both symbolizing the social consent for new Constitution and saying to political parties 'we are ready for a new constitution', and applying-requesting the democratic initiative period to revive for the solution of the Kurdish problem. (*Radikal*, 26 September 2010)

Keyman interpreted the results of the referendum as the symbol of the social consent for a new constitution for Turkey and the solution of the Kurdish problem. This discursively constructs a common consent for the AKP's formation of post-Kemalist nation-state identity. As might be expected, there were different motivations from all sides to try and achieve an agreement for a new citizenship definition. For instance, the leftist circles wanted to transform certain political continuities rooted in the military-coup constitution. They said, 'not enough, but yes' to the draft due to the fact they were not interested in who were reforming the nation-state identity, but they were interested in the attempt of erasing the political traces of 1980. In this context, how Kurdish identity should be represented, included or excluded in the new constitutional citizenship is one of the main contents of New Turkey's national identity. Although the general intention seems to solve the gangrenous issue, the political culture, the way of doing politics and the political struggle cannot bring about the building of mutual confidence on both sides. With the aim of finding out how the Turkish media represented and reproduced this political struggle through different supporter discourses on the Kurdish Initiative based on different ideological stands, the following section focuses on the coverage of Islamist *Zaman*, leftist *Radikal* and liberal *Taraf* on this topic.

The AKP's Kurdish Initiative in the post-Kemalist discourse

Islamist nationalist discourse in the Turkish press is apparently a supporter of the AKP's Kurdish Initiative. In terms of discursive construction of collective 'we-group', *Zaman*'s columnist Mumtazer Turkone uses a positive self-representation strategy for integration of Kurds in 'we all' and 'ourselves': 'It's the Kurds themselves who will eradicate the terrorist swamp and we all need to trust Kurds and I mean we need to trust ourselves.' He (*Zaman*, 17 January 2010) adds: 'The initiative on the other hand deserves constructive and enriching language and contribution. As terror is a result if the agents disappear the terrorism will be vaporised by itself.' The strategy of rationalization appears by indicating terror as a result of the problem not just the problem itself. The causal reasons should be found out and fought against to end terror as the outcome of the Kurdish problem. More significantly, he underlines the necessity of the specific positive language use in discussion on the Initiative in order to have positive results.

He questions the strict and aggressive discourse of the ethno-nationalist MHP through the argumentation of the MHP profits arising from the 'Kurdish uprising' and 'the blood of terror'. Here, discursively, 'uprising' is a remarkable description of the Kurdish problem. Turkone (*Zaman*, 9 January

2011) justifies his argument in noting that they use the mosque courtyards where the funerals of martyrs are held, as a meeting place, and demands 'how many votes does a funeral cost?' suggesting this is the main reason for the escalation of terrorism. Therefore, he argues that MHP ethno-nationalism and Kurdish leftist nationalism are constitutive of each other. They feed and reconstruct each other: 'Kurdish question nurtured and raised the Kurdish nationalism (*ulusalcilik*). Yet would not the Kurdish question and nationalism strengthen the MHP as an anti-thesis? Aren't these two contradictions getting power from each other?' As has been demonstrated, argumentation patterns are based on the strategy of emphasizing the negative common features of both sides. While opposing the MHP, Turkone (*Zaman* 17 June 2011) openly showed his support for the government and argued that 'AK party is the only party both for Turks and Kurds'. In the context of the domestic power struggle, these examples illustrate how Islamists and Kurds aimed to collaborate to construct a post-Kemalist nation-state identity, s the Kurdish Initiative was a historical attempt for the solution of the problem, Apart from him, Turan Alkan (*Zaman*, 25 December 2010) directly stated: 'Kurdish Initiative was a right policy.' He noted that what was targeted was right; but the reason it could not reach its destination was because the government did not prepare society and there was a panic of the opposition, 'what if the initiative works?'.

This argument can be deduced from the leftist author and academician Murat Belge's comments on the nature of opposition in Turkey: 'The whole aim of "opposition" in today's crisis is by any means to remove this government, the party of this government and the social population who created them from power.' He amalgamates this point with why the government's intention to find a 'peaceful' and 'democratic' solution for the Kurdish problem came across with non-striking intense opposition. Without any exceptional viewpoints, they were opposed to whatever the government had to offer on the solution. In addition, he addresses the impatience shown on the government's 'democratic initiative':

> I had said that the people who expect results from the 'initiative' in two days couldn't think of asking 'What did you do? What did you succeed?' to the ones who bring the events to these days, for twenty-five years, by making 'cross-border' operations, by burning a village in one day and a forest in another day, by making laws. (*Taraf*, 28 December 2009)

In Murat Belge's article the temporal dimension of the problem is touched on by the negative narrative of the experiences of the past twenty-five years. By illustrating what had been done before, he justifies his criticism on the impassioned attitude of some sides about the government's attempt to sort out the longstanding historical problem in a few days. For many reasons, one can assume that he is right on this argumentation if one looks at the negative representations of AKP's initiative in the context of the common political future in both Turkish nationalist and Kurdish nationalist discourse. By examining Aysel Tugluk's expression (*Radikal*, 18 September 2011), it may be argued that not just the MHP and the CHP (ethno-nationalists and Kemalist nationalists), but also Kurdish nationalists did not contribute to the discursive reconstruction process of the will to live together: 'No one deceives himself, this process leads to civil war. And at the end of the process, will the desire and the ideal to live together remain? Do not remain! A famous phrase: "When the blood is shed, the redemption must be paid!"' In this expression, the language of war is justified by the strategy of balancing one crime with another. Causal explanations such as the lack of living together are shifting responsibility to the 'others'. The 'redemption' metaphor refers the cost of violence as retaliation. This discourse reproduces the never-ending cycle of violence in the Kurdish question and legitimizes it by blaming others.

In this context, the liberals, leftists and social democrats turn debating on the AKP's and the PKK's U-turn to the non-functional military solution which has been tried for twenty-five years. While negotiations behind closed doors are not working for the peace, the last circumstances spring to mind, more polarization and crystallization in Turkish politics. Ahmet Altan presented this point with the allegory of hungry cavemen in order to criticize other political parties copycatting the extreme nationalist MHP politics in the peacebuilding process:

> They are making a hash of peace, dipping their hands into the peace like three cavemen trying to share a cake with cream. As in the fights of those hungry moments every time, 'the wildest' one likens everyone to himself. As the wildest in this fight is the MHP, it is common attitude to be like the MHP. The AKP, CHP and PKK imitate the MHP. (*Taraf*, 25 August 2009)

In addition, Altan commented on his disappointment with the Kurdish contribution to the 'democracy initiative' with the argument that it is just a representative of a particular region or ethnic group and it is silenced on the common issues of Turkey:

> While there was a cut-throat 'battle of democracy' in Turkey, it was breaking our hearts that the Kurds were standing aside and did not get involved in the fight as if the democracy was only interesting the Turks. Kurdish politicians were just expressing the problems related to their race and their regions, and they were keeping silent in the face of our common problems, just like Erbakan lovers before February 28 with a strange 'communitarianism'. (*Taraf,* 28 February 2010)

Interestingly, he uses the illustration of Islamists before the postmodern military intervention of 28 February 1997 for describing the present Kurdish politicians. The matter with Kurdish politicians is pointed out as not being a Turkey's party, merely a regional party. As noted before, the Islamists could become the majority party with the AKP's revisionism and conservative democracy discourse. Otherwise, they would keep on being representative of a specific Islamist community. Tayyip Erdogan's AKP succeeded by being the voices of others with the discourse of 'democracy for everyone', which was also convincing both the liberal and leftist sides. During the last decade Prime Minister Erdogan has been arguing that they are against ethnic nationalism. But the tone of Sunni Islamism in their discourse has become more perceptible day by day. Finally in 2012, he declared their four principles in Adana: 'one state, one nation, one flag and one religion'. He underlined that he did not include 'one language'. After the opposing comments, the party members said, 'one religion' might be a tongue slip.

More problematically, the dominance of security and its fight against terrorism discourse turned Turkey's democracy into a downhill battle, using the cases of Ergenekon, Balyoz and KCK to apply the general term of 'terrorism' to the new Penal Code effectuated in 2006. In the cases of Ergenekon and Balyoz, hundreds of people (mostly army officers and journalists) were taken into custody (Rodrik 2011). In the case of the KCK, the same happened to the Kurdish people (mostly politicians and journalists). The polarized political situation in 'the *war* of all *against* all' lost them the chance of peacebuilding once again. As Ahmet Insel wrote in *Radikal* (23 October 2011) questioning of the legitimacy of violence is difficult in Turkey due to the fact that both parties – the state and the PKK – are becoming anti-politics in the case of the

Kurdish problem: 'The idea that the solution to this "gangrenous problem" will be achieved with an extremely bloody fight seems to have dominated both parties. Both parties are demanding an absolute allegiance to itself. Both parties are firmly hugging the concept of "just war". The politics of violence is destroying the politics.'

In contrast to the blaming 'others' strategy used in most of the media discourse, in the *Radikal* newspaper, Fuat Keyman (11 September 2011) strategically employed constructive discourse on the topos of 'responsibility' which has a unity and solidarity-enhancing function in the Kurdish issue. He underlined the importance of a new constitution-writing process for equal citizenship as a chance to build the democratic and peaceful collective present and future of Turkey. He invited the AKP and the BDP to behave responsibly towards the Kurdish problem, to establish the will of a common present and tomorrow on the basis of 'peace, democratic negotiations/equality/justice/conscience/language', by taking lessons from the pains and mistakes of the past. The necessity of learning from common past experiences was expressed by Keyman in making use of the transformation strategy. On how to change the on-going struggle, from a social democracy perspective he offered a specific language use in peacebuilding, a language of equality, justice and conscience. Beyond others, this is an alternative, pluralist imagination of Turkey.

Conclusions

The thematic content of discourses on Turkish national identity contains the construction of a collective past, present and future; a common physical geography and borders; and a common culture. The concept of a Turkish nation as an imagined community is built on these elements in the different discourses. Using this perspective of the nation, in this chapter, the discourse analysis as the methodological framework of study is applied to investigate how these contents of Turkish national identity are generated and reproduced through Turkish media discourse in the context of Turkey's European Union membership and the Kurdish problem. This aspires to show the multiple faces of Turkey from a national and an international level; official and oppositional; constitutional and cultural models of identity in relation to the internal power struggle in the 2000s, particularly giving rise to the power of two traditional 'others' of the Kemalist state: Islam and Kurds. Based on this essential assumption, it is discovered that there is not one simple understanding of the EU and Turkish identity construction depending on the context of Turkey's Kurdish question. Here, the main argumentations of different discursive constructs of Turkish national identity are outlined and the strategies applied in these constructions are summarized as the findings of the detailed linguistic analysis of the case study.

The detailed discourse-analytical investigation of Kemalist discourse of Turkish nationalism from the *Cumhuriyet* newspaper provides the Kemalist conceptualization of nation and self-perception in the selected context. Regarding issues such as the common national past, they refer to the Kemalist legacy and its institutions. In the discursive construct of the common present, they address Turkey's membership of the EU with a concern for preserving the secular identity of state and its guardian army. With the belief in the AKP's instrumentation of the EU adaptation process in order to cloak its Islamist agenda in the discourse of freedom and democracy, they perceive the EU process as a 'threat' to the regime of the state, to unity of the nation, its independence and sovereignty. Moreover, they argue that the EU harmonization is misappropriated by the Kurds for realization of their opposing demands to Turkey. Regarding the Kurdish question, the EU was represented as 'external other', while European integration was at the top of Turkey's agenda. While non-European and Muslim identity discourses were becoming dominant in the last decade, public support and political agenda for the EU lost attention in Turkish media. In addition, the 'blamed others' have been redefined in 2009 as the United States, the West or global actors.

Kemalist discourse addresses 'homogenization' under Turkish identity and citizenship by the strategy of perpetuation and justification. This homogeneity point is also common in the ethno-nationalist discourse of the MHP. However, the ethno-nationalists do not underline secularism or Kemalism; but Turkic and Muslim characters of the nation which can be described as populist nationalism. The best-selling *Hurriyet* newspaper is chosen to illustrate this perspective of the Turkish nation. Despite the fact that some *Hurriyet* authors criticize what is happening in Turkey from different perspectives, *Hurriyet* tends to be more populist in parallel with government policies in assuming that it represents a majority mentality and an imagined collective everyday life culture in the focused timeline.

In contrast to Kemalist discourse, the self-perception of Islamist discourse positions Turkey culturally as a part of the Muslim world. They focus on

Muslimhood in the discursive construction of their difference from the West. However, they argue that they are in favour of Turkey's bid for EU membership in terms of common values, mainly democracy. In the data analysis, it is seen that this democracy discourse is instrumentalized by the Islamists in order to justify transformation of the Kemalist nation-state's secularism and citizenship policies. With a reference to Muslimhood, 'Islam has one nation' discourse is used in opposition to the Kemalist state's unequal identity policies, particularly its relationship with the Kurds. Therefore, they seem to be supporters of EU conditionality in consolidation of Kurdish rights. However, *Zaman's* coverage of the headscarf issue apparently indicated that they lost interest in being a part of the Union since they could not get what they expected from the EU, namely support of religious freedom in Turkey. Certainly, they put Islam at the heart of their view of the world and relationships with the others. Because of that, secularist politics of the Kemalist state are defined as 'armed tyranny' to Muslim people. They make a distinction between the Kemalist state and the Muslim nation. Based on this, they offer a commemoration and reconstruction of the state's Islamic identity as a solution to Turkey's problems. They even see the AKP's self-identification of 'conservative democrat' rather than 'Islamic' as the problem; it is not enough to provide a common identity and sense of belonging among Muslims. In a nutshell, they argue that 'Islam is the answer' in relation to the internal and external others of Turkey, although this concept of the nation still maintains the situation of 'all animals are equal, but *some* animals are *more equal than others*', not including the rights of the secularists, non-Muslims and LGBTs. By decoding this paradox, this book makes an original contribution to the literature through analysing Turkey's new identity with a specific focus on the concept of 'national identity' and power struggle of different Turkish nationalisms. It reveals how the notions of Turkish nation-state identity are naturalized with the references to the majority's religion.

In addition to the other findings, this case study found out that as Islamists, the liberal-leftists' main motivation in supporting reforms was the necessity of transformation in the Kemalist state structure. Therefore, they endorsed the AKP's attempts in the reformation process. Indeed, all discourses of the Turkish nation identity claimed to be in favour of democratization. However, the content of the concept was diverse in the extent to which they wanted it for the 'others' who do not think, do not live, or do not dress, like them.

Reformation in state-society relations, state-military relations or state-minorities relations requires redefinition of power relations. This inevitably reveals who resist and who encourage the changes in discursive construction of Turkish nation-state identity while empowering traditional disadvantaged groups of the state. On this point, the pluralist perspectives of liberal-leftists and social democrats, as seen in *Taraf* and *Radikal*, do not exclude some specific groups or define new others in the nation formation for the sake of satisfying the majority's identity demands. Related argumentation patterns demonstrate that this pluralist view of the world reverberates through the AKP's Kurdish Initiative. It demonstrates why these groups have been supporters in the AKP's pro-Kurdish Initiative and pro-reconstitution campaigns. Recently, what is particularly remarkable is the AKP's emphasis on the Islamic character of Turkey and reluctance in vitalizing reforms have shifted the perceptions of liberal-leftists, social democrats and the socialist wing of the Kurdish movement in the changing power relations in Turkey. Unfortunately, a new process widens the fault lines between the sides; namely Turks versus Kurds; Islamists versus Secularists.

Foreign policy challenge: the debate of the axis shift in Turkish foreign policy

This case study empirically argues that Turkish national identity and foreign policy discourses are reproductive and constitutive of each other. The comparative perspective on Turkish media observes the articulation of Turkey's post-Kemalist identity across multiple discourses, not just within official discourse. By highlighting linkages between domestic and foreign policymaking, this section aims to demonstrate the domestic debate on Turkey's international identity and whether there is a shift in the orientation of the country, namely from Westernization to neo-Ottomanism or Islamization. The time period of the discourse analysis ends in 2011, and therefore does not cover emerging challenges of Turkish democracy and Turkish foreign policy during the political uprisings of the Arab world.

On the axis shift debate Turkish prime minister Erdogan answered the comments (*Taraf*, 11 June 2010): 'We not only share the same geography with the Arabs, but breathe also the same air or live the same seasons, we share the same history, we have the feeling of a common culture, common civilization.' He further stated (*Taraf*, 13 June 2010, p. 8): 'Foreign newspapers claiming this serves Israel. Who are you serving for then?' Apparently, the definition of 'we' in Turkey's official discourse has been changed by discursively addressing a common political past, present and culture with the Arabs. For instance, the Prime Minister went to Kuwait and Qatar and addressed to the common future with the Muslim countries (*Hurriyet*, 16 January 2011): 'We are together, that's enough for us!' and added: 'If obstacles are removed, fifty-seven Islamic countries will become self-sufficient with their production, technology and brain power'. The Prime Minister both caressed the soul of the hosts with these words and blinked at the conservative votes inside.

Nevertheless, it was argued by the Kemalist circle that Turkey disregarded the relationships with the EU in its foreign policy since Turkey's European Union process had been suspended in 2006. Thus, Middle East politics occupied a privileged place in Turkish foreign policy as the times of the Ottoman Empire. On the issue, the President of the Turkish Republic, Abdullah Gul (*Taraf*, 15 June 2010) stated that it is either 'lack of knowledge or a bad will' if one commented on Turkey's relationship with Muslim countries as a deviation of axis. Turkey participated in 98 per cent of the decisions given by the EU in foreign policy. According to him, nothing was more nonsense than discussing Turkey's axis by looking at its relationship with its neighbour or any other country in its region.

Among the newspapers that are analysed in this research, the Kemalist *Cumhuriyet* claimed that there has been an axis shift in Turkish foreign policy's Western orientation. *Cumhuriyet* empowered this opposing stand by referring to oppositional political actors such as Onur Oymen from the Kemalist CHP who declared that Turkey was playing a leading role in radical Islamic countries (*Cumhuriyet*, 12 June 2010). Deniz Bolukbasi from the MHP said that under AKP's power, Turkey was experiencing a backbone deviation not an axis deviation. Ahmedinejad, Hizbullah's leader Nasrallah and Hamas's leader Haniye were in Erdogan's photo frame. In relation to the resistance to change in Turkey's identity, it was not surprising that *Cumhuriyet* occasionally quoted from the members of ethno-nationalist MHP, who had the same strong concerns in preserving Turkish national identity as the Kemalists. It was reported that the leader of MHP, Devlet Bahceli, stated the centre had gone away from Ankara many years ago and that it had already become affiliated with the axis of Erivan, Erbil, Brussels and Washington.

While the official state discourse is changing and redefining the relationship with other nations, it is important to observe what alternative perspectives think about it in order to see the big picture of Turkey from a wider political discourse. Therefore, this section is devoted to doing a media analysis in an effort to shed light on the power struggle on redefining Turkey's identity in international relations. While opposition parties express their unrest against AKP's relationship with the Islamic world, some other political actors in Turkey's big picture such as big business patrons, liberals, leftists and even most of the Kurdish people, were seen supporting government policies and positioning themselves in changing power relations up until 2011. For instance, it was reported (*Taraf*, 17 June 2010) that businessmen in the East Mediterranean thought that it was wrong to evaluate Turkey's recent intense cooperation with the Arab world as an 'axis deviation'. It was presented as extending Turkey's sphere of influence. Kazim Celiker (*Taraf*, 15 June 2010) justified Turkey's relations with these countries in the AKP period by noting that the axis inevitably deviated towards the trade as the consequence of the global crisis. The developments in the global economy played a great role in Turkey's turning towards the Middle East and Far East (*Taraf*, 20 June 2010). It was reported that Philip Gordon, Deputy National Security Advisor to US Vice-President Kamala Harris, said (*Taraf*, 13 June 2010): 'Turkey's role in the Middle East is not a preference against the West; it is a part of its foreign policy.' The liberal press supported AKP government's policies, especially its foreign policy activism, with news headlines such as (*Taraf*, 15 June 2010): 'The EU approval to Turkey's axis', reporting Stefan Fule put an end to the comments on Turkey's axis has deviated, it has moved away from the West with these words: 'I don't think Turkey's steps are in conflict with the EU membership process.' In the liberal discourse, we see the strategy of justification and perpetuation for ongoing transformation in Turkey and Turkey's relationships with other countries. That means, the liberal press contributed to reconstruction of Turkey's post-Kemalist nation-state identity.

Concerning this new political atmosphere in Turkey, the following section analyses Kemalist arguments in the axis shift debate as the opposition discourse, then it turns to analyse other discourses advocating the official discourse and concluding with remarks relating to the new emerging challenges of TFP.

The Kemalist discourse on the New Turkish foreign policy: the Islamization of Turkey

In this context of Turkey's partnership with other countries, Oztin Akguc (*Cumhuriyet*, 25 July 2010) suggested Turkey should remain neither in the axis of the West nor Arab-Islam. Turkey should be in its own axis and should move in the direction of its own axis: 'It cannot be successful in that if it follows the EU, obeys the USA or walks through the Arab-Islam states... Main theme of our National Anthem is in the line "I have lived freely for all eternity". To live freely can be managed by forming its own axis, not by deviating towards the axis of the East.' Lexical choices in the text underline national sovereignty and the will of independence. This argumentation is justified with the lyrics of the Turkish National Anthem. The selected sentence of 'I have lived freely for all eternity' discursively reproduces the image of the Turkish nation that has never lived under any other state's political authority in its history. This also reconstructs the main motto of the Kemalist nation-state: 'Turks have no friends, but Turks.' This discourse simultaneously serves to give us a deeper understanding why some argue there has been a paradigm shift in Turkey's relations with others in terms of the New Turkish foreign policy's principles of 'zero problem with neighbours'. This point requires more analysis, thus, first the discursive construction of resistance to this paradigm shift will be revealed, and then the discourses with the strategy of transformation will be analysed to complete a bigger picture of the power struggle in maintaining and changing Turkish identity.

Huner Tuncer (*Cumhuriyet*, 31 January 2011) interpreted the so-called change in Turkish foreign policy as leaving Ataturk's honourable foreign policy. He asserted that 'Ataturk's Turkey', which only trusted in its own power and stood on its own two feet in an international community, has been changed and taken its power from dependency on foreign countries. All Kemalist values are consciously neglected, internal and external policies are attempted to give a new shape in the direction of AKP's Islamic values and beliefs. He confirmed this argumentation with the example of ignoring Ataturk's 'peace at home, peace in the world' principal while being so close to the Arab countries in the Middle East.

On extending relations with Turkey's neighbours, Cuneyt Arcayurek (*Cumhuriyet*, 17 April 2010) reminded what Davutoglu said in a meeting with the Arabs: 'Jerusalem will become a capital city in the near future. We'll go there altogether and perform prayers in Al-Masjid Al-Aqsa.' However, he held a critical stand on where the new path in foreign policy might take Turkey:

> There is no doubt the river is flowing again, but its bed has been changed. Now it is flowing towards the East not the West. Certainly, the Arabs will say that 'water' (RTE) has found its way! Angrily he is asking: 'What's this hatred against the Arabs?' Then he is trying to justify the Arabs. According to him, the historical fact that the Arabs cooperated with the British in the First World War and stabbed Turkey in the back is just a 'local event' in that period. Let's think where the new way will lead us.

In this passage, the river metaphor is used to refer to Turkish foreign policy. The shift in the river's bed and where the water goes are descriptive of the East regarding Turkey's current relationship with the Arabs. More significantly, the Turkish prime minister Recep Tayyip Erdogan is using the reference to water as those responsible for the change, reiterating this by using his initials, 'RTE' rather than his full name. 'Water has found its way' means Erdogan moves naturally towards the Muslim countries. Arcayurek opposes his discursive reconstruction of historical narrative on the Turkish-Arabian relations in repeating the Kemalist national history discourse that argues the Arabs betrayed Turks in the First World War. Based on this treacherous image of the Arabs in the common political past, he raises a sceptical question on what these events may mean in the common political future.

Similarly, Guray Oz (*Cumhuriyet*, 16 June 2010) criticizes the reinvention of the past in the context of the relationships between Turkish and Arab peoples. Oz identifies pro-Islamist reconstruction of common political past and present with the Arabs as an outcome of 'consciousness deviation', which is the main method of axis shift that has been realized step by step and sometimes silently since 2002. What is worth noting is that he makes a distinction between different debates of axis shift in Turkish politics. For him, it is not about improving trade relationships with Arab countries or the United States, Russia, and China. But, when the values, human rights, democratic rights are in question, it matters where Turkey heads. The situation of the journalists, intellectuals and the system of the law show that it leads to dictatorship governance in the Middle East:

If the journalists and numerous intellectuals accused of terrorism cannot be released and the judge of the court is not listened to, if more and more suits are brought against the journalists among whom is the author of what you are reading now, this means the human rights part of the axis deviation has greatly improved and has come a long way towards a quite acceptable dictatorship governance in the Middle East.

To justify his argument of 'consciousness deviation', he reminds how Erdogan has employed this in the case of Iraq. According to him, the people forget about AKP's submission of the Permit of March 1st to the Assembly and now they support the shift in Erdogan's USA discourse. Erdogan brings to account and blames the United States: 'We haven't forgotten the widows in Iraq, what you have done there?' This means Erdogan controls and manipulates what people know and believe about Turkey's relations with the other nations. It challenges AKP's New Turkey rhetoric.

Like Guray Oz, Emre Kongar (*Cumhuriyet*, 12 June 2010) argued that Turkey's axis has already deviated from a modern and democratic Western country to a 'Middle Eastern authoritative-totalitarian country' both internally and externally. He claimed that internal structural changes and the political facts experienced during the eight years of AKP government have driven Turkey to this shift. Concepts like Ataturk, Kemalist, Kemalism, laicism, struggle against reaction have started to be used in the same meaning with a pro-coup mind-set and defenders of these concepts are starting to be treated as criminals. 'Conservative' policies have clearly been put into practice from the dressing style of society to the food-beverage culture through central government, the state and municipalities; for example, drinking and buying alcoholic drinks have become a problem especially in small cities. Mechanisms have been established to track, listen to and record everybody anywhere and at any time. These tracking and listening records which are signs of an 'authoritative-totalitarian' regime alone have been leaked to the media sometimes in the form of a legal disguise and sometimes through completely illegal ways; nothing is left as the private life of an individual. These alone are enough to see that Turkey has deviated to an authoritative-totalitarian regime from a democratic one, but there are more other indicators. The media has been directed by economic and financial measures, a fully supportive media group has been created and a few independent media have been threatened with large tax penalties. Media members, intellectuals, university lecturers, rectors, educators, politicians and even jurisdiction members have been imprisoned and their period of detention has been transformed into a prison sentence despite the protests of all the bodies of lawyers. Jurisdiction has become open to the pressures of the political power and media and suggestions that will put the superior organs of jurisdiction totally under the auspices of politics have been submitted for referendum.

Emre Kongar's points give comprehensive clues as to why the Kemalists want to maintain Turkey's Western identity and resist 'Islamization' of the country by the AKP. This demonstrates how a discourse on foreign policy may work in preserving a national identity or provide a justification for a change. It is because a decision on the EU or cooperation with the Muslim countries is directly related to 'Which Turkey do people want to live in, a democratic or an authoritarian one?' or 'How do they want to live?' and 'With whom?'

In this context, the next text illustrates the everyday production of nationhood through the debate of 'axis shift' in Turkish foreign policy. Deniz Kavukcuoglu (*Cumhuriyet*, 27 April 2011) stated that the face of the AKP government had long been turned towards the Middle East instead of the West. He claimed this changed the image of national lands and cities. He used the metaphor of the pitch-black clouds to describe the AKP government's 'political Islamist hegemony' over Istanbul with ugly skyscrapers and seven-stars hotels of 'uncouthness' which allured sheiks, emirs, sultans, kings. This Kemalist discourse exhibits the strategy of resistance to transform 'beautiful Istanbul into Arabia'. In his language use, 'Arabization' of Istanbul is negatively portrayed with the concepts of ugliness and uncouthness, which can be seen as a humiliation of Arab culture. Here, the image of Arab and Middle East are represented as the 'others' of Turkey through the stereotypical construction of political Islam with the metaphor of black clouds. Contrary to that, 'enlightenment' emphasis discursively constructs Turkey's distinctive situation and national difference from the Arab countries. Kavukcuoglu expressed his unrest about Arabic and Islamic influence on Turkey through a specific emphasis on Istanbul. He noted how this changed his feeling of belonging:

> Until recently, when they asked me, 'Where are you from?' I said, 'I'm from Istanbul'. It was true, indeed. I was born and grew up in Istanbul. But now I answer this as, 'I'm from Izmir'. This city where I go to at least once a year,

where my parents and grandparents were born and grew up is still warmer, closer to me. Above all, it is more enlightened.

This quotation contains highly personalized phrases (me, I said, I answer) and it conveys a rigid conception of Turkey through the expression of Izmir's uniqueness with its enlightenment. He distinguished Izmir from Istanbul and other parts of the country. Here, the symbolic meaning of city and city life is remarkable in order to understand the reproduction of power relationship in everyday life. Izmir, one of the Western cities of Turkey, is known as the castle of Kemalism or 'non-Muslim Izmir' in Islamist discourses. Therefore, the shift in his feeling of belonging to a city from Istanbul to Izmir seems a personal sentiment, this nevertheless rhetorically symbolizes secularist nationalist resistance to Islamization. Based on this observation on the changing city life and his feeling of belonging, Kavukcuoglu ends his passage with a call to regain consciousness right away, feed and foster hope, transfer and extend it to cities, protest again reaction, get out of the darkness and arrive at light. Then remain there forever, just like Izmir.

The advocate media: the expanded axis in Turkish foreign policy

An overview on the developments in Turkish foreign policy in the first decade of the 2000s demonstrates that neo-Islamist elites were successful in the integration of Turkey to neo-liberal politics and globalization. Therefore, it can be said that pragmatism dominated Turkey's media discourse and the media became like the advocate of government's policies. Moreover, in order to support government policies, the opinions from economic and business sectors that were parallel to the official state discourse were covered in the media. By analysing the debate on Turkish foreign policy's axis shift from Western orientation in Turkish media, this section shows that foreign policy discourse represents the domestic power struggle and reconstruction of Turkey's post-Kemalist nation-state identity.

In order to have a deeper understanding of the 'We are all interested' discourse and Islamist definition of 'we', the following text presents a justification of the argument in noting 'we feel responsible for other Muslims in Turkey's socio-cultural geography' (*Zaman*, 20 November 2010). In the text, the borders of Turkey's socio-cultural geography are mapped in the Balkans, Caucasians,

Middle Asia, the whole of the Middle East and the middle of Africa. This definition of geography is based on the Islamic historical past of the nation in the Ottoman Empire lands of Anatolia, Middle East, North Africa, Balkans and the Caucasians. Otherwise, this map would include Malaysia or Indonesia which have Muslim populations too.

> Political geography of Turkey is as defined in the National Pact; socio-cultural geography extends to Balkans, Caucasians, Middle Asia, whole of the Middle East and the middle of Africa. All pleasant and unpleasant events on this geography have an influence on our people. We feel sorry for a Caucasian tribe, to the people of Palestine and Iraq just as we feel sorry for Bosnia. We feel responsible for all this geography. The region is under the invasions and pressures of foreign powers today, this increases anger in Turkey. What does feeling sorry for the people of Bosnia, Chechnya, Palestine, Lebanon and Iraq have to do with 'ethnic nationalism' or 'racist chauvinism'?

Opposing the Kemalist understanding of Turkey's political geography, which was defined in the National Pact, this text discursively constructs Islamist understanding of 'our people' based on the aforementioned Turkey's socio-cultural geography. This new imagination relocated Turkey in its neighbourhood and inspired New Turkish foreign policy in redefinition of who are the foreigners of the nation. As noted in previous sections, Turkish foreign minister Ahmet Davutoglu's culturalist *Strategic Depth* perspective on Turkish foreign policy has brought redefinitions in Turkey's international identity and its relationship with other nations. Davutoglu argued that Turkey would not insist on being Western. It embraced Turkey's position at the crossroads of civilizations and targeted embracing Turkey's political, economic and cultural reach within a multi-lateral foreign policy and rhythmic diplomacy. This vision entailed rehabilitation of the Ottoman era in a way predicated on two pillars of *historical depth* and *geographical depth*. This example shows how the Turkish media represent, reproduce and reconstruct the new discourse of Turkish foreign policy.

Related with the debate, the Muslim conservative newspaper *Zaman* (1 January 2010) reported that Turkish people believed there was no shift in Turkish foreign policy's Western orientation. According to USAK's survey, 80 per cent of people supported progress in relationship with neighbouring countries. Ihsan Dagi wrote (*Zaman*, 15 June 2010, p. 12) about why the axis shift debate was on the political agenda. He argued that the AKP transformed the Kemalist-militarist regime by the help of the West. Those who blamed the Islamist AKP for turning its face to the East aimed to effect the West and position the West on the side of the Kemalist-militarists again. Dagi (*Zaman*, 20 February 2009) used the phrase 'silent revolution' for what the AKP brought to Turkey's external relations. He defined it as a liberal transformation that was based on cooperation, negotiation and multi-lateralism. Essentially, he claimed if one looked at Turkey through Kemalist eyes, its language use and practice, the liberal transformation could be understood. In this Kemalist traditional narrative, Turkey was surrounded by its enemies. This security discourse was instrumentalized for establishing, legitimizing, reproducing and maintaining a militarist social and political order. For the sake of keeping security against invented internal enemies, the regime victimized democracy, law and pluralism which were seen as luxurious and risky demands. Dagi indicated that the authority of militarist political culture fell by a new perspective on other states and people. The perspective changed from 'everybody is a potential enemy' discourse to 'everybody is a potential partner for cooperation' discourse. According to his analysis, this was liberalization of Turkish foreign policy by redefinition of its privileged principles as democracy and economic development. Therefore, it was argued that it was not the axis deviation.

On these emerging developments, Mehmet Ali Birand wrote that the previous world order is no longer present (*Hurriyet*, 20 October 2010). For him, the times when the USA and Europe looked down on Turkey and managed the world are all in the past. The new world order is being established and Turkey is trying to find its own place in this new order. With a departure from this belief, he found the axis shift debate exaggerated (*Hurriyet*, 16 June 2010): 'Erdogan took two steps, we all protested... Some of us are frightened.' He noted what was behind the worries, the deviation which began with foreign policy might continue internally with the deviation in the secular system. He advised: 'We shall not frighten ourselves in vain.' He believed no-one, even those among the most radical Islamists, would like to see an economically downfallen Turkey dealing with the war between the Turks and the Kurds. Turkey cannot go anywhere by promoting anti-Westernism.

In *Radikal*, Eyup Can (12 June 2010) asked whether Turkey was falling out with the USA and caring for the Middle East Union more than the European Union as the 're-awakening of new Ottomanism'. In his opinion, Foreign

Minister Davutoglu is neither a typical Islamist nor a romantic Ottomanist. He supported the objective of Turkey's new target, whereby the Middle East Union intends to turn this generation into a generation of complete security and economic integration. Here, Can reproduces the official discourse emphatically in the same way as the discourse of government representatives. When the AKP came to power, they consciously distanced themselves from the traditions of Turkey's mainstream Islamist movement, National Outlook, rather they reformed a conservative discourse, encapsulating centre-right parties' sentiments. Despite the fact that neo-Ottomanism does not appear in Davutoglu's 'Strategic Depth' approach, the historical depth means that the Ottoman Empire and its cultural focus is high on Muslim solidarity, particularly Sunni Islam (Oktem 2013: 78).

On the debate of neo-Ottomanism in Turkish foreign policy, Cengiz Candar (*Radikal*, 30 June 2010) supported Turkey's newly emerging identity in international relations. He reminded us first of *New York Times* columnist Stephen Kinzer's words on the re-rise of Turkey in the new century, particularly on the old Ottoman geography. Kinzer focused on Turkey's strategic importance of being at the centre of the great Eurasia land. He stressed Turkey's location and strategic potential provided by its ability to integrate into the Ottoman heritage, Islamism and democracy successfully. Candar further quoted from Obama's speech in the Turkish Grand National Assembly:

> The ones discussing about the future of Turkey are wondering whether you will be pulled towards one way or the other. I guess they don't seize understanding of one thing: Turkey's greatness comes from its ability to stay at the centre of everything. Here (in Turkey), the West and the East are not separating from each other. Just the opposite, they are coming together.

This example shows that new Turkish foreign policy discourse reconstructs its nation-state identity discourse and reinforces its new geographical imagination. It also illustrates international support of the AKP's imagination of Turkey which constitutes a challenge of Kemalist nation-state discourse. Turkish media frequently reproduced Davutoglu's understanding of Turkey's place and its 'global role' in the world. Cengiz Candar proved these roles of Turkey in noting that Turkey was trying to relieve the tensions between Iran and the United States, Syria and Iraq, Armenia and Azerbaijan. No diplomats other than Turks were accepted in Tehran, Washington, Moscow, Tiflis, Damascus and Cairo. No other country was respected by Hamas, Hezbollah and Taliban while maintaining good relationships with Israel, Lebanon and Afghanistan governments. Using these argumentations, it was claimed that the world needs Turkey as a country to undertake the role of a mediator, peacemaker and arbitrator. Moreover, Candar noted that the country that could not solve its Kurdish problem could not ensure 'civil peace' and would not be able to reach any 'strategic skyline'. Turkish law still restricts freedom of expression and the minorities are not protected completely, either. While Turkey is on its way to become one of the indispensable forces in the world, there is one important obstacle it has to pass – it's time to manage its own country. Undoubtedly, this perspective on 'peace' confirms the main assumption of this research in validating the link between Turkey's identity constructions in relation to insider and outsider *others* of the nation-state.

Davutoglu's 'zero problems with neighbours' formula in the language of diplomacy and democratization built an inclusive platform for both Turkey's neighbours abroad and at home (Fisher Onar 2012: 72). Soft power of Turkey in foreign policy in embracing economic liberalism empowered the AKP's legitimacy in pursuit of democratic initiatives for traditional domestic others of the Turkish nation-state, Islamists and Kurds. This was why it was given 56 per cent support in its nationwide referendum for constitutional reform in September 2010. The rhetorical shifts of government from democracy discourse to security discourse came out, the limits of Sunni-Islamic conservative change, consolidating parties' power, conservative values and interests in politics rather than aiming at democracy for whole people. Therefore, the main challenges facing Turkey have been the tendency of a conservative majoritarian populism, which has produced strong anxiety in the secularist and liberal people of the country as was seen in the Gezi Park Protests in 2013. The *democratic depth* appears to lack the ingredient for ensuring different lifestyles and rights of the others that constitute half of the population.

Beyond the domestic challenges, political movements and transitions in the Arab world continue to put Turkish foreign policy to a serious test in terms of balancing its regional and global policies. The main challenge of Turkey's foreign policy in the Middle East is facing its relations with the United States, Israel, Iran and Syria. For instance, on the one hand Turkey improved its relations with Russia and Iran due to its energy and security interests; on the other hand, Turkey found itself in the opposition camp to them as an outcome of their diverse approaches to the Syrian uprising. The Syrian regime's brutal reaction to the demonstrators has damaged the AKP government's ties with President Bashar al-Assad and its economic and cultural engagement with Syria. Turkey's democracy discourse and soft power policy failed in the Syria test. Since 2011, the AKP government has shifted to a security discourse towards the emerging challenges in domestic and external affairs.

Conclusions

Different conceptualizations of Turkish international identity employ different inclusion and exclusion categories, which involve different actors in the 'we' group and 'they' group. On this assumption, the first case study showed that religion and different interpretations of it shift the discursive construction of Turkish identity and antagonisms. The second case study revealed how these antagonisms project different foreign policies; therefore, it moved the issue of Turkey's post-Kemalist identity formation into Turkey's European integration debate and redefinition of Turkey's external relations. Lastly, this case study demonstrated that the concepts of foreign policy, which are embedded in the news discourse, construct and shift New Turkey's identity depending on the domestic power struggle. It analysed how foreign policy discourse in the Turkish media constructs and challenges emerging post-Kemalist Turkish nation-state identity and the power struggle on definition of this identification. It focused on the representations of 9/11 and the Iraq War in order to trace conceptualizations of Turkey's international identity, in particular its Western, Middle Eastern, Muslim and secular identities. In this way, it argued that there are competing Turkish national identity discourses, which map Turkey and its relations with other nations in various ways.

This case study showed that Turkish media reminded and constructed Muslimhood of Turkish nation. The findings confirmed that Turkey has been searching for its new place in the new world order, in particular in the changing dynamics of the Middle East. The Turkish media defined a pivotal role for Turkey in transformation of the region. Thus, the majority of the reporting and columnists interpreted that Turkish foreign policy has not shifted its Western orientation, but has expanded its axis. The post-Kemalist reimagination of Turkey is just challenged by the Kemalist discourse of *Cumhuriyet* newspaper. The representation of the foreign policy issues in the media involves representing boundaries which mark the inclusion and exclusion, or who belongs, to the unity. The examples showed that the Arabs are one of the external others in the Kemalist identity discourse. On the other hand, the new state discourse of Turkey constructs a sameness discourse and stresses the common cultural and historical roots of Muslim countries. In addition, neo-liberal, pragmatic politics of Islamist AKP government helped to improve Turkey's relationship within its Muslim neighbourhood.

For a general evaluation of the axis shift in Turkish Foreign Policy, the examples from *Zaman, Taraf, Hurriyet* and *Radikal* indicate that the Turkish media supported the AKP and its policies in foreign relations. It is a fact that Muslim intellectuals, liberal democrats and socialists came to the point of consensus for a democratic transformation and wanted to distance themselves from Kemalist authoritarianism and 'isolationism'. The reimagination of the nation during the last decade shows that Turkey's engagement with neo-liberal politics satisfied some liberals and they seemed eager to portray Turkey as the 'Western country of the Middle East' (Birand, *Hurriyet*, 25 March 2011). However, this general support can be read as growing self-censorship (Arsan 2013) and there has been widespread silence in the Turkish media due to increasing government pressures and Erdogan's intolerance against the dissident voices of the media. However, the warnings for 'peace at home' as a condition of 'peace in the borders and abroad' appear in drawing the limits of support in line with AKP's reimagination of Turkey.

4

Conclusion

The literature on Turkey's new identity is mostly built upon the AKP's influence in Turkish politics which focuses on the role of Islam and Ottoman heritage in its discourse. In contrast, this study focused on the concept of nationalism and contributed to the literature of Contemporary Turkish Studies by being the first to apply Ruth Wodak's Discourse-Historical Approach to the 'process' of the power struggle in the discursive construction of Turkish nation-state identity in the Turkish media. In this regard, the analytical research agenda examined how Turkish national identity in domestic and foreign policy constructions articulated by the Turkish media reinforced or contested with each other in maintaining and transforming the Kemalist nation-state identity in the second term of the AKP government between 2007 and 2011, which witnessed two national referendums, the Presidential Referendum in 2007 and the Constitutional Referendum in 2010, as the milestones of domestic power struggle. By focusing on this power struggle, it can be argued that this book developed an analytic and critical reading of post-Kemalist Turkish politics and its challenges.

With these aims, the first chapter of the book was devoted to building the historical background for studying Turkey's identity. Since the main assumption in the Turkish case is that there are multiple Turkish nationalisms rather than an essentialist, single Turkish nationalism, the historical overview, and the literature on Turkish nationalism in Chapter 1 examined the origins and developments in different versions of Turkish nationalisms. It demonstrated that the historical fear of Kemalism defines two domestic others as the untrustworthy citizens of the Kemalist nation-state. During the nation-building era of the Republicanists, the new secular regime fought against an Islamist and Kurdish resistance; thus, the Islamists and Kurds were defined as the domestic 'others' and as 'threats' to the regime and modern Turkish identity. International support for the

AKP's policies and Kurdish demands contributed to darken the reactionary tone of the Kemalist discourse, as part of the domestic power struggle on the post-Kemalist reformation of Turkey's identity. It argued that the AKP's new imagination of the nation has played the main role in redefining the Turkish nation and the relationship of Turks with domestic and international others. Kemalist nation-state identity has been challenged by two traditional domestic others of the state, Islamists and Kurds. Moreover, the AKP's foreign policy discourse is asserted as the third challenge of Kemalist nation-state identity.

Chapter 2 outlined the theoretical and methodological framework for analysing the struggle on over redefining Turkey's international identity in media discourse. By taking a critical stand, Ruth Wodak's Discourse-Historical Approach formed the methodological framework for investigating the different discursive construction of thematic identities in the case of Turkey. This theoretical part assumed that discourse affects the way in which people define and talk about identity politics and how they express their ideologies, perspectives on the world, and social relations. It argued that different perspectives on the nation construct 'sameness' and 'difference' between groups and the identification of 'we' and 'they'. This framework for studying Turkish national identity construction in the domestic and international context made it possible to bring out the tension in maintaining and changing Turkish identity. It also showed that the media is a site where both official state discourse and opposing discourses could be studied as the parts of the investigation of Turkey's post-Kemalist identity transformation.

On these assumptions, Chapter 3 empirically showed that there is no 'single' Turkish nationalism and there has been an emergence of post-Kemalist nation-state identity through the power struggle between different narratives of the Turkish nation under the AKP government. All case studies contributed to present diverse Turkish national narratives in different imaginations of common political past, present and future. The case studies revealed both how the traditional others of the Kemalist nation-state could create a common consent in the construction of New Turkey and how it has been challenged during the transformation. Shedding a light on this process of historical change is crucial for a deeper understanding of contemporary Turkish politics, in particular, for the understanding of emerging new self/other relationships of Turkey which is a unique example in the relationship between religion, nationalism and foreign policy in International Relations.

With a departure from the fact that the media provide readily accessible and useful data in the form of ideologically diverse language usages, the book then moved on to an empirical study of how they imagine the nation and the different ways in which they define Turkish identity depending on their particular perspectives, the context and the on-going power struggle in Turkey. The Discourse-Historical Approach showed that specific language usages established power relations and served or challenged hegemonies in the context of the construction of a post-Kemalist nation-state identity in Turkey. The key question concerned how Turkish media discursively re/constructs Turkey's international identity. It discussed both the national and international dimensions in three of the thematic case studies in Chapter 3. The rationale was to throw light on the interaction between national identity and foreign policy by bringing out how media discourse links the two. In this context, the following section overviews the findings of the analysis and links them to contemporary Turkish politics.

The construction of the post-Kemalist nation-state identity

The book has examined the form taken by challenges to Turkey's Kemalist identity, focusing in particular on the AKP's pro-Islamist discourse, Kurdish discourse, and foreign policy discourse. It concluded that not only has the AKP's Muslim nationalism reconstructed New Turkish foreign policy, but also New Turkish foreign policy discourse has reconstructed the Turkish nation's Muslim identity and reinforced Muslim nationalism. The media analysis empirically showed that there is a clash of different narratives of the Turkish nation-state within a complex interdependence between Islam, secularism, modernism and Westernization in Turkey. The study has also made an important contribution to discourse analysis in politics by making use of Critical Discourse Analysis and making sense of diversity; the complexity of the identity of Turkey said much about both the religious and cultural dimensions of International Relations, in particular, contemporary Turkish studies and Middle East studies.

The outcomes of foreign policy decision making directly influence the daily lives of individuals. What people think about themselves and others is reproduced in the media and considered in foreign policymaking. In contrast to the state-centric explanations that are dominant in the literature of Turkish foreign policy, this study approached Turkish politics from a media perspective. The work responded to this gap by paying attention to the national tension on the definition of Turkey's identity through analysing discursive practices as fostering or reinforcing relations of domination in the media.

Furthermore, the Turkish case has assumed even greater importance during the period of writing this book. Identity politics and the rhetoric of 'blaming others' in different national imaginations have become pervasive in Turkish politics and society. Moreover, political parties have benefited from the polarization of the electorates. Identity matters have been instrumentalized to cloak the social, economic and political problems of Turkey. It seems that banal nationalism has been difficult to overcome and a 'daily plebiscite' of living together peacefully has been lost in Turkey (Ozkirimli 2014). In this context, this book may raise awareness of the tensions, as part of the processes by which identity is constructed, and discriminatory practices committed for the sake of political interests.

To highlight how the study has contributed to academic scholarship concerning the struggle over Turkey's identity, theoretical and methodological assumptions of the research will be revisited in Section 4.2. It outlines the key themes and issues revealed by an application of Critical Discourse Analysis to the case of Turkey. Then, the empirical findings will be connected in the content of the discursive constructs of Turkish national identity in domestic and international contexts in the first decade of the 2000s. In summary, this study is perhaps the first academic attempt to examine the discursive construction of Turkish nation-state identity within wider political and thematic discourses, comparing how being Turkish has been discursively articulated in relation to the domestic power struggle. Since these events are still relatively recent, these analyses remain provisional, even if the study has highlighted the complex and dynamic processes that lie behind the emergence of New Turkey.

Theoretical contribution: media, nationalism, foreign policy triangle

This project took its theoretical inspiration from three disciplines: nationalism studies, foreign policy analysis and media studies. Using a Foucauldian perspective on the concept of the 'discourse' served to link the notions of media, nationalism and foreign policy. A theoretical starting point is an approach that accepts nationalism as an ideology; as patterns of belief, practice, assumption, habit and representation that are reproduced discursively (Wodak et al. 1999) by the state and its institutions but also in the daily lives of citizens in everyday conversations (Billig 1995). Based on this assumption, the concept of nation is defined as a mental construct of the imagination of the nation (Anderson 1983) in people's minds, embedded in ideological power relations, politics and everyday language. It is argued that an imagined unity is based on recognition and opposition in the definition of 'us' and 'them', by promoting a sense of belonging together in a historical narrative (Wodak et al. 1999). Beyond official state discourse, there are multiple understandings of nationhood in political discourse according to different identities and ideologies that diversely imagine national uniqueness and difference towards 'others'. From the perspective of foreign policy analysis, it is also assumed that nation-state identity is constructed in interaction with both domestic and international 'others' rather than simply one or the other (Campbell 1998; Neumann 1999; Diez 2001; Hansen 2006; Waever 2006). Three case studies on discursive practices of differentiation and exclusion in the media articulated construction of the national identity and its self/other relations within and outside the borders of Turkey.

Based on this discursive approach to national identity and foreign policy, this study has argued that Turkish national identity is discursively constructed and that a fundamental conflict has existed between competing nationalist discourses in Turkish society over the definition of what Turkish identity should be and how to place Turkey in the world. Examination of these changing and contrasting definitions of 'Turkishness' has shed light on the struggle between the domestic actors and ideologies and illuminated competing views of the world that differ concerning Turkey's regional and world role. In so doing, the study has made an original contribution to the study of contemporary Turkish studies. With a specific focus on the media, expanding the focus beyond official state discourse to a wider set of actors within debate indicated how and why dominant Muslim conservative and opponent political discourses changed as a consequence of the transformation of power relations with the AKP government. Thus, the research broadened the analytical scope to media discourse in order to demonstrate the clash of discursive constructions of Turkish national identity by considering the major 'symbiotic antagonisms of nationalisms' (Kadioglu and Keyman 2011) in Turkish politics.

The empirical contribution: the reimagination of Turkey

The detailed investigation of the three case studies has confirmed the central claim of this thesis; namely, that there are different and context-determined narratives on the Turkish nation that highlight different interpretations of Turkey's common past, present and future, and common territory. Analysing Turkish media discourse has revealed the diversity of political discourses on the issues of Turkish national identity and foreign policy, based on people's positions and perspectives on the world. The analysis undertaken reveals that the power struggle in Turkey has been more than the secular-Islamic dichotomy (Somer 2010a, b, 2011); it is the clash of different national imaginations. The Discourse-Historical Approach made it possible to highlight how each Turkish nationalism uses constructive strategies to express the specific narrative of the nation, to determine who belongs to the Turkish nation, and their understandings of common history and the future. Significantly, by highlighting certain intertextual themes such as Turkishness, Kurdishness and Muslimhood in Turkey's national identity and foreign policy discourse in the press, the findings of the study demonstrate the limitations and borders in mapping post-Kemalist Turkey both in the national and international contexts.

In the selected historical process, the media witnessed and mirrored the Kemalist resistance to Islamic reformation in Turkey's identity. In this context, this study found that the main pillars of Kemalist Turkish nation-state identity have been challenged by the AKP's new imagination of Turkey. Secularism has been confronted by the normalization of civil-military relations and the abolition of bans on Islamic symbols in public institutions in the universities, hospitals and parliament. Moreover, Kemalist Turkey asserted that every citizen of the Republic is a Turk or a 'future Turk', specifically the Muslim peoples of Anatolia. This left Kurdish identity as not recognized in Kemalist politics. However, Islamists in power changed the state discourse on the Kurdish problem by acknowledging Kurdish rights. The dominant ideology was changing, and Kemalist Turkey's definition of nation and citizenship was challenged by Kurdish and Islamist identities.

Within this context, this study has shown how the Turkish media has contributed to the AKP's changing power relations and reimagination of the nation based on the formation of a new historical and geographical Ottomanism as this study defines the post-Kemalist narrative of the nation.

The Turkish media played a role in forming, constructing and distributing a new narrative of the nation and creating a general consent for new policies. This reformation in nation-state discourse has opened the way for economic, cultural and political good relationships with countries in the Middle East region and adapted Turkey's Islamists to international cooperation. This brought about a new look for Islamists and enhanced their soft power to convince different groups on decision making. Hence, the liberal nationalist discourse has become allied with the AKP in the transformation of Kemalist nation-state identity.

Furthermore, the data made it possible to see the slippery character of the link between these competing narratives. Especially, the ethnic-nationalist understanding of nation and citizenship has been addressed instrumentally when it is required politically in other nationalist discourses. Even this tactical addressing produces a new concept in Turkish politics as 'MHPlesmek' which means resembling, mimicking radical ethnic-nationalist party, the MHP. On the other hand, Kemalist secular nationalism, Islamist and liberal nationalisms and their reformations also appear within the selected timeframe.

In this context, the empirical findings reported above gave important clues about selective ideological readings of the common political past directly played a role in the definition of domestic and external others of Turkey. For instance, on one side Islamist nationalism constructs its discourse on Ottoman history and Islamic heritage, while on the other side secularists construct a national discourse on the Republican times, M. Kemal Ataturk's principles and heritage. These insights also illuminated the shape of these diverse discourses and their perspectives on foreign policy issues, specifically in the case of Turkish foreign policy's axis shift.

The analysis originally makes clear that Islamist discourse in the media constructs Turkey as the 'other' of the West from a historical and cultural perspective. According to the Kemalist secularist perspective, Turkish culture and nation are a part of the modern European family; being a part of the West or Europe means being a member of 'contemporary civilization' for them. Nevertheless, the coverage of the *Cumhuriyet* newspaper demonstrated that the memory of the Independence War against the Western powers is still alive in the Kemalist minds. This means that, in principle, they are pro-Western but naturally they are also sceptical as to its outcome. The domestic power struggle on the redefinition of Turkey's identity enhanced this scepticism and caused them to be inward-looking. They believed that the newly emerging narrative of the nation and the dress of the state was Islamic and was a threat to the Kemalist secular regime and lifestyles.

Similarly, in the case of Kurdish Initiative, the Sèvres Syndrome and the memory of Independence War against the European powers have played a role in the construction of their Euro-sceptic discourse in terms of their common political past with the European countries and the common political present and future with Europe. Kemalist discourse could not adapt itself to the democratization and globalization process due to the security concerns related to the Kurdish identity politics, in particular the fear of Islamic reactionism and separation of the country. Secularism is a 'must' for the Kemalist nation-state imagination; it is the only way of modernization, enlightenment, science and civilization. Despite the fact that secular nation-state identity was built in a top-down process by the Kemalist state, the case of the presidential election in 2007 shows that the secularist way of life has been accepted and has been internalized by the secularist circles and became a part of Turkish national identity.

Analysing language use in the data revealed an important result in the identification of three main strategies used in the discursive construction of national identity: constructive strategies, strategies of perpetuation or justification, and strategies of transformation. According to the findings, the Kemalist nationalist perspective used the strategies of perpetuation to resist changes to the dominant narrative in the 2000s. Supporters of this perspective hold a secularist, modernist, enlightenmentalist approach to Turkey's identity and its place in the world. Based on their belief that AKP was backed by foreign powers, their foreign policy discourse had a sceptical outlook and anti-imperialist leftish colouring against the West.

Islamists at the beginning of the new millennium have succeeded in adapting themselves globally and economically by becoming allies with neo-liberal world politics. Islamists in the power have used the strategy of transformation to break the Kemalist status quo and hegemony in the nation-state discourse and bureaucracy. The analysis indicated that *Zaman*'s Islamic perspective of the nation is not ethnic-nationalist toward the Muslim nations, but it would be xenophobic to non-Muslims and discriminatory to secularists, non-believers and LGBTs. The instances from *Hurriyet*, *Radikal* and *Taraf* newspapers demonstrated that liberals tended to corroborate AKP's pragmatist policies as was seen in the case of the 'axis shift' debate in Turkish foreign policy. In general, there was a lack of social and ethical perspectives for promoting rights and civil liberties for the others. Looking at the representation of the core elements in the discursive construction of Turkish identity in Turkish media, among the newspapers, *Radikal* was the only one that could have the pluralist perspective in three case studies.

The first case study on the presidential elections in 2007 showed the perception of Turkish identity in an everyday context in both citizenship and religion-based elements. The presidential elections case contributed to a fruitful observation on contested conceptualizations of the Turkish nation and the fact they contained culture and religion-based elements. What explicitly occurs in the data is that Islamists expressed their rejection of Republican assertive secularist politics by directly indicating that they was responsible for present political problems. In terms of a common political past, the legacy of the Turkish nation-state was represented negatively by the Islamists, liberal and leftist circles. Muslim conservative *Zaman*'s columnists referred to the multi-cultural Ottoman Period to justify their argumentation and oppositional perspective on the Kemalist nation-state whenever they mention the Republican period and its secularist policies. With a self-victimizing strategy, they hold a victim thesis that argues the Sunni majority is a victim of the Kemalist nation-state. They argued that the state suppressed the lifestyles and beliefs of religious Turks. The universities did not accept female students wearing headscarves, the courts regularly banned Islamist political parties, and the military constantly intervened to maintain suppression. This victim thesis points to the core element of the Islamic perspective on Turkish national identity which constructs Kemalists as the 'others' of their identity. Under the AKP government, secular Turks and bureaucracy lost their privileged positions in the centre and had to take second place. But the post-Kemalist nation-state under Sunni-Muslim conservative nationalism has defined new others and victims of the state.

Similarly, in the second case study, the 'blaming others strategy' was used in terms of referring to the origins of Turkey's Kurdish problem. What was particularly remarkable in this debate was that Islamists and liberals highlighted the Kemalist denial of Kurdish culture and language in the public sphere. Like Islamists, Kurds were portrayed as the victims of Turkey's Republican past and on the assessment of current political problems. Assertive secularist policies and military-state structure were directed to justify the demand for transformation in new constitution-writing and consolidation of democracy in parallel with the EU reforms. Regarding this post-Kemalist transformation, the AKP used democracy discourse to change the laws introduced following the 1980 military coup and also had the support of left-wing and right-wing citizens in the Constitutional Referendum in September 2010. The liberals and the majority of Kurds have taken the side of the AKP in democratic transformation. However, the more challenges the AKP faced, the more it mimicked the Kemalist methods for suppression of the opposition.

In the third case study on Turkish foreign policy, the linguistic instances from *Cumhuriyet* point out the Kemalist belief that the AKP follows the Islamic agenda in foreign policy as well. With a strategy of resistance to change and othering the Arabs, improving relations with the Islamic countries in the Middle East is called Arabization of Turkey. Also, Muslim conservative *Zaman*'s columnists contributed to reconstructing the new foreign policy discourse with the new geographic imagination of Turkey which addressed the Ottoman legacy and constructed a responsibility discourse related to Muslim peoples in the Ottoman territory. The conception of 'self' in Turkey's foreign policy widened its boundaries with this new imagination. Other newspapers' coverage represented common support for AKP's pragmatist and economy-based policies in the Middle East. Since 2011 the dynamic international relations have reconstructed the image of the AKP and Turkey. In particular, political transformations and challenges of Middle East uprisings contributed to the significance of Turkey's domestic peace.

Erdogan's New Turkey and its challenges

In 2002, the charter members of AKP as the reformist wing of Turkey's Islamists departed from the anti-Western National Outlook movement and moved towards the US-based Fetullah Gulen's liberal Islamist movement. This gave a moderate Islamic country image to Turkey or a democratic 'model' for a liberal political system able to incorporate an Islamic party. The AKP with a discourse on conservative democracy backed by international actors such as the United States and the EU had strong implications at both national and international levels. In its first term, the AKP brought a paradigmatic change in the democratization of Kemalist nation-state discourse with the help of the Europeanization process. In its second term, the AKP consolidated its Muslim conservative politics both in domestic and international politics under the shadow of a domestic power struggle. The AKP aimed to end the Kemalist nature of the Republic, thus it reduced the power of the Turkish army in politics, thus utilized the power of the Gulenist network in the Turkish judiciary and governed the Ergenekon trials for this purpose, which led to the imprisonment of many journalists, writers and military officers, including General Ilker Basbug.

Since its third victory in the general elections in 2011, the AKP government has openly articulated a mission for social engineering in the pursuit of bringing up religious generations based on a conservative Sunni view of social morality that privileges the Sunni Hanefi Turks (Yesilada and Rubin 2013). The repression of the Gezi Park protests in the summer of 2013 was the last straw that broke the camel's back in the Turkish political sphere. These developments have realized the Islamists' fears of secular-Westernist people and confirmed the anxieties of Kemalist circles. It can be said that the domestic struggle has turned from the matter of who governs Turkey to who has the power of maintaining different lifestyles in a highly polarized society (Keyman 2014).

Moreover, it began to be questioned whether the Turkish model offered by AKP is good for democracy and the future of Turkey (Taspinar 2014). Indeed, the new Turkish model, the so-called post-Kemalist Turkey, has had the paradoxes of adopting the authoritarian legacy of its Kemalist predecessors and drawing new religious fault lines which constitute illiberal models both for Turkish democracy and the countries in political transition in the Arab world.

During the Arab uprisings, the Erdogan government followed the same Sunni line in foreign policy (Ozkan 2014; Uzgel 2013). The main challenge Turkey's foreign policy in the Middle East is facing is its relations with the United States, Russia, Israel, Iran and Syria. For instance, on one hand, Turkey improved its relations with Iran due to its energy and security interests; while on the other hand, Turkey found itself in the opposition camp to Iran due to the difference of their approaches to the Syrian uprising. The Syrian regime's brutal reaction to the demonstrators has damaged the AKP government's ties with President Bashar al-Assad and their economic and cultural engagement with Syria. Turkey's democracy discourse and soft power policy failed in the Syria test.

Onis (2013) pointed out two main challenges of majoritarian democracy in the age of the AKP's New Turkey. First, a consensus and mutual toleration need to be constructed among the secularists and religious conservatives in public life, and pluralism should be protected under the law for every citizen, particularly for the minorities. Second, a compromise needs to be built on the matter of territorial unity of the Turkish state and the political rights of the Kurdish citizens. This means something should be done beyond the cultural and group rights of Kurds. About Turkey's transformation, Omer Taspinar (2014: 49) called it 'the end of the Turkish model' which referred to its positive democratic image replaced by authoritarianism in domestic politics, cronyism, and corruption in the economy and deadlock in foreign policy. Unfortunately, Erdogan's 'new brave Turkey' (Akkoyunlu 2013) began to mimic the authoritarian methods of the old Kemalist nation-state. The state's ideological apparatus such as the media, the educational institutions, and jurisdiction have been restructured to strengthen the government's power and its mission in every aspect of life. Illiberal anti-terrorism laws and routine imprisonments have been used for suppression of opposition voices coming from students, journalists, politicians and civil society activists alike (Ozbudun 2014). That means the Erdogan government's way of dealing with social diversity and the demands of plurality has become problematic and signals a democratic deficit both at home and abroad. Emerging challenges have made the Erdogan administration authoritarian against its opponents, which have caused it to lose support from leftists and liberals. As a result, the national media and opposition became dysfunctional for a powerful democracy.

Moreover, an open clash between Turkey's Islamists appeared in December 2013 as a major earthquake in the political agenda of Turkey which exhibited the difference between the perspectives of Islamists, their conservatisms, and their practices of power politics (Taspinar 2014b). New power struggles of Islamists on the top of the power hill have determined the country's politics since the Gulenist failed coup attempt of 15 July 2016. Therefore, a further research arena would focus on observation of different nationalist perspectives of Islamic discourses in Turkey.

This research can be inspiring for using Critical Discourse Analysis in the identity politics of International Relations. In particular, the Turkish experience in both Islam and secularism with the clash of different narratives of the nation offers lessons for other countries in the Middle East and North Africa seeking to transform identity and power politics. Also, the social media would be useful to broaden the understanding of the daily construction of national identities, renegotiation of definitions, and perceptions on the self and other categories in politics. One of the aims of this study was to open a channel for more discussion on the political polarizations in Turkey rather than provide definitive answers. Hopefully, new studies and attempts would contribute to open the ways to break the fear wall and censorship that can lead Turkey to have a free press and academia for the construction of a common discourse of justice and freedom.

Bibliography

Achugar, M. (2004), 'The Events and Actors of 11 September 2001 as Seen from Uruguay: Analysis of Daily Newspaper Editorials', *Discourse & Society*, 15: 291.

Ahmad, F. (1993), *The Making of Modern Turkey*, London: Routledge.

Akboga, S. (2014), 'Turkish Civil Society Divided by the Headscarf Ban', *Democratization*, 21 (4): 610–33.

Akcura, Y. (1976), *Üç Tarz-ı Siyaset*, Ankara: Türk Tarih Kurumu Basımevi.

Akkor Gul, A. (2006), 'Turkish Prime Time Television: Mass Culture and Tabloidization', *Istanbul University Communication Faculty Journal*, 25: 33–55.

Akkor Gul, A. (2011), 'Monopolization of media ownership as a challenge to the Turkish television broadcasting system and the European Union', *Ankara Avrupa Çalışmaları Dergisi*, 10 (2): 27–46.

Akkoyunlu, K. (2013), 'Erdogan's "Brave New Turkey" Looks to Past and Future', *Al-Monitor*, 3 April.

Akser, M. and B. Baybars-Hawks (2012), 'Media and Democracy in Turkey: Toward a Model of Neoliberal Media Autocracy', *Middle East Journal of Culture and Communication*, 5: 302–21.

Aksoy, S. Z. (2009), 'The Prospect of Turkey's EU Membership as Represented in the British Newspapers: The Times and The Guardian, 2002–2005', *Journal of European Studies*, 39 (4): 469–506.

Aktar, A. (2000), *Varlık Vergisi ve 'Türkleştirme' Politikaları, (Capital Tax and 'Turkification' Policies)*, Istanbul: Iletisim Yayınları.

Aktar, A. (2006), *Türk Milliyetçiliği, Gayrimüslimler ve Ekonomik Dönüşüm, (Turkish Nationalism, non-Muslims and Economical Transformation)*, İstanbul: İletişim Yayınları.

Alaranta, T. (2011), *Kemalism, Enlightenment, and Legitimacy: The Reproduction of Secularist National Identity in Turkey*, London: Lambert.

Alden, C. and A. Aran (2011), *Foreign Policy Analysis: New Approaches*, London: Routledge.

Alexander, M. (2006), 'The Strategic Depth Doctrine of Turkish Foreign Policy', *Middle Eastern Studies*, 42 (6): 945–64.

Altunisik, M. B. (2009), 'Worldviews and Turkish Foreign Policy in the Middle East', *New Perspectives on Turkey*, 40: 169–92.

Altunisik, M. B. and L. G. Martin (2011), 'Making Sense of Turkish Foreign Policy in the Middle East under AKP', *Turkish Studies*, 12 (4): 569–87.

Anderson, B. (1983), *Imagined Communities: Reflections on the Origin and Spread of Nationalism*, London: Verso.

Aras, B. (2009), 'Davutoglu Era in Turkish Foreign Policy', *Insight Turkey*, 11 (3): 127–42.

Aras, B. and H. Fidan, (2009), 'Turkey and Eurasia: Frontiers of a New Geographic Imagination', *New Perspectives on Turkey*, 40: 193–215.

Aras, B. and A. ve Gorener (2010), 'National Role Conceptions and Foreign Policy Orientation: The Ideational Bases of the Justice and Development Party's Foreign Policy Activism in the Middle East', *Journal of Balkan and Near Eastern Studies*, 12 (1): 73–92.

Aras, B. and R. K. Polat (2007), 'Turkey and the Middle East: Frontiers of the New Geographic Imagination', *Australian Journal of International Affairs*, 61 (4): 471–88.

Argun, B. (1999), 'Universal Citizenship Rights and Turkey's Kurdish Question', *Journal of Muslim Minority Affairs*, 19 (1): 85–103.

Arsan, E. (2013), 'Savaşı ve Barışı Çerçevelemek: Türk ve Kürt Basınında 'Öteki Acının' Tanıklığı' (Framing the War and Peace), *'Medyada Barış Mümkün mü?' Konferansı*, 18 Nisan, Boğaziçi Üniversitesi, Barış Eğitimi Uygulama ve Araştırma Merkezi.

Arsan, E. (2014), 'Radikal İki de Düştü', (Radikal II is lost, too), *Evrensel*, 20 June.

Atasoy, Y. (2009), *Islam's Marriage with Neo-Liberalism: State Transformation in Turkey*, London: Palgrave Macmillan.

Atay, T. (2013), 'The Clash of "Nations" in Turkey: Reflections on the Gezi Park Incident', *Insight Turkey*, 15 (3): 39–44.

Aydin, U. U., ed. (2015), *Neoliberal Muhafazakar Medya (Neoliberal Conservative Media)*, Istanbul: Ayrıntı Yayınları.

Aydin-Duzgit, S. (2011), 'Avrupa Birliği-Türkiye İlişkilerine Postyapısalcı Yaklaşım: Almanya Örneğinde Dış Politika ve Söylem Analizi', *Uluslararası İlişkiler Dergisi*, 8 (29): 49–70.

Aydin-Duzgit, S. (2014), 'Unravelling European Union Foreign Policy through Critical Discourse Analysis: Guidelines for Research', in C. Carta and S. F. Morin (eds), *EU Foreign Policy through the Lens of Discourse Analysis: Making Sense of Diversity*, NY: Ashgate.

Azak, U. (2010), *Islam and Secularism in Turkey: Kemalism, Religion and the Nation State*, London: IB Tauris.

Baker, P. and T. McEnery (2005), 'A Corpus-based Approach to Discourses of Refugees and Asylum Seekers in UN and Newspaper Texts', *Journal of Language and Politics*, 4 (2): 197–226.

Baker, P., C. Gabrielatos, M. Khosravinik, M. Krzyżanowski, T. McEnery and R. Wodak (2008), 'A Useful Methodological Synergy? Combining Critical Discourse Analysis and Corpus Linguistics to Examine Discourses of Refugees and Aasylum Seekers in the UK Press', *Discourse Society*, 19: 273.

Balabanova, E. (2007), *Media, Wars and Politics Comparing the Incomparable in Western and Eastern Europe*, England: Ashgate Publishing Company.

Bali, R. N. (2000), *Bir Türkleştirme Serüveni 1923-1945 (A Turkification Episode 1923-1945)*, Istanbul: İletişim Yayınları.

Bali, R. N. (2006), 'The Politics of Turkification during the Single Party Period', in H. Kieser (ed.), *Turkey Beyond Nationalism*, London-New York: I.B. Tauris.

Bali, R. N. (2012), *The Wealth Tax (Varlık Vergisi), Affair: Documents from the British National Archives*, Istanbul: Libra Kitapçılık.

Bamford, J. (2005), *A Pretext for War: 9/11, Iraq, and the Abuse of America's Intelligence Agencies*, New York: Anchor Books.

Barlow, D. M. and B. Mills (2009), *Reading Media Theory: Thinkers, Approaches and Contexts*, New York: Pearson Longman.

Barnett, J. (2008), 'Peace and Development: Towards a New Synthesis', *Journal of Peace Research*, 45 (1): 75–89.

Barras, A. (2009), 'A Rights-Based Discourse to Contest the Boundaries of State Secularism? The Case of the Headscarf Bans in France and Turkey', *Democratization*, 16 (6): 1237–60.

Beck, S. and M. Downing (2003), *The Battle for Iraq: BBC News Correspondents on the War Against Saddam*, Baltimore, MD: Johns Hopkins University Press.

Bell, A. and P. Garrett (1998), 'Media and Discourse: A Critical Overview', in A. Bell and P. Garrett (eds), *Approaches to Media Discourse*, 1–20, Oxford: Blackwell.

Bennett, W. L. (2007), *When the Press Fails: Political Power and the News Media from Iraq to Katrina (Studies in Communication, Media, and Public Opinion)*, Chicago: University of Chicago Press.

Berkes, N. (1964), *The Development of Secularism in Turkey*, New York: Routledge.

Bertrand, I. and P. Hughes (2004), *Media Research: Audiences, Institutions, Texts*, New York: Palgrave Macmillan.

Bhargava, R., ed. (1998), *Secularism and Its Critics*, Oxford: Oxford University Press.

Bilgic, E. E. and Z. Kafkaslı (2013), *Gencim, Özgürlükçüyüm, Ne İstiyorum? Diren Gezi Parkı Anket Sonuç Raporu (I am Young, Pro-Liberty, what do I want? Report on the Results of the Gezi Parkı Survey)*, Istanbul: Bilgi Üniversitesi Yayınları.

Bilgin, P. (2005), 'Turkey's Changing Security Discourses: The Challenge of Globalisation', *European Journal of Political Research*, 44: 175–201.

Bilgin, P. (2008), 'The Politics of Security and Secularism in Turkey: From the Early Republican Era to EU Accession Negotiations', in Dietrich Jung and Catharina

Raudvere (eds), *Religion, Politics, and Turkey's EU Accession*, 139–56, London: Palgrave.

Bilgin, P. (2009), 'Securing Turkey Through Western-oriented Foreign Policy', *New Perspectives on Turkey*, 40: 105–25.

Bilgin, P. (2011), 'Security Dimension: A Clash of Security Cultures? Differences Between Turkey and European Union Revisited', in A. E. Cakir (ed.), *Fifty Years of EU-Turkey Relations: A Sisyphean Story* (Routledge Advances in European Politics), New York: Routledge.

Bilgin, P. and A. Bilgic (2011), 'Turkey's "New" Foreign Policy toward Eurasia', *Eurasian Geography and Economics*, 52 (2): 173–95.

Billig, M. (1995), *Banal Nationalism*, London: Sage.

Billig, M. (2009), 'Reflecting on a Critical Engagement with Banal Nationalism: Reply to Skey', *The Sociological Review*, 57 (2): 347–52.

Bora, T. (2003), 'Nationalist Discourses in Turkey', *The South Atlantic Quarterly*, 102 (2/3): 433–51.

Bora, T. (2011), 'Nationalist Discourses in Turkey', in A. Kadioglu and F. Keyman (eds), *Symbiotic Antagonisms: Competing Nationalisms in Turkey*, Utah: The University of Utah Press.

Bora, T. and K. Can (2004), *Devlet ve Kuzgun: 1990'lardan 2000'lere MHP (State and Raven: From 1990s to 2000s the MHP)*, Ankara: Iletisim Yayinlari.

Boydstun, A. E. (2013), *Making the News: Politics, the Media, and Agenda Setting*, Chicago and London: University of Chicago Press.

Boyt-Barret, O. and T. Rantanen (2001), 'News Agency Foreign Correspondents', in J. Tunstall (ed.), *Media Occupations and Professions*, Oxford: Oxford University Press.

Bozdaglioglu, Y. (2003), *Turkish Foreign Policy and Turkish Identity: A Constructivist Approach*, London: Routledge.

Bozdogan, S. and R. Kasaba (1997), *Rethinking Modernity and National Identity in Turkey*, Seattle and London: University of Washington Press.

Breuilly, J. (1994), *Nationalism and the State*, University of Chicago Press.

Brubaker, R. (1998), *Citizenship and Nationhood in France and Germany*, MA: Harvard University Press.

Bruter, M. (2005), *Citizens of Europe? The Emergence of a Mass European Identity*, Basingstoke: Palgrave Macmillan.

Buckingham, L. (2013), 'Mixed Messages of Solidarity in the Mediterranean: Turkey, the EU and the Spanish Press', *Discourse & Society*, 24 (2): 186–207.

Burcoglu, N. K. (1999), *The Image of the Turk in Europe from the Declaration of the Republic in 1923 to the 1990s*, Istanbul: The Isis Press.

Burroughs, E. (2015), 'Discursive Representations of "Illegal Immigration" in the Irish Newsprint Media: The Domination and Multiple Facets of the "Control" Argumentation', *Discourse & Society*, 26 (2): 165–83.

Buzan, B., O. Waever and J. de Wilde (1998), *Security: A New Framework for Analysis*, Boulder: Rynne Lienner.

Cagaptay, S. (2002), 'Reconfiguring the Turkish Nation in the 1930s', *Nationalism and Ethnic Politics*, 8 (2): 67–82.

Cagaptay, S. (2013), 'Defining Turkish Power: Turkey as a Rising Power Embedded in the Western International System', *Turkish Studies*, 14 (4): 797–811.

Calhoun, C. (1994), *Social Theory and the Politics of Identity*, Oxford: Blackwell Publishers Ltd.

Cam, A. and I. Sanlier-Yuksel (2015), 'Turkiye'de Medya'nın 2002 Sonrası Dönüşümü: Ekonomi Politik Bir Yaklaşım' (Transformation of Turkish Media after 2002: An Economy-politics Approach), in U. U. Aydin (ed.), *Neoliberal Muhafazakar Medya (Neoliberal Conservative Media)*, Istanbul: AyrintiYayinlari.

Campbell, D. (1998), *Writing Security, United States Foreign Policy and the Politics of Identity*, Manchester: Manchester University Press.

Canan-Sokullu, E. (2011), 'Turcoscepticism and Threat Perception: European Public and Elite Opinion on Turkey's Protracted EU Membership', *South European Society and Politics*, 6 (3): 483–97.

Canefe, N. (2002), 'Turkish Nationalism and Ethno-symbolic Analysis: The Rules of Exception', *Nations and Nationalism*, 8 (2): 133–55.

Canefe, N. (2008), 'Turkish Nationalism and the Kurdish Question: Nation, State and Securitization of Communal Identities in a Regional Context', *South European Society & Politics*, 13 (3): 391–8.

Canefe, N. and T. Bora (2003), 'The Intellectual Roots of Anti-European Sentiments in Turkish Politics: The Case of Radical Turkish Nationalism', *Turkish Studies*, 4 (1): 127–48.

Carta, C. and S. F. Morin, eds (2014), *EU Foreign Policy Through the Lens of Discourse Analysis: Making Sense of Diversity*, New York: Routledge

Casanova, J. (2011), 'The Long, Difficult, and Tortuous Journey of Turkey into Europe and the Dilemmas of European Civilization', *Constellations*, 13 (2): 234–47.

Casier, M. and J. Jongerden, eds (2011), *Nationalisms and Politics in Turkey, Political Islam, Kemalism and the Kurdish Issue*, London and New York: Routledge.

Celik, A. and A. Blum (2007), 'Future Uncertain: Using Scenarios to Understand Turkey's Geopolitical Environment and Its Impact on the Kurdish Question', *Ethnopolitics*, 6 (4): 569–83.

Cerutti, F. and S. Lucarelli, eds (2008), *The Search for a European Identity: Values, Policies and Legitimacy of the European Union*, London: Routledge.

Checkel, J. T. and P. J. Katzenstein (2009), *European Identity*, Cambridge and New York: Cambridge University Press.

Chilton, P. (2004), *Analysing Political Discourse: Theory and Practice*, London and New York: Routledge.

Chilton, P. (2013), *Time: Language, Cognition, and Reality*, Oxford: Oxford University Press.

Chomsky, N. (2012), 'On Turkey', Interview with David Barsamian, *Armenian Weekly*, 2 September.

Chouliaraki, L. (2000), 'Political Discourse in the News: Democratizing Responsibility or Aestheticizing Politics?' *Discourse & Society*, 11: 293.

Christensen, C. (2007), 'Concentration of Ownership, the Fall of Unions and Government Legislation in Turkey', *Global Media and Communication*, 3 (2): 179.

Christensen, M. (2010), 'Notes on the Public Sphere on a National and post-National Axis: Journalism and Freedom of Expression in Turkey', *Global Media and Communication*, 6 (2): 177–97.

Ciddi, S. (2008), 'The Republican People's Party and the 2007 General Elections: Politics of Perpetual Decline', *Turkish Studies*, 437–55.

Cinar, A. (2005), *Modernity, Islam, and Secularism in Turkey: Bodies, Places, and Time*, Minneapolis: The University of Minnesota Press.

Cirakman, A. (2011), 'Flags and Traitors: The Advance of Ethno-nationalism in the Turkish Self-image', *Ethnic and Racial Studies*, 34 (11): 1894–912.

Cizre, U. (2004), 'Problems of Democratic Governance of Civil-military Relations in Turkey and the European Union Enlargement Zone', *European Journal of Political Research*, 43: 107–25.

Cizre-Sakallioglu, U. (1998), 'Kurdish Nationalism from an Islamist Perspective: The Discourses of Turkish Islamist Writers', *Journal of Muslim Minority Affairs*, 18 (1): 73–89.

Clarke, M. (1996), 'Foreign Policy Analysis: A Theoretical Guide', in S. Stavridis and C. Hill (eds), *Domestic Sources of Foreign Policy: West European Reactions to the Falklands Conflict West European Reactions to the Falklands Conflict*, Oxford: Berg Publishing.

Clary-Lemon, J. (2010), '"We're not Ethnic, We're Irish!": Oral Histories and the Discursive Construction of Immigrant Identity', Discourse & Society, 21 (1): 5–25.

Coban, F. (2012), 'Turkey's Europeaness Question in the Turkey and EU Relations', in M. Tunçoku and G. Baba (eds), *Memorium Book of Didem Yaman*, Canakkale: COMU.

Cohen, B. (1965), *The Press and Foreign Policy*, Princeton University Press.

Cohen, B. (1972), *The Public's Impact on Foreign Policy*, Little Brown.

Colakoglu, N. M. (2018), *Dunya Basininda Ataturk (Ataturk in the World Press)*, Ist: Dogan Kitap.

Connolly, W. (2000), *Why I am Not a Secularist*, Minneapolis: University of Minnesota Press.

Cottle, S. and Lester, L. (2011), *Transnational Protests and the Media*, Oxford: Peter Lang.
Criss, N. B. (2010), 'Dismantling Turkey: The Will of the People?', *Turkish Studies*, 11 (1): 45–58.
Cumhuriyet (13 October 2005), Başbakan Kimi Temsil Ediyor?
Cumhuriyet (13 October 2005), Dursun Atılgan: 'İhanet Cephesi' İşbaşında
Cumhuriyet (20 October 2005), Başkent İçin Kara Leke.
Cumhuriyet (27 October 2005), Oktay Akbal: Çılgın Türkler'den Şaşkın Türklere!
Cumhuriyet (27 October 2005), Türban Yasağı İşlemiyor.
Cumhuriyet (03 December 2005), Çağın Neresindeyiz?
Cumhuriyet (31 December 2005), Müfettişten Atatürk'e Hakaret.
Cumhuriyet (08 June 2006), Uğur Demir: 'TRT, AKP'nin Çiftliği'.
Cumhuriyet (30 January 2007), Usta Yazar Ayla Kutlu, 'Nasıl bir Cumhurbaşkanı' İstediği Sorusuna şu Yanıtı Veriyor.
Cumhuriyet (14 April 2007), Tehlikenin Farkındayız.
Cumhuriyet (23 April 2007), Erdal Atabek: İki Ayrı Türkiye (mi Var?)
Cumhuriyet (30 April 2007) Mustafa Balbay: Mevzu Vatansa Gerisi Teferruat.
Cumhuriyet (24 July 2007a), Sonuçlar Dünya Basınında. AB'nin Yorumları: 'Türkiye'de Ilımlı İslam Kazandı'.
Cumhuriyet (24 July 2007b), Merkez Sağda Hasar Büyük.
Cumhuriyet (30 July 2007), AKP'nin Seçim Başarısı Bir Ölçüde Merkez Sağın Çöküşü Üzerine Sağlanmıştır.
Cumhuriyet (30 July 2007), Emre Kongar: Nasıl Oldu? Ne Yapmalı?
Cumhuriyet (17 January 2008), Deniz Som: Sessiz Sedasız (!)
Cumhuriyet (16 January 2010), Güray Öz: Bilinç Kayması.
Cumhuriyet (17 April 2010), Cüneyt Arcayürek: Su Yolunu Bulmuş.
Cumhuriyet (17 April 2010), Devlet Bahçeli Genişlemeyi Özetledi.
Cumhuriyet (12 June 2010), Emre Kongar: Çağdaş Demokrasiden Ortadoğulu Otoriter-Totaliter Rejime Doğru.
Cumhuriyet (12 June 2010), Türkiye'nin BM Güvenlik Konseyi'nde İran'dan yana tavır koyması, Başbakan Recep Tayyip Erdoğan'ın Arap dünyasına dönük mesajları 'eksen kayması' tartışmalarını da beraberinde getirdi.
Cumhuriyet (23 July 2010), Suheyl Batum: 28 Şubat ve 27 Nisan.
Cumhuriyet (25 July 2010), Öztin Akgüç: Türkiye'nin Ekseni.
Cumhuriyet (22 November 2010), Erol Manisalı: Keynes, Sistem ve Siyasal Partilerimiz.
Cumhuriyet (30 January 2011), AKP Oyun Kurmaya Çalışırken Oyuncak Oluyor.
Cumhuriyet (31 January 2011), Hüner Tuncer: Dış Politikamızda Eksen Kayması.
Cumhuriyet (27 April 2011), Deniz Kavukçuoğlu: Karanlıktan Aydınlığa.
Cumhuriyet (07 May 2011), Ali Sirmen: İpleri Geren Gerene.

Cumhuriyet (18 August 2011), Bahçeli, şunları kaydetti: 'Açılım denilen yıkım projesine son verilmeli ve bu projenin koordinatörü olan ilgili Başbakan Yardımcısı acilen istifa etmelidir.'

Cumhuriyet (01 November 2011), Belçika'nın başkenti Brüksel'de terör olaylarını kınamak için düzenlenen mitingde, Avrupa Parlementosu binası önüne üzerinde Çukurca şehitlerinin fotoğrafları bulunan 26 tabut bırakıldı.

Cusinamo-Love, M. (2003), 'The New Bully Pulpit: Global Media and Foreign Policy', in M. Rozell and J. Mayer (eds), *Media Power, Media Politics*, 257–89, Maryland: Rowman & Littlefield Publishers.

Dagi, I. (2005), 'Transformation of Islamic Political Identity in Turkey: Rethinking the West and Westernization', *Turkish Studies*, 6 (1): 21–37.

Davutoglu, A. (1994), *Civilizational Transformation and the Muslim World*, Istanbul, Turkey: Bilim ve Sanat Vakfı Yayınları.

Davutoglu, A. (1997), 'The Clash of Interests: An Explanation of the World (Dis) Order', *Perceptions: Journal of International Affairs*, 2 (4): 1–17.

Davutoglu, A. (2000), 'Philosophical and Institutional Dimensions of Secularisation: A Comparative Analysis', in Azzam Tamimi and John L. Esposito (eds), *Islam and Secularism in the Middle East*, 170–208, New York: New York University Press.

Davutoglu, A. (2001), *Stratejik Derinlik: Turkiye'nin Uluslararasi Konumu (Strategic Depth: Turkey's International Position)*, Istanbul, Turkey: Kure Yayinlari.

Davutoglu, A. (2008), 'Turkey's Foreign Policy Vision: An Assessment of 2007', *Insight Turkey*, 10 (1): 77–96.

De Fina, A. et al. (2006), *Discourse and Identity*, Cambridge: Cambridge University Press.

De Jong, W. et al. (2005), *Global Activism, Global Media*, London: Pluto Press.

Dekavalla, M. (2010), 'Tax, War and Waiting Lists: The Construction of National Identity in Newspaper Coverage of General Elections after Devolution', *Discourse &Society*, 21: 638.

Delanty, G. (1995), *Inventing Europe Idea, Identity, Reality*, London: Macmillan.

Delanty, G. and C. Rumford (2005), *Rethinking Europe: Social Theory and the Implications of Europeanization*, London: Routledge.

Deringil, S. (1991), 'Legitimacy Structures in the Ottoman State: The Reign of Abdulhamid II (1876–1909)', *International Journal of Middle East Studies*, 23: 345–59.

Deringil, S. (2007), 'The Turks and 'Europe': The Argument from History', *Middle Eastern Studies*, 43 (5): 709–23.

Deutsch, K. W. (1953), *Nationalism and Social Communication: An Inquiry into the Foundations of Nationality*, New York: John Wiley&Sons.

Devereux, E. (2009), *Understanding the Media*, London: Sage.

Diez, T. (2001), 'Europe as a Discursive Battleground: European Integration Studies and Discourse Analysis', *Cooperationand Conflict*, 36 (1): 5–38.

Diez, T. (2004), 'Europe's Others and the Return of Geopolitics', *Cambridge Review of International Affairs*, 17 (2): 319–35.

Donmez, R. O. (2007), 'Nationalisms in Turkey: Political Violence and Identity', *Ethnopolitics*, 6 (1): 43–65.

Donmez, R. O. (2011), 'The Justice and Development Party's Perspective of Social Exclusion: Between Societal Security and Morality', *Middle East Critique*, 20 (1): 67–80.

Donmez, R. O. and P. Enneli, eds (2011), *Societal Peace and Ideal Citizenship for Turkey*, Plymouth: Lexington Books.

Duran, B. (2006), 'JDP and Foreign Policy as an Agent of Transformation', in H. Yavuz (ed.), *The Emergence of a New Turkey: Democracy and the AK Party*, 281–305, Utah: The University of Utah Press.

Duran, B. (2013), 'Understanding the AK Party's Identity Politics: A Civilizational Discourse and Its Limitations', *Insight Turkey*, 15 (1): 91–109.

Eisenstein, E. L. (1979), *The Printing Press as an Agent of Change: Communications and Cultural Transformations in Early-Modern Europe*, Cambridge: Cambridge University Press.

Eligur, B. (2010), *The Mobilization of Political Islam in Turkey*, New York: Cambridge University Press.

Ergil, D. (2009), *Kürtleri Anlamak: Güvenlik Politikalarından Kimlik Siyasetine (Understanding the Kurds: From Security Policies to Identity Politics)*, Istanbul: Timas Yayıncılık.

Erzan, R., K. Kirişçi and H. Yılmaz (2002), 'EU and Public Opinion in Turkey', in *Turkish Economic and Social Studies Foundation (TESEV)*, İstanbul.

Fairclough, N. (1995a), *Critical Discourse Analysis: Papers in the Critical Study of Language*, New York: Longman Publishing.

Fairclough, N. (1995b), *Media Discourse*, London: Edward Arnold.

Fairclough, N. (2001), *Language and Power*, London: Longman.

Fairclough, N. (2003), *Analysing Discourse: Textual Analysis for Social Research*, London: Routledge.

Fairclough, N. and R. Wodak (1997), 'Critical Discourse Analysis', in Teun A. van Dijk (ed.), *Discourse as Social Interaction*, 2, 258–84, London: Sage.

Fidan, H. (2010), 'Turkish Foreign Policy Towards Central Asia', *Journal of Balkan and Near Eastern Studies*, 12 (1): 109–21.

Finlayson, A. (1999), *Language in: Contemporary Social and Political Theory: An Introduction*, 47–68, Buckingham: Open University Press.

Finlayson, A., ed. (2003), *Contemporary Political Thought: A Reader and Guide*, Edinburgh University Press/New York University Press.

Finlayson, A., ed. (2009), *Democracy and Pluralism: The Political Thought of William E. Connolly*, London: Routledge.

Finlayson, A. (2011), 'Cameron, Culture and the Creative Class: The Big Society and the Post- bureaucratic Age', *The Political Quarterly*, 82: 35–47.

Finlayson, A. and J. Valentine, eds (2002), *Politics and Poststructuralism*, Edinburgh: Edinburgh University Press.

Fisher Onar, N. (2009a), 'Echoes of a Universalism Lost: Rival Representations of the Ottomans in Today's Turkey', *Middle Eastern Studies*, 45 (2): 229–41.

Fisher Onar, N. (2009b), *Neo-Ottomanism, Historical Legacies, and Turkish Foreign Policy*, EDAM/German Marshall Fund Working Paper Series, 2009/3.

Fisher Onar, N. (2011a), 'Constructing Turkey Inc.: The Discursive Anatomy of a Domestic and Foreign Policy Agenda', *Journal of Contemporary European Studies*, 19 (4): 463–73.

Fisher Onar, N. (2011b), 'Continuity or Rupture? The Historiography of the Ottoman Past and Its Political Uses', in K. Nicolaidis and B. Sebe (eds), *Echoes of Colonialism*, 139–53, Cambridge: Cambridge University Press.

Fisher Onar, N. (2012), "Democratic Depth': The Missing Ingredient in Turkey's Domestic/Foreign Policy Nexus?' in K. Oktem et al. (eds), *Another Empire? A Decade of Turkey's Foreign Policy under the Justice Development Party*, 61–77, Istanbul: Istanbul Bilgi University Press.

Fisher Onar, N. and M. Müftüler-Bac (2011), 'The Adultery and Headscarf Debates in Turkey: Fusing "EU-niversal" and "alternative" modernities?', *Women's Studies International Forum*, 34 (5): 378–89.

Flowerdew, J., David C. S. Li and S. Tran (2002), 'Discriminatory News Discourse: Some Hong Kong Data', *Discourse& Society*, 13: 319.

Fokas, E. (2008), 'Islam in the Framework of Turkey–EU Relations: Situations in Flux and Moving Targets', *Global Change, Peace & Security: formerly Pacifica Review: Peace, Security & Global Change*, 20 (1): 87–98.

Forchtner, B. (2011), 'Critique, the Discourse-historical Approach, and the Frankfurt School', *Critical Discourse Studies*, 8 (1): 1–14.

Foucault, M. (1972), *The Archaeology of Knowledge*, New York: Pantheon.

Fowler, R. (1991), *Language in the News: Discourse and Ideology in the Press*, London: Routledge.

Gambetti, Z. (2009), 'İktidarın Dönüşen Çehresi: Neoliberalizm, Şiddet ve Kurumsal Siyasetin Tasfiyesi' (Transformation of the Power's Face: Neoliberalism, Violence and Elimination of Institutional Policies), *İstanbul Üniversitesi Siyasal Bilgiler Fakültesi Dergisi*, 40: 143–64.

Gans, H. J. (2003), *Democracy and the News*, New York: Oxford University Press.

Gee, J. (2005), *An Introduction to Discourse Analysis*, London: Routledge.

Gellner, E. (1983), *Nations and Nationalism*, Ithaca: Cornell University Press.

Gencel Bek, M. (2004), 'News Reporting in Turkish Television and Tabloidisation', *İletişim Araştırmaları*, 2 (1): 9–38.

Gilboa, E. (2002), *Media and Conflict: Framing Issues, Making Policy, Shaping Opinions*, Leiden: Martinus Nijhoff.

Gillespie, M. (2005), *Media Audiences*, Maidenhead: Open University Press.

Gillespie, M. and J. Toynbee (2006), *Analysing Media Texts*, New York: Open University Press.

Golding, P. and P. Harris (1997), *Beyond Cultural Imperialism: Globalization, Communication and the New International Order*, London: SAGE Publications.

Gole, N. (2000), *Muhendisler ve Ideoloji (Engineers and Ideology)*, Istanbul: Metis.

Goody, J. (2005), *Avrupa'da İslam Damgası (Islam Stigma in Europe)*, Istanbul: Etkileşim Yayınları.

Goving, N. (2004), 'Media Coverage: Help or Hindrance in Conflict Prevention', in S. Badsey, (ed.), *The Media and International Security*, London: Frank Coss.

Gunes, C. (2009), 'Kurdish Politics in Turkey: Ideology, Identity and Transformations', *Ethnopolitics*, 8 (2): 255–62.

Gungor, N., ed. (2010), *Cumhuriyet Döneminde İletişim: Kurumlar, Politikalar (Communication in the Republican Era: Institutions, Policies)*, Ankara: Siyasal Kitapevi.

Gunter, M. (2000), 'The Continuing Kurdish Problem in Turkey after Öcalan's Capture', *Third World Quarterly*, 21 (5): 849–69.

Gunter, M. (2007), 'Turkey's Floundering EU Candidacy and Its Kurdish Problem', *Middle East Policy*, 14 (1): 117–23.

Guveli, A. (2011), 'Social and Economic Impact of the Headscarf Ban on Women in Turkey', *European Societies*, 13 (2): 171–89.

Guven, İ. (2010), 'Globalisation, Political Islam and the Headscarf in Education, with Special Reference to the Turkish Educational System', *Comparative Education*, 46 (3): 377–90.

Habermas, J. (1989), *The Structural Transformation of the Public Sphere: An Inquiry into a Category of Bourgeois Society*, Cambridge, MA: MIT Press.

Habermas, J. (2008), 'Notes on Post-Secular Society', *New Perspectives Quarterly*, 25 (4): 17–29.

Hale, W. (2012) *Turkish Foreign Policy since 1774*, London: Routledge.

Hale, W. and E. Ozbudun (2010), *Islamism, Democracy and Liberalism in Turkey: The Case of the AKP*, London: Routledge.

Hallin, D. C. and P. Mancini (2004), *Comparing Media Systems: Three Models of Media and Politics*, New York: Cambridge University Press.

Hammond, P. (2007), *Media, War and Postmodernity*, New York: Routledge.

Hanioglu, M. S. (1995), *The Young Turks in Opposition*, NY: Oxford University Press

Hanioglu, M. S. (2001), *Preparation for a Revolution: The Young Turks, 1902–1908*, NY: Oxford University Press.
Hanioglu, M. S. (2011), 'Üç Milliyetçilik (Three Nationalisms)', *Sabah*, 29 May.
Hansen, L. (2006), *Security as Practice: Discourse Analysis and the Bosnian War*, London: Routledge.
Hansen, L. and O. Waever (2001), *European Integration and National Identity: The Challenge of the Nordic States*, London: Routledge.
Heper, M. (2008), *State and Kurds in Turkey: The Question of Assimilation*, Basingstoke: Palgrave Macmillan.
Heper, M. (2011), *Türkiye'nin Siyasal Hayatı: Tarihsel, Kurumsal ve Karşılaştırmalı Açıdan, (Turkey's Political History: Historical, Institutional and Comparative Perspectives)*, Istanbul: Dogan Kitap.
Herman, E. S. and N. Chomsky (2002), *Manufacturing Consent: The Political Economy of the Mass Media*, New York: Pantheon.
Hill, C. (2003), *The Changing Politics of Foreign Policy*, Basingstoke: Palgrave Macmillan.
Hill, C. and W. Wallace (1996), 'Introduction: Actors and Actions', in C. Hill (ed.), *The Actors in Europe's Foreign Policy*, London: Routledge.
Hjelm, T. (2014), 'National Piety: Religious Equality, Freedom of Religion and National Identity in Finnish Political Discourse', *Religion*, 44 (1): 28–45.
Hobsbawm, Eric J. (1991), *Nations and Nationalism since 1789*, Cambridge: Cambridge University Press.
Hojelid, S. (2010), 'Headscarves, Judicial Activism, and Democracy: The 2007-8 Constitutional Crisis in Turkey', *The European Legacy*, 15 (4): 467–82.
Holsti, O. R. (1992), 'Public Opinion and Foreign Policy: Challenges to the Almond-Lippmann Consensus Mershon Series: Research Programs and Debates', *International Studies Quarterly*, 36 (4): 439–66.
Huntington, S. P. (2002), *The Clash of Civilizations and the Remaking of World Order*, New York: Free.
Hurriyet (26 September 2005), Baydemir: Bayrak Tüm Yurttaşların Ortak Değeri.
Hurriyet (29 September 2005), Emin Çölaşan: Hezimetin Başlangıcı.
Hurriyet (22 November 2005), Emin Çölaşan: Elden Çıkan Güneydoğu.
Hurriyet (29 November 2005), Cüneyt Ülsever: Şemdinli Üzerinden Irak.
Hurriyet (11 April 2006), Mehmet Ali Birand: Ali Babacan Aranıyor (!)
Hurriyet (14 January 2007), Bülent Arınç: Dindar Cumhurbaşkanı Seçeceğiz.
Hurriyet (15 April 2007), Ahmet Hakan: Ey Tayyip Erdoğan!.. Ey Deniz Baykal!
Hurriyet (15 April 2007), Bekir Coşkun: Güzel Günler Göreceğiz Çocuklar…
Hurriyet (25 April 2007), Bekir Coşkun: Demokrasiyi Soytarılaştırmak.
Hurriyet (22 July 2007), Deniz Baykal: Biz Değil Merkez Sağ Çöktü.
Hurriyet (22 July 2007), Recep Tayyip Erdoğan: Hepimizi Birleştiren Ortak Değer ve Hedeflerimiz Var.

Hurriyet (24 July 2007), Bekir Coşkun: Utangaç Seçmen.
Hurriyet (24 July 2007), Cengiz Çandar: Türkiye Yanılmadı, Yanıltmadı.
Hurriyet (24 July 2007), Hadi Uluengin: Sivil Zafer.
Hurriyet (28 July 2007), Mehmet Barlas: Orada Bir Köy Yok Uzakta… O Köy Artık Kente ve İktidara Geldi.
Hurriyet (24 August 2007), Özdemir İnce: Türban ve Göstergebilim.
Hurriyet (26 August 2007), Özdemir İnce: Laikçilik ve Kalpazanlık.
Hurriyet (29 August 2007), Cüneyt Ülsever: Ayrışan Türkiye.
Hurriyet (09 November 2007), Ulusu: Sevr ile AP Kararları Aynı.
Hurriyet (21 September 2009), Dönüş Gövde Gösterisine Döndü.
Hurriyet (22 October 2009), CHP Genel Başkanı Deniz Baykal: 'Teröristler Kahraman Haline Dönüştü…"
Hurriyet (16 June 2010), Mehmet Ali Birand: Gerçek Eksen Kayması Öyle Değil Böyle Olur.
Hurriyet (22 June 2010), Bahçeli: AKP Küresel Siyasi Taşerondur.
Hurriyet (20 October 2010), Mehmet Ali Birand: Bakışlar Hızla Türkiye'ye Dönüyor.
Hurriyet (16 January 2011), Cüneyt Ülsever: Biz Bize Yeteriz!
Hurriyet (25 March 2011), Mehmet Ali Birand: Türkiye Orta Doğu'nun 'Batılı ülkesi' Olduğunu Gösterdi.
Hurd, E. S. (2011), 'A Suspension of (dis)belief: The Secular-Religious Binary and the Study of International Relations', in C. Calhoun, M. Juergensmeyer and J. VanAntwerpen (eds), *Rethinking Secularism*, Oxford: Oxford University Press.
Hurd, E. S. (2012), 'International Politics after Secularism', *Review of International Studies*, 38: 943–61.
Hutchinson, J. (2000), 'Ethnicity and Modern Nations', *Ethnic and Racial Studies*, 23 (4): 651–69.
Hutchinson, J. and A. D. Smith (1995), *Nationalism*, Oxford: Oxford University Press.
Icduygu, A., D. Romano, and I. Sirkeci (1999), 'The Ethnic Question in an Environment of Insecurity: The Kurds in Turkey', *Ethnic and Racial Studies*, 22 (6): 991–1010.
Inalcik, H. (1997), *Economic and Social History of the Ottoman Empire*, New York: Cambridge University Press.
Inalcik, H. (1998), 'Türkiye Cumhuriyeti ve Osmanlı', (Turkish Republic and the Ottomans), *Doğu Batı*, 5.
Inthorn, S. (2007), *German Media and National Identity*, New York: Cambria.
Jäger, S. and F. Maier (2009), 'Theoretical and Methodological Aspects of Foucauldian Critical Discourse Analysis and Dispositive Analysis', in R. Wodak and M. Meyer (eds), *Methods of CDA*, 34–61, London: Sage.

Jenks, J. (2006), *British Propaganda and News Media in the Cold War*, Edinburgh: Edinburgh University Press.

Jepperson, R., A. Wendt and P. J. Katzenstein (1996), 'Norm, Culture and Identity in National Security', in P. Katzentein (ed.), *The Culture of National Security*, New York: Columbia University Press.

Kadioglu, A. (2011), 'Twin Motives of Turkish Nationalism', in A. Kadıoglu and F. Keyman (eds), *Symbiotic Antagonisms: Competing Nationalisms in Turkey*, 33–57, Utah: The University of Utah Press.

Kadioglu, A. (2012), 'Limits of Conservative Change: Reform Choreography of the Justice and Development Party', in K. Oktem, et al. (eds), *Another Empire? A Decade of Turkey's Foreign Policy under the Justice Development Party*, Istanbul: Istanbul Bilgi University Press.

Kadioglu, A. and F. Keyman, eds (2011), *Symbiotic Antagonisms: Competing Nationalisms in Turkey*, Utah: The University of Utah Press.

Kalaycioglu, E. (2002a), 'State and Society in Turkey: Democracy, Development and Protest', in Amyn B. Sajoo (ed.), *Civil Society in the Muslim World*, 247–72, London: I. B. Tauris.

Kalaycıoglu, E. (2002b), 'The Motherland Party: The Challenge of Institutionalization in a Charismatic Leader Party', *Turkish Studies*, 3 (1): 41–61.

Kalaycioglu, E. (2010), 'Justice and Development Party at the Helm: Resurgence of Islam or Restitution of the Right-of-Center Predominant Party?', *Turkish Studies*, 11 (1): 29–44.

Kalaycıoglu, E. (2012), 'Kulturkampf in Turkey: The Constitutional Referendum of 12 September 2010', *South European Society and Politics*, 17 (1): 1–22.

Kamali, M. (2006), *Multiple Modernities, Civil Society and Islam: The Case of Iran and Turkey*, Liverpool: Liverpool University Press.

Kamrava, M. (1998), 'Pseudo-democratic Politics and Populist Possibilities: The Rise and Demise of Turkey's Refah Party', *British Journal of Middle Eastern Studies*, 25 (2): 275–301.

Kandiyoti, D. (2012), 'The Travails of the Secular: Puzzle and Paradox in Turkey', *Economy and Society*, 41 (4): 513–31.

Kanra, B. (2009), *Islam, Democracy and Dialog in Turkey*, Aldershot: Ashgate.

Karasipahi, S. (2009), *Muslims in Modern Turkey: Kemalism, Modernism and the Revolt of the Islamic Intellectuals*, London: I.B.Tauris & Co Ltd.

Katzenstein, P., ed. (1996), *The Culture of National Security: Norms and Identity in World Politics*, New York: Columbia University Press.

Kavakci-Islam, M. (2010), *Headscarf Politics in Turkey: A Postcolonial Reading*, Basingstoke: Palgrave Macmillan.

Kaya, A. and F. Kentel (2005), *Euro Türkler: Türkiye ile Avrupa Birliği Arasında Köprü mü Engel mi (Euroturks: Are They a Bridge or a Barrier Between the EU and Turkey?)*, Istanbul: Bilgi Universitesi Yayınları.

Kaya, R. and B. Cakmur (2010), 'Politics and the Mass Media in Turkey', *Turkish Studies*, 11 (4): 521–37.

Kayali, H. (1997), *Arabs and Young Turks: Ottomanism, Arabism, and Islamism in the Ottoman Empire, 1908–1918*, Berkeley: University of California Press.

Keohane, R. and J. Nye (1997), *Power & Interdependence*, New York: Pearson.

Keyman, E. F. (2007a), 'Modernity, Secularism and Islam: The Case of Turkey', *Theory, Culture, & Society*, 24 (2): 215–34.

Keyman, E. F., ed. (2007b), *Remaking Turkey: Globalization, Alternative Modernities, and Democracy*, Lanham: Lexington Books.

Keyman, E. F. (2011), 'Nationalism in Turkey: Modernity, State, and Identity', in A. Kadıoglu and F. Keyman (eds), *Symbiotic Antagonisms: Competing Nationalisms in Turkey*, 10–33, Utah: The University of Utah Press.

Keyman, E. F. (2014), 'The AK Party: Dominant Party, New Turkey and Polarization', *Insight Turkey*, 16 (2): 19–31.

Keyman, E. F. and A. Icduygu, eds (2005), *Citizenship in a Global World: European Questions and Turkish Experiences*, London: Routledge.

Keyman, E. F. and Z. Onis (2007), *Turkish Politics in a Changing World: Global Dynamics and Domestic Transformations*, Istanbul: Istanbul Bilgi University Press.

Kieser, H. L., ed. (2008), *Turkey Beyond Nationalism*, London: I. B. Tauris.

Kirisci, K. (2011), 'The Kurdish Issue in Turkey: Limits of European Union Reform', *South European Society and Politics*, 16 (2): 335–49.

Kocan, G. and A. Oncu (2004), 'Citizen Alevi in Turkey: Beyond Confirmation and Denial', *Journal of Historical Sociology*, 17 (4): December.

Koenig, T., S. Mihelj, J. Downey and M. Gencel Bek (2006), 'Media Framings of the Issue of Turkish Accession to the EU', *Innovation: The European Journal of Social Science Research*, 19 (2): 149–69.

Kologlu, O. (1993), *Türkiye'de Basın (The Press in Turkey)*, Istanbul: İletişim Yayınları.

Krzyzanowski, M. (2009), 'Discourses About Enlarged and Multilingual Europe: Perspectives from German and Polish National Public Spheres', in P. Stevenson and J. Carl (eds), *Language, Discourse and Identity in Central Europe*, Basingstoke: Palgrave Macmillan.

Krzyzanowski, M. (2010), *The Discursive Construction of European Identities: A Multi-level Approach to Discourse and Identity in the Transforming European Union*, Frankfurt am Main: Peter Lang.

Krzyzanowski, M. (2011), '(Mis)Communicating Europe? On Deficiencies and Challenges in Political and Institutional Communication in the European Union', in B. Kryk-Kastovsky (ed.), *Intercultural Communication Past and Present*, Amsterdam/Philadelphia: John Benjamins.

Krzyzanowski, M. and R. Wodak (2009), *Politics of Exclusion: Debating Migration in Austria*, New Brunswick: Transaction Press.

Kubálková, V. (2001), *Foreign Policy in a Constructed World*, Routledge.

Kula, O. B. (2006), *Avrupa Kimliği ve Türkiye (European Identity and Turkey)*, Istanbul: Buke Yayıncılık.

Kumrular, O. (2008), *Türk Korkusu (Turkophobia)*, Istanbul: Doğan Kitap.

Kuran Burcoglu, N. (2011), 'The Impact of Islamic Sects on Education and the Media in Turkey', *International Journal of Cultural Policy*, 17 (2): 187–97.

Kuru, A. T. (2007), 'Passive and Assertive Secularism: Historical Conditions, Ideological Struggles, and State Policies Toward Religion', *World Politics*, 59: 568–94.

Kuru, A. T. and A. Stepan (2012), 'Laicite as an "Ideal Model" and a Continuum: Comparing Turkey, France and Senegal', in Ahmet T. Kuru and Alfred Stepan (eds), *Democracy, Islam, and Secularism in Turkey*, New York: Columbia University Press.

Kuru, A. T. and A. Stephan, eds (2012), *Democracy, Islam, and Secularism in Turkey (Religion, Culture, and Public Life)*, New York: Columbia University Press.

Kushner, D. (1977), *The Rise of Turkish Nationalism, 1876–1908*, London: Frank Cass.

Kuyucu, A. T. (2005), 'Ethno-religious "Unmixing" of 'Turkey": 6–7 September Riots as a Case in Turkish Nationalism', *Nations and Nationalism*, 11 (3): 361–80.

Lapid, Y. and F. Kratochwil, eds (1997), *The Return of Culture and Identity in IR Theory*, Lynne Rienner: Boulder.

Larrabee, F. S. (2013), 'Turkey's New Kurdish Opening', *Survival: Global Politics and Strategy*, 55 (5): 133–46.

Larsen, H. (1997), *Foreign Policy and Discourse Analysis: France, Britain and Europe*, London: Routledge.

Larsen, H. (2014), 'Continuity or Change in National Foreign Policy Discourses post-Lisbon? The Case of Denmark', in C. Carta and J. F. Morin (eds), *EU Foreign Policy Through the Lens of Discourse Analysis: Making Sense of Diversity*, Farnham: Ashgate.

Lewis, B. (2002), *The Emergence of Modern Turkey*, Oxford: Oxford University Press.

Li, J. (2009), 'Intertextuality and National Identity: Discourse of National Conflicts in Daily Newspapers in the United States and China', *Discourse & Society*, 20 (1): 85–121.

Livingston, S. (1990), 'Interpreting a Television Narrative: How Different Viewers See a Story', *Journal of Communication*, 40 (1): 72–85.

Livingston, S. (1997), 'Clarifying the CNN Effect: An Examination of Media Effects According to Type of Military Intervention', Research Paper R-18, Kennedy School of Government, Harvard University. Cambridge, MA: Harvard University Press.

Madianou, M. (2002), *Mediating the Nation: News, Audiences and Identities in Contemporary Greece*, PhD thesis, University of London School of Economics and Political Science.

Maksudyan, N. (2005), *Türklüğü Ölçmek: Bilimkurgusal Antropoloji ve Türk Milliyetçiliğinin Irkçı Çehresi 1925-1939 (Measuring Turkishness: Science-fictional Anthropology and the Racist Face of Turkish Nationalism 1925–1939)*, Istanbul: Metis Yayınları.

Mardin, S. (1973), 'Center-periphery Relations: A Key to Turkish Politics?', *Daedalus*, 102 (1): Post-Traditional Societies, 169–90.

Mardin, S. (1991), *Turkiye'de Din ve Siyaset (Religion and Politics in Turkey)*, Istanbul, Turkey: İletişim Yayınları.

Mardin, S. (2006), *Religion, Society, and Modernity in Turkey*, New York: Syracuse University Press.

Mayr, A., ed. (2008), *Language and Power: An Introduction to Institutional Discourse*, London: Continuum.

McCombs, M. (2014), *Setting the Agenda: Mass Media and Public Opinion*, Cambridge: Polity Press.

McLean, H. (2014), 'Cracks in the Creative City: The Contradictions of Community Arts Practice', *International Journal of Urban and Regional Research*, 38 (6): 2156–73.

Mcnair, B. (1998), *The Sociology of Journalism*, London: Arnold.

McQuail, D. (2000), *Mass Communication Theory*, London: SAGE.

McSweeney, B. (1999), *Security, Identity, and Interests: A Sociology of International Relations*, Cambridge: Cambridge University Press.

Mearsheimer, J. (2001), *The Tragedy of Great Power Politics*, New York: W. Norton & Company.

Mermin, J. (1999), *Debating War and Peace: Media Coverage of U.S. Intervention in the Post-Vietnam Era*, Princeton: Princeton University Press.

Mihelj, S. (2011), *Media Nations: Communicating Belonging and Exclusion in the Modern World*, London: Palgrave Macmillan.

Miller, D., ed. (2003), *Tell Me Lies: Propaganda and Media Distortion in the Attack on Iraq*, London: Pluto Press.

Miller, D. (2007), *Media Pressure on Foreign Policy: The Evolving Theoretical Framework*, New York: Palgrave Macmillan.

Molina, P. S. (2009), 'Critical Analysis of Discourse and of the Media: Challenges and Shortcomings', *Critical Discourse Studies*, 6 (3): 185–98.

Morgenthau, H. (1993), *Politics Among Nations: The Struggle for Power and Peace*, New York: McGraw-Hill Companies.

Morley, D. (1992), *Television, Audiences and Cultural Studies*, London: Routledge.

Morley, D. and C. Brunsdon (1999), *The Nationwide Television Studies*, London and New York: Routledge.

Morris, C. (2005), *The New Turkey: The Quiet Revolution on the Edge of Europe?* London: Granta.

Muftuler Bac, M. (2005), 'Turkey's Political Reforms and the Impact of the European Union', *South European Society and Politics*, 10 (1): 17–31.

Muftuler Bac, M. and Y. Gursoy (2010), 'Is There a Europeanization of Turkish Foreign Policy? An Addendum to the Literature on EU Candidates', *Turkish Studies*, 11 (3): 405–27.

Murinson, A. (2006), 'The Strategic Depth Doctrine of Turkish Foreign Policy', *Middle Eastern Studies*, 42 (6): 945–64.

Murray, C. and K. Schroder (2003), *Researching Audiences: A Practical Guide to Methods in Media Audience Analysis*, London: Bloomsbury Academic.

Narbone, L. and N. Tocci (2007), 'Running Around in Circles? The Cyclical Relationship Between Turkey and the European Union', *Journal of Southern Europe and the Balkans Online*, 9 (3): 233–45.

Natali, D. (2004), 'Ottoman Kurds and Emergent Kurdish Nationalism', *Critique: Critical Middle Eastern Studies*, 13 (3): 383–7.

Natali, D. (2005), *The Kurds and the State: Evolving National Identity in Iraq, Turkey, and Iran*, Syracuse: Syracuse University Press.

Negrine, R. (2008a), *The Transformation of Political Communication: Continuation and Changes in Media and Politics*, New York: Palgrave Macmillan.

Negrine, R (2008b), 'Imagining Turkey: British Press Coverage of Turkey's Bid for Accession to the European Union in 2004', *Journalism*, 9 (5): 624–45.

Negrine, R., et al. (2008), 'Turkey and the European Union: An Analysis of How the Press in Four Countries Covered Turkey's Bid for Accession in 200', *European Journal of Communication*, 23 (1): 47–68.

Neumann, I. B. (1999), *Uses of the Other: 'The East' in European Identity Formation*, Minneapolis: University of Minnesota Press.

Neumann, I. B. and O. Wæver, eds (1997), *The Future of International Relations: Masters in the Making?* London: Routledge.

Neyzi, L. (2002), 'Remembering to Forget: Sabbateanism, National Identity, and Subjectivity in Turkey', *Comparative Studies in Society and History*, 44 (1): 137–58.

Nightingale, V. (2011), *The Handbook of Media Audiences (Global Handbooks in Media and Communication Research)*, Oxford: Wiley-Blackwell.

Nikolaev, A. G. and E. A. Hakanen, (2006), *Leading to the 2003 Iraq War: The Global Media Debate*, New York: Palgrave Macmillan.

Noyon, J. (2003), *Islam, Politics and Pluralism: Theory and Practice in Turkey, Jordan, Tunisia and Algeria*, Royal Institute for International Affairs/Chatham House.

Nye, J. (2002), *The Paradox of American Power: Why the World's Superpower cannot Go It Alone*, New York: Public Affairs.

Nye, J. (2004), *Soft Power: Means to Success in World Politics*, USA: Public Affairs.

Oguzlu, T. (2008), 'Middle Easternization of Turkey's Foreign Policy: Does Turkey Dissociate from the West?' *Turkish Studies*, 9 (1): 3–20.

Oguzlu, T. (2013), 'Making Sense of Turkey's Rising Power Status: What Does Turkey's Approach Within NATO Tell Us?' *Turkish Studies*, 14 (4): 774–96.

Oguzlu, T. and M. Kibaroglu (2009), 'Is the Westernization Process Losing Pace in Turkey: Who's to Blame?', *Turkish Studies*, 10 (4): 577–93.

O'heffernan, P. (1991), *Mass Media and American Foreign Policy: Insider Perspectives on Global Journalism and the Foreign Policy Process*, Norwood: Ablex Publishing.

Okte, F. (1951), *Varlık Vergisi Faciası (The Catastrophe of the Turkish Capital-Tax)*, Istanbul: Nebioğlu Yayınları.

Oktem, K. (2011), *Angry Nation: Turkey since 1989*, London: Zed Books.

Oktem, K. (2013), *Domestic and Foreign Policy Dimensions of the Challenges Facing Turkey*, SEESOX: Oxford.

Oktem, K. et al. (2010), *Turkey's Engagement with Modernity: Conflict and Change in the 20th Century*, London: Palgrave Macmillan.

Onis, Z. (2003a), 'Globalization, Democratization and the Far Right: Turkey's Nationalist Action Party in Critical Perspective', *Democratization*, 10 (1): 27–52.

Onis, Z. (2003b), 'Domestic Politics, International Norms and Challenges to the State: Turkey-EU Relations in the post-Helsinki Era', *Turkish Studies*, 4 (1): 9–34.

Onis, Z. (2001), 'Political Islam at the Crossroads: From Hegemony to Co-existence', *Contemporary Politics*, 7 (4): 281–98.

Onis, Z. (2004), 'Turgut Ozal and His Economic Legacy: Turkish Neo-Liberalism in Critical Perspective', *Middle Eastern Studies*, 40 (4): 113–34.

Onis, Z. (2007), 'Conservative Globalists Versus Defensive Nationalists: Political Parties and Paradoxes of Europeanization in Turkey', *Journal of Southern Europe and the Balkans*, 9 (3): 247–61.

Onis, Z. (2009), *The New Wave of Foreign Policy Activism in Turkey: Drifting Away from Europeanization?* Copenhagen: DIIS.

Onis, Z. (2011), 'Multiple Faces of the "New" Turkish Foreign Policy: Underlying Dynamics and a Critique', *Insight Turkey*, 13 (1): 47–65.

Onis, Z. (2013), 'Sharing Power: Turkey's Democratization Challenge in the Age of the AKP Hegemony', *Insight Turkey*, 15 (2): 103–22.

Onis, Z. and S. Yilmaz (2009), 'Between Europeanization and Euro-Asianism: Foreign Policy Activism in Turkey During the AKP Era', *Turkish Studies*, 10 (1): 7–24.

Oran, B. (1990), *Ataturk Milliyeciligi (Ataturk Nationalism)*, Ankara: Bilgi Yayinevi.

Oran, B. (2004), *Türkiye'de Azınlıklar (Minorities in Turkey)*, Istanbul: İletişim Yayınları.

Oran, B. (2011), *Turkish Foreign Policy: 1919–2006*, Salt Lake City: University of Utah Press.

Oran, B. (2013), *Turk Dış Politikası, Cilt III: 2001–2012*, Istanbul: İletişim Yayınları.

Ors, B. and A. Komsuoglu, (2007), 'Turkey's Armenians: A Research Note on Armenian Identity', *Nationalism and Ethnic Politics*, 13 (3): 405–29.

Ozbudun, E. (2006), 'From Political Islam to Conservative Democracy: The Case of the Justice and Development Party in Turkey', *South European Society and Politics*, 11 (3): 543–57.

Ozbudun, E. (2009), *Democratization and the Politics of Constitution-making in Turkey*, Budapest: Central European University Press.

Ozbudun, E. (2014), 'AKP at the Crossroads: Erdogan's Majoritarian Drift', *South European Society and Politics*, 19 (2): 155–67.

Ozcan, M. (2008), *Harmonizing Foreign Policy: Turkey, the EU and the Middle East*, England: Ashgate.

Ozcan, M. (2011), 'From Distance to Engagement: Turkish Policy Towards the Middle East, Iraq and Iraqi Kurds', *Insight Turkey*, 13 (2): 71–92.

Ozkan, B. (2014), 'Turkey, Davutoglu and the Idea of Pan-Islamism', *Survival: Global Politics and Strategy*, 56 (4): 119–40.

Ozkirimli, U. (2000), *Theories of Nationalism: A Critical Introduction*, Hampshire: Palgrave.

Ozkirimli, U. (2005), *Contemporary Debates on Nationalism: A Critical Engagement*, New York: Palgrave.

Ozkirimli, U. (2011), 'The Changing Nature of Nationalism in Turkey: Actors, Discourses, and the Struggle for Hegemony', in A. Kadioglu and F. Keyman (eds), *Symbiotic Antagonisms: Competing Nationalisms in Turkey*, 82–103, Utah: The University of Utah Press.

Ozkirimli, U. (2014), 'The "Three Turkeys": Making Sense of 30 March Local Elections', *Huffpost*, 8 April.

Ozkirimli, U. and S. Sofos (2008), *Tormented by History: Nationalism in Greece and Turkey*, London: C Hurst & Co Publishers Ltd.

Ozoglu, H. (2004), *Kurdish Notables and the Ottoman State*, New York: State University of New York.

Ozyurek, E. (2006), *Nostalgia for the Modern: State Secularism and Everyday Politics in Turkey*, Durham, NC: Duke University Press.

Parker, O. (2009), 'Cosmopolitan Europe and the EU-Turkey Question: The Politics of a Common Destiny', *Journal of European Public Policy*, 16 (7): 1085–101.

Poulton, H. (1997), *The Top Hat, the Grey Wolf, and the Crescent: Turkish Nationalism and the Turkish Republic*, New York: New York University Press.

Prentice, S. (2010), 'Using Automated Semantic Tagging in Critical Discourse Analysis: A Case Study on Scottish Independence from a Scottish Nationalist Perspective', *Discourse& Society*, 21: 405.

Protess, D. and M. McCombs (1991), *Agenda Setting: Readings on Media, Public Opinion, and Policymaking (Routledge Communication Series)*, New York: Routledge.

Radikal (14 April 2007), Sezer: Rejim Tehdit Altında, Gül: Halk Bunlara İnanmıyor.

Radikal (20 May 2007), Baskin Oran: Antiemperyalizm.

Radikal (23 July 2007a), Bu da Halkın Muhtırası.

Radikal (23 July 2007b), 'Orijinal Demokrasi'nin Zaferi.

Radikal (23 July 2007c), Mahfi Eğilmez: Başarının Temel Unsuru Ekonomi.

Radikal (23 July 2007d), Haluk Şahin: 'Demokrasime Dokunma'.

Radikal (19 August 2007), İsmet Berkan: Fransız Ordusu Gibi mi Olacak?

Radikal (30 August 2007), Hasan Celal Güzel: 'Gül devri' ve Yeni Dönem.

Radikal (08 September 2007), Murat Belge: Üçüncü Millet.

Radikal (22 October 2009), Dağdakilerin Hepsi Gelsin.

Radikal (22 October 2009), Havai Fişek ve Kutlama Ateşleriyle Karşıladılar.

Radikal (23 October 2009), Cengiz Candar: Kör Olmayın.

Radikal (17 January 2010), Aysel Tuğluk: Gösteri Siyaseti ve Gerçek.

Radikal (25 January 2010), Sırrı Süreyya Önder: Senin Yurdun Neresi?

Radikal (12 June 2010), Eyüp Can: ABD ve Türkiye: Dost mu Düşman mı?

Radikal (30 June 2010), Cengiz Çandar: İki Türkiye; İkisi de Türkiye…

Radikal (06 July 2010), Nuray Mert: II. Abdülhamid, AKP ve Muhalefet.

Radikal (26 September 2010), Fuat Keyman: Uzlaşmaya Çağrı.

Radikal (08 November 2010), Sırrı Süreyya Önder: Naylondan Kelepçe, Kanlı Kına.

Radikal (11 September 2011), Fuat Keyman: Silahlar Sussun, Söz Bitmesin.

Radikal (18 September 2011), Aysel Tuğluk: Sahiden Bildiğiniz Gibi Değil.

Radikal (02 October 2011), Aysel Tuğluk: Gerekenler Yapılacaktır.

Radikal (23 October 2011), Ahmet Insel: Nihai Hesaplaşma Arzusu.

Radikal (20 November 2011), Ahmet Insel: Kadim Ankara Kriterlerinin Dönüşü.

Reisigl, M. and R. Wodak (2001), *Discourse and Discrimination: Rhetorics of Racism and Antisemitism*. London: Routledge.

Richardson, J. E. (2007), *Analysing Newspapers: An Approach from Critical Discourse Analysis*, New York: Palgrave Macmillan.

Robinson, P. (2002), *The CNN Effect: The Myth of News, Foreign Policy and Intervention*, London: Routledge.

Robinson, P. (2004), 'Researching US Media-State Relations *and* Twenty-First Century Wars', in S. Allan and B. Zelizer (eds), *Reporting War: Journalism in Wartime*, London and New York: Routledge.

Rodrik, D. (2011), 'Ergenekon and Sledhammer: Building or Undermining Rule of Law', *Turkish Policy Quarterly, Spring*, 10 (1): 99–109.

Romano, D. (2006), *The Kurdish Nationalist Movement: Opportunity, Mobilization, and Identity*, Cambridge: Cambridge University Press.

Rosenau, J. (1980), *The Scientific Study of Foreign Policy*, New York: Nichols Publishing Company.

Ruddock, A. (2000), *Understanding Audiences: Theory and Method Paperback*, London: SAGE Publications Ltd.

Rulikova, M. (2004), 'The Influence of pre-accession Status on Euroscepticism in EU Candidate Countries', *Perspectives on European Politics and Society*, 5 (1): 29–60.

Rumelili, B. (2011), 'Turkey: Identity, Foreign Policy, and Socialization in a Post-Enlargement Europe', *Journal of European Integration*, 33 (2): 235–49.

Rumford, C. and Turunc, H. (2011), 'Identity Dimension: Postwesternisation: A Framework for Understanding Turkey-EU Relations', in A. E. Cakir (ed.), *Fifty Years of EU-Turkey Relations: A Sisyphean Story (Routledge Advances in European Politics)*, New York: Roudledge.

Said, E. (1977), *Orientalism*, London: Penguin.

Saideman, S. (2002), 'Conclusion: Thinking Theoretically about Identity and Foreign Policy', in Shibley Telhami and Michael Barnett (eds), *Identity and Foreign Policy in the Middle East*, 169–201, Ithaca: Cornell University Press.

Saracoglu, C. (2009), '"Exclusive Recognition": The New Dimensions of the Question of Ethnicity and Nationalism in Turkey', *Ethnic and Racial Studies*, 32 (4): 640–58.

Saracoglu, C. (2013), 'AKP, Milliyetçilik ve Dış Politika: Bir Milliyetçilik Doktrini Olarak Stratejik Derinlik', *Alternatif Politika*, 5 (1): 52–68.

Sarigil, Z. (2007), 'Europeanization as Institutional Change: The Case of the Turkish Military', *Mediterranean Politics*, 12 (1): 39–57.

Sarigil, Z. (2010), 'Curbing Kurdish Ethno-nationalism in Turkey: An Empirical Assessment of pro-Islamic and Socio-economic Approaches', *Ethnic and Racial Studies*, 33 (3): 533–53.

Sarwar, K. (2006), *America and Europe after 9/11 and Iraq: The Great Divide*, Westport: Praeger.

Sayari, S. (2007), 'Towards a New Turkish Party System?' *Turkish Studies*, 8 (2): 197–210.

Schiffrin, D., D. Tannen and H. Hamilton, eds (2001), *The Handbook of Discourse Analysis*, Oxford: Blackwell Publishers Ltd.

Schmidt, V. A. (2007), 'Trapped by Their Ideas: French Élites' Discourses of European Integration and Globalization', *Journal of European Public Policy*, 14 (7): 992–1009.

Schmidt, V. A. (2008), 'Discursive Institutionalism: The Explanatory Power of Ideas and Discourse', *Annual Review of Political Science*, 11: 303–26.

Schneeberger, A. (2009), 'Constructing European Identity Through Mediated Difference: A Content Analysis of Turkey's EU Accession Process in the British Press', *Journal of Media and Communication*, 1: 83–102.

Schudson, M. (1999), *The Power of News*, Cambridge, MA: Harvard University Press.

Seib, P. (2006), *Beyond the Front Lines: How the News Media Cover a World Shaped by War*, New York: Palgrave Macmillan.

Seib, P. (2008), *The Al Jazeera Effect: How the New Global Media are Reshaping World Politics*, Lincoln: Potomac Books Inc.

Seib, P. (2011), *Global Terrorism and New Media: The post Al-Qaeda Generation*, New York: Routledge.

Seib, P., ed. (2012), *Al Jazeera English: Global News in a Changing World*, New York: Palgrave Macmillan.

Semetko, H. and M. Scrammell, eds (2012), *The SAGE Handbook of Political Communication*, New York: SAGE Publications Ltd.

Shafer, B. C. (1955), *Nationalism: Myth and Reality*, New York: Harcourt, Brace and World.

Shaw, M. (1996), *Civil Society and Media in Global Crises*, London: Pinter.

Skey, M. (2009), 'The National in Everyday Life: A Critical Engagement with Michael Billig's Thesis of Banal Nationalism', *The Sociological Review*, 57 (2): 331–46.

Skey, M. (2011), *National Belonging and Everyday Life: The Significance of Nationhood in an Uncertain World*, Basingstoke: Palgrave.

Smith, A. D. (2000), *Myths and Memories of the Nation*, Oxford: Oxford University Press.

Smith, A. D. (2001), *Nationalism: Theory, Ideology, History*, Oxford: Blackwell.

Smith, A. D. (2009), *Ethno-symbolism and Nationalism: A Cultural Approach*, London and New York: Routledge.

Smith, D. and S. Wright, (1999), *Whose Europe? The Turn Towards Democracy*, Oxford: Blackwell.

Smith, T. W. (2005), 'Between Allah and Ataturk: Liberal Islam in Turkey', *The International Journal of Human Rights*, 9 (3): 307–25.

Somer, M. (2005), 'Mainstream Discourse on Kurds Resurgence and Remaking of Identity: Civil Beliefs, Domestic and External Dynamics', *Comparative Political Studies*, 38: 591.

Somer, M. (2007), 'Moderate Islam and Secularist Opposition in Turkey: Implications for the World, Muslims and Secular Democracy', *Third World Quarterly*, 28 (7): 1271–89.

Somer, M. (2010a), 'Democratization, Clashing Narratives, and "Twin Tolerations" between Islamic-Conservative and Pro-Secular Actors', in Marlies Casier and Joost

Jongerden (eds), *Nationalisms and Politics in Turkey: Political Islam, Kemalism and the Kurdish Issue*, 28–48, New York: Routledge.

Somer, M. (2010b), 'Media Values and Democratization: What Unites and What Divides Religious-Conservative and Pro-Secular Elites?', *Turkish Studies*, 11 (4): 555–77.

Somer, M. (2011), 'Toward a Non-standard Story: The Kurdish Question and the Headscarf, Nationalism, and Iraq', in A. Kadioglu and F. Keyman (eds), *Symbiotic Antagonisms: Competing Nationalisms in Turkey*, 253–89, Utah: The University of Utah Press

Somer, M. and G. L. Evangelos (2010), 'Turkey's New Kurdish Opening: Religious Versus Secular Values', *Middle East Policy*, 17 (2): 152–65.

Soroka, S. (2003), *Agenda-Setting Dynamics in Canada*, Vancouver: University of British Columbia Press.

Soykut, M. (2007), *Avrupa'nın Birliği ve Osmanlı Devleti (The Union of Europe and the Ottoman State)*, Istanbul: Bilgi Üniversitesi Yayınları.

Soysal, M. (1999), 'The Kurdish Issue: A Turkish Point of View', *The International Spectator: Italian Journal of International Affairs*, 34 (1): 11–17.

Sozen, A. (2010), 'A Paradigm Shift in Turkish Foreign Policy: Transition and Challenges', *Turkish Studies*, 11 (1): 103–23.

Sozeri, C. and Z. Guney (2011), *The Political Economy of the Media in Turkey: A Sectoral Analysis*, İstanbul: TESEV Democratization Program Media Studies Series.

Stepan, A. (2011), 'The Multiple Secularisms of Modern Democratic and Non-democratic Regimes', in C. Calhoun, M. Juergensmeyer and J. Van Antwerpen (eds), *Rethinking Secularism*, 114–44, Oxford: Oxford University Press.

Stokes, J. (2003), *How to Do Media & Cultural Studies*, London: Sage Publications Ltd.

Street, J. (2011), *Mass Media, Politics, and Democracy*, New York: Palgrave Macmillan.

Sullivan, J. L. (2012), *Media Audiences: Effects, Users, Institutions, and Power*, London: SAGE Publications.

Taki, M. and L. Coretti (2013), 'The Role of Social Media in the Arab Uprising – Past and Present', *Westminster Papers in Communication and Culture*, 9 (2): 1–22.

Tamer, A. (2004), *İrade-i Milliye: Kurtuluş Savaşının İlk Resmi Yayını*, Istanbul: Tüstav.

Tank, P. (2005), 'Political Islam in Turkey: A State of Controlled Secularity', *Turkish Studies*, 6 (1): 3–19.

Tank, P. (2006), 'Dressing for the Occasion: Reconstructing Turkey's Identity?' *Southeast European and Black Sea Studies*, 6 (4): 463–78.

Taraf (08 June 2009), Ayhan Aktar: Türkiye, Sadece Türklerin midir?

Taraf (17 August 2009), Cihan Aktaş: Dağa Çıkan Kürt.
Taraf (25 August 2009), Ahmet Altan: Savaş Tımarhanesi.
Taraf (24 October 2009), Murat Belge: Şov Yapmak.
Taraf (28 December 2009), Murat Belge: Yirmibeş Yılın Birikimi.
Taraf (28 February 2010), Ahmet Altan: Kürtler ve Demokrasi.
Taraf (11 June 2010), Türkiye'nin Ekseni İnsan.
Taraf (13 June 2010), Eksen Kayması Kara Propaganda.
Taraf (13 June 2010), Türkiye'nin Doğu'ya Kaydığı Tezi Bir Fantezi.
Taraf (14 June 2010), Sezin Oney: Eksen Kaymıyor, Kilitler Açılıyor.
Taraf (15 June 2010), Gül: Biraz Tartışılsın.
Taraf (15 June 2010), Kazım Çeliker, Eksen Ticarete Doğru Kaydı.
Taraf (15 June 2010), Türkiye'nin Eksenine AB Onayı.
Taraf (17 June 2010), Eksen Yerinde Hedef Büyüdü.
Taraf (20 June 2010), Çin 10 Yıl Sonra Büyük Abi Olacak.
Taraf (23 October 2010), Ahmet Altan: Rota.
Taraf (08 January 2011), Ahmet Altan: Bu nasıl rejim kardeşim?
Taraf (03 February 2011), Arapların Özlemi Türkiye.
Taraf (04 February 2011), Olaylar Türkiye'nin Önemini Gösterdi.
Taraktas, B. (2008), 'Comparative Approach to Euroscepticism in Turkey and Eastern European Countries', *Journal of Contemporary European Studies*, 16 (2): 249–66.
Taspinar, O. (2004), *Kurdish Nationalism and Political Islam in Turkey Kemalist Identity in Transition*, New York: Routledge.
Taspinar, O. (2014a), 'The End of the Turkish Model', *Survival: Global Politics and Strategy*, 56 (2): 49–64.
Taspinar, O. (2014b), 'The Conflict within Turkey's Islamic Camp', *Global Turkey in Europe: Commentary*, 20, November.
Taylor, P. M. (1997), *Global Communications, International Affairs, and the Media since 1945*, New York: Routledge.
Taylor, P. M. (1999), *British Propaganda in the Twentieth Century: Selling Democracy*, Edinburgh: Edinburgh University Press.
Taylor, P. M. (2004), 'The Military and the Media: Past, Present and Future', in S. Badsey (ed.), *The Media and International Security*, London: Frank Coss.
Tekin, B. (2008), 'The Construction of Turkey's Possible EU Membership in French Political Discourse', *Discourse & Society*, 19 (6): 727–63.
Tekin, B. (2010), *Representations and Othering in Discourse: The Construction of Turkey in the EU Context*, Amsterdam/Philadelphia: John Benjamins B. V.
Tezcur, G. M. (2009), 'Kurdish Nationalism and Identity in Turkey: A Conceptual Reinterpretation', *European Journal of Turkish Studies*, 10: 1–21.

The International Committee to Protect Journalists report (2013). https://cpj.org/data/imprisoned/2020/?status=Imprisoned&start_year=2013&end_year=2020&group_by=location

Tileaga, C. (2005), 'Accounting for Extreme Prejudice and Legitimating Blame in Talk about the Romanies', *Discourse &Society*, 16: 603.

Tilly, C. (1990), *Coercion, Capital, and European States, AD 990–1990*, Oxford: Wiley-Blackwell.

Tocci, N. (2005), 'Europeanization in Turkey: Trigger or Anchor for Reform?' *South European Society and Politics*, 10 (1): 73–83.

Tocci, N. (2007), *The EU and Conflict Resolution*, London: Routledge.

Toktas, S. and B. Aras (2009), 'The EU and Minority Rights in Turkey', *Political Science Quarterly*, 124 (4): 697–720.

Toprak, B. (2009), *Being Different in Turkey: Religion, Conservatism, and Otherization: Research Report on Neighbourhood Pressure*, İstanbul: Bogazici University.

Turner, B.S. and B. Zengin-Arslan, (2013), 'State and Turkish Secularism: The Case of the Diyanet', in B. S. Turner (ed.), *The Religious and the Political: A Comparative Sociology of Religion*, Cambridge: Cambridge University Press.

Uslu, N. et al. (2005), 'Turkish Public Opinion Toward the United States in the Context of the Iraq Question', *MERIA (Middle East Review of International Affairs)*, 9 (3): 75–107.

Uzer, U. (2011), 'The Genealogy of Turkish Nationalism: From Civic and Ethnic to Conservative Nationalism in Turkey', in A. Kadioglu and F. Keyman (eds), *Symbiotic Antagonisms: Competing Nationalisms in Turkey*, 103–33, Utah: The University of Utah Press

Uzgel, I. (2013), 'Riots, Resistance and Repression: Notes on the Gezi Protests', *The Kurdish Yearbook of International Relations*, 43: 197–206.

Van Dijk, T. A. (2005), *Racism and Discourse in Spain and Latin America*, Amsterdam: John Benjamins B.V.

Van Dijk, T. A. (2009), *Society and Discourse: How Social Contexts Influence Text and Talk*, Cambridge: Cambridge University Press.

Van Leeuwen, T. and R. Wodak (1999), 'Legitimizing Immigration Control: A Discourse-Historical Analysis', *Discourse Studies*, 1 (1): 83–119.

Verney, S. (2007), 'The Dynamics of EU Accession: Turkish Travails in Comparative Perspective', *Journal of Southern Europe and the Balkans*, 9 (3): 307–22.

Verney, S. (2011), 'Euroscepticism in Southern Europe: A Diachronic Perspective', *South European Society and Politics*, 16 (1): 1–29.

Verney, S. and K. Ifantis, eds (2009), *Turkey's Road to European Union Membership: National Identity and Political Change*, Abingdon: Routledge.

Wæver, O. (1990), 'Three Competing Europes: German, French, Russian', *International Affairs*, 66 (3): 477–93.

Wæver, O. (1998), 'The Sociology of a Not So International Discipline: American and European Developments in International Relations', *International Organization*, 52 (4): 687–727.

Waever, O. (2001), 'Identity, Communities and Foreign Policy: Discourse Analysis as Foreign Policy Theory', in L. Hansen and Ole Waever (eds), *European Integration and National Identity: The Challenge of the Nordic States*, London: Routledge.

Waever, O., ed. (2006), *European Integration and National Identity: The Challenge of the Nordic States*, London: Routledge.

Wallace, W. (1998), 'Book Review: Larsen, H. (1997), Foreign Policy and Discourse Analysis: France, Britain and Europe', *International Affairs*, 74 (3): 681.

Waltz, K. N. (1979), *Theory of International Politics*, Reading: Addison-Wesley Publishing.

Waltz, K. N. (2001), *Man, the State and War: A Theoretical Analysis*, New York: Columbia University Press.

Weiss, G. and R. Wodak, eds (2003), *Critical Discourse Analysis: Theory and Interdisciplinarity*, London: Palgrave Macmillan.

Went, A. (1999), *Social Theory of International Politics*, Cambridge: Cambridge University Press.

White, J. (2013), *Muslim Nationalism and the New Turks*, Princeton: Princeton University Press.

Widdowson, Henry G. (2004), *Text, Context, Pretext: Critical Issues in Discourse Analysis*, Oxford: Blackwell.

Wilmer, F. (2002), *The Social Construction of Man, the State and War: Identity, Conflict, and Violence*, New York: Routledge.

Wiltse, E. C. (2008), 'The Gordian Knot of Turkish Politics: Regulating Headscarf Use in Public', *South European Society and Politics*, 13 (2): 195–215.

Wittek, P. (1952), 'Le Role des Tribus Turgues dans l'Empire Ottoman', in *Melanges Georges Smets*, Brussels: ULP, 665–76.

Wodak, R. (1989), *Language, Power and Ideology*, Amsterdam: John Benjamins Publishing Company.

Wodak, R. (2001), 'The Discourse-Historical Approach', in R. Wodak and M. Meyer (eds), *Methods of Critical Discourse Analysis*, 63–75, London: Sage.

Wodak, R. (2011a), '"Us" and "Them": Inclusion/exclusion-discrimination via Discourse', in G. Delanty, R. Wodak and P. Jones (eds), *Migration, Identity, and Belonging*, 54–77, Liverpool: Liverpool University Press.

Wodak, R. (2011b), *The Discourse of Politics in Action: Politics as Usual*, Basingstoke: Palgrave.

Wodak, R., ed. (2012a), *Critical Discourse Analysis (SAGE Benchmarks in Language and Linguistics), 1–4*, London: SAGE Publications Ltd.
Wodak, R. (2012b), 'Language, Power and Identity', *Language Teaching*, 45 (2): 215–33.
Wodak, R. and M. Meyer (2005), *Methods of Critical Discourse Analysis*, London: Sage.
Wodak, R. and G. Weiss, eds (2007), *Critical Discourse Analysis: Theory and Interdisciplinarity*, UK: Palgrave Macmillan.
Wodak, R. et al., eds (2013), *Right-Wing Populism in Europe: Politics and Discourse*, London: Bloomsbury Academic.
Wodak, R., R. Cillia, M. Reisigl and K. Liebhart, (1999), *The Discursive Construction of National Identity*, Edinburgh: Edinburgh University Press.
Wolfsfeld, G. (2004), *Media and the Path to Peace*, Cambridge: Cambridge University Press.
Wong, R. (2005), 'The Europeanization of Foreign Policy', in C. Hill and M. Smith (eds), *International Relations and the European Union*, Oxford University Press.
Yavuz, M. H. (1998), 'A Preamble to the Kurdish Question: The Politics of Kurdish Identity', *Journal of Muslim Minority Affairs*, 18 (1): 9–18.
Yavuz, M. H. (2001), 'Five Stages of the Construction of Kurdish Nationalism in Turkey', *Nationalism and Ethnic Politics*, 7 (3): 1–24.
Yavuz, M. H., ed. (2006), *The Emergence of a New Turkey: Democracy and the AK Party*, Salt Lake City: University of Utah Press.
Yavuz, M. H. (2009), *Secularism and Muslim Democracy in Turkey*, Cambridge: Cambridge University Press.
Yegen, M. (2007a), '"Jewish-Kurds" or the New Frontiers of Turkishness', *Patterns of Prejudice*, 41 (1): 1–20.
Yegen, M. (2007b), 'Turkish Nationalism and the Kurdish Question', *Ethnic and Racial Studies*, 30 (1): 119–51.
Yegen, M. (2009), "Prospective-Turks' or 'Seudo-Citizens': Kurds in Turkey', *The Middle East Journal*, 63 (4): 597–615.
Yegen, M. (2011), 'Banditry to Disloyalty: Turkish Nationalisms and the Kurdish Question', in A. Kadioglu and F. Keyman (eds), *Symbiotic Antagonisms: Competing Nationalisms in Turkey*, Utah: The University of Utah Press.
Yesilada, B. and B. Rubin, ed. (2013), *Islamization of Turkey Under the AKP Rule*, New York: Routledge.
Yesiltas, M. (2013), 'The Transformation of the Geopolitical Vision in Turkish Foreign Policy', *Turkish Studies*, 14 (4): 661–87.
Yilmaz, H. (2007), 'Turkish Identity on the Road to the EU: Basic Elements of French and German Oppositional Discourses', *Journal of Southern Europe and the Balkans Online*, 9 (3): 293–305.

Yilmaz, H. (2009), 'Problems of Europeanization and European Perceptions of Turkey as a Future Member State', *Promotion of the Civil Society Dialogue between European Union and Turkey*, Universities Grant Scheme (Contract No: TR0604.01-03/070).

Yilmaz, H. (2014), *Identities, Kurdish Problem and Solution Process in Turkey: Perceptions and Attitudes in Public Opinion*, Istanbul: Acik Toplum Vakfi ve Bogazici Universitesi.

Yust, K. (1995), *Kemalist Anadolu Basini (Kemalist Anatolian Press)*, Ankara: Çagdas Gazeteciler Dernegi.

Yuval-Davis, N. (1993), 'Gender and Nation', *Ethnic and Racial Studies*, 16: 421–32.

Zaman (14 January 2007), Halkın Çogu Sezer'in Düşüncelerini Paylaşmıyor.

Zaman (22 January 2007), Emine Dolmacı: Sezer'in Cumhurbaşkanlığı Tanımı: Devlete Kalkan, İcraate Fren.

Zaman (14 April 2007), Tuncay Özkan'ın Provokasyonu ADD'i Bile Kızdırdı.

Zaman (14 April 2007a), Vahap Coşkun: Şuna Demokrasiyi Sindirmek Bize Ağır Geliyor Desenize.

Zaman (14 April 2007b), ADD'liler 'Darbeci' Diye Anılmaktan Rahatsız.

Zaman (22 April 2007), Mustafa Armağan: Atatürk Türkiyesinin Hitler Almanyasına Ekonomik Bağı.

Zaman (23 April 2007), Malatya'daki Cinayetler Dini Motifli Değil.

Zaman (23 July 2007), Dünya Sonuçtan Memnun: Demokrasi için Büyük Başarı.

Zaman (20 February 2009), İhsan Dağı: Eksen Kayması mı, Liberal Dönüşüm mü?

Zaman (17 January 2010), Mumtazer Türköne: Tarihin 'Açılım'ı

Zaman (15 June 2010), İhsan Dağı: Eksen Tartışması Neden Gündemde?

Zaman (08 November 2010), Ali Bulac: Önümüzdeki Badire!

Zaman (25 December 2010), Turan Alkan: Sizi Yaramazlar Sizi.

Zaman (28 December 2010), Mumtazer Türköne: Kürt Sorunu Çözülür.

Zaman (09 January 2011), Mumtazer Türköne: MHP ve Kürt Sorunu I: Anti-Kürtçülük.

Zaman (17 June 2011), Mumtazer Türköne: Kürt Sorunu Çözülecek mi?

Zaman (31 July 2011), Mumtazer Türköne: 'Yeni Türkiye' Hepimize Hayırlı Olsun.

Zaman (28 October 2011), Mumtazer Türköne: Kürt Sorununda Paradigmayı Değiştirmek.

Zaman (25 November 2020), Hepimiz Sorumluyuz!

Zubaida, S. (1996), 'Turkish Islam and National Identity', *Middle East Report*, April-June: 10–15.

Zubaida, S. (2009), *Islam, the People, and the State: Political Ideas and Movements in the Middle East*, London: IB Tauris.

Zubaida, S. (2011), *Beyond Islam: A New Understanding of the Middle East*, London: IB Tauris.

Zucconi, M. (2009), 'The Impact of the EU Connection on Turkey's Domestic and Foreign Policy', *Turkish Studies*, 10 (1): 25–36.

Zurcher, E. J. (1993), *Turkey: A Modern History*, London: I. B. Tauris.

Zurcher, E. J. and H. Van der Linden (2007), *The European Union, Turkey and Islam*, Amsterdam: Amsterdam University Press.

Index

(For other named sources, discussed in each chapter, see the Bibliography)

AKP   3–6, 10, 27, 29, 33, 35, 39, 42, 43, 45–7, 69, 71–3, 78–80, 84, 85, 87, 88, 90, 91, 93, 94, 96–100, 104, 105, 107–13, 115–23, 125, 126, 129–33, 135–7, 139–46
  conservatism   4, 24, 25, 35, 90, 146
  majoritarian democracy   146
  neo-Islamist elites   126
  opposition   19, 33, 35, 42, 62, 69, 80, 84, 85, 87, 90, 91, 96, 104, 109, 114, 117, 119, 120, 122, 131, 138, 143–6
Al Jazeera effect   52
Anatolia   2, 13, 14, 16, 19, 31, 93, 128, 140
anti-Western   14, 34, 109, 129, 144
  Christian West   14
Ataturkist Ideas Organisation   94, 95

banal nationalism   50, 54, 70, 138
Berkes, Niyazi   22
boundaries   16, 56, 62, 75, 86, 133, 144

centre-right parties   35, 130
citizenship   2, 16, 20, 29, 31, 69, 71, 86, 97, 100, 102, 103, 107, 112, 113, 118, 119, 140, 141, 143
civic nationalism   20, 57
civilization   9, 38, 39, 43, 47, 121, 141, 142
CNN effect   52
Cold War   6, 9, 10, 26, 30, 32, 37, 38, 44, 46, 47, 52, 55, 62, 72
collective identity   32, 37
collective national consciousness   107
Constitutional Court   26, 85, 96
Contemporary Turkey Studies
  Cagaptay, Soner   17
  Canefe, Nergis   11, 15, 17, 34, 41, 65, 71
  Gokalp, Ziya   22

Gole, Nilufer   25
Hanioglu, Sukru   15, 17
Heper, Metin   16, 18
Inalcik, Halil   12, 17
Lewis, Bernard   9, 12–14, 21, 23
Mardin, Serif   10, 17, 19, 73
Copenhagen School   62
Critical Discourse Analysis   7, 61, 63, 64, 66, 69, 81, 83, 137, 138, 146, *see also* Discourse-Historical Approach; Ruth Wodak; Teun Van Dijk

Discourse-Historical Approach   50, 64, 66, 77, 135–7, 140, *see also* discursive strategies; Ruth Wodak
  anthroponymy   79
  dehumanization   108
  historicity   5, 67
  intertextuality   82
  lexical units   79, 94, 102
  linguistic means and realisations   77
  linguistic production   64
  metaphor   88, 102, 115, 124, 126
  negative representation   115
  relativization   106
  sameness and difference   79
  solidarity-enhancing function   117
  temporal references   79
discrimination   20, 21, 27, 31, 67, 68, 80
  discriminatory discourses   4
  exclusionary practices   20
discursive strategies   68, 77–9
  blaming others strategy   143
  strategies of nomination   79
  strategies of perpetuation   78, 98, 142
  strategies of transformation   78, 142
  strategy of justification   106, 122
  trivialization strategy   94, 95, 111
diversity   3, 10, 30, 35, 54, 55, 66, 67, 75, 83, 106, 137, 140, 146

Index

emancipation 23, 46, 64, 84, 86, 107
Enlightenment 1, 23, 36, 126, 127, 142
equal citizenship 57, 117, *see also* civic-nationalism; pluralism; rights-based citizenship
ethnic nationalism 58, 73, 116, 128
Eurasia 46, 130
European identity 9, 35, 41, 68
   anti-EU discourse 41
   Euro-skepticism 41, 42, 109, 142
   Euro-skeptic narrative 40
Europeanization 3, 29, 35, 39, 44, 47, 72, 111, 145
   democratization 3, 4, 33, 52, 119, 131, 142, 145
   new constitution-writing 117, 144
   Penal Code 39, 70, 116
   reforms 3, 15, 19, 23, 39, 71, 85, 119, 120, 144
European Union 2, 33, 34, 39–41, 66, 83, 117, 121, 129
   Copenhagen Summit 37
   Customs Union 38, 40
   EU conditionality 39, 71, 119
   harmonization 39, 71, 118
   human rights and democracy 34
   privileged partnership 40, 41

foreign policy analysis 6, 7, 59, 61, 138, 139
   Campbell, David 6, 62, 139
   constructivist approach 4, 60
   discursive institutionalism 61
   Larsen, Henrik 63
   Morgenthau, Hans 59
   neo-realism 60
   postmodernism 49
   post-structuralism 61
   Waever, Ole 61, 62, 82, 139 (*see also* Copenhagen School)
free-market economy 25
French Revolution 17

globalization 4, 31, 32, 49, 109, 110, 112, 127, 142
Grand National Assembly 20, 23, 72, 130

Huntington, Samuel 9, 38, 44

Imagined Communities 50, 54, 55, 59, 70
industrialization 18, 55

inequality 63, 67, 68, 80, 82
Islamism 14, 15, 130
   headscarf 85, 87, 88, 91, 92, 94, 95, 103, 104, 119
   Islamic brotherhood 25, 29
   Islamist nationalism 73, 90, 141
   Islamization 42, 87, 90, 94, 111, 120, 123, 126, 127
   Moderate Islamic Republic of Turkey 110, 111
   political Islam 1, 10, 24, 25, 69, 90, 126
   Sunni Islam 2, 25, 116, 130

Kemalism 5, 16, 118, 125, 127, 135
   Kemalist army-state 102, 105
   Kemalist narrative 7, 11, 12, 83, 99, 140
   Kemalist nationalism 16, 73, 90, 94, 99, 110
   Kemalist nation-state identity 6, 9–11, 31, 35, 47, 72, 73, 75, 77, 84, 90, 97, 98, 100, 102, 112, 114, 122, 127, 135–7, 141
   Kemalist resistance 140
Kurdish question 1, 28–32, 34, 35, 78, 100, 101, 107–9, 114, 115, 118
   anti-Kurdish discourse 25
   KCK 116
   Kurdish ethno-nationalism 30
   Kurdish identity 19, 28–30, 73, 80, 105, 113, 140, 142
   Kurdish Initiative 29, 80, 84, 100, 107–11, 113, 114, 120, 142
   Kurdishness 33, 101, 103, 140
   Kurdish Opening 77
   Kurdish Teali Cemiyeti 28
   Kurdistan Workers' Party 29
   Ocalan, Abdullah 29, 32, 105, 106, 111
   peacebuilding 109, 115–17
   terror problem 29, 30

laicism 27, 80, 110, 111, 125
liberalization 32, 42, 69, 129
liberal nationalism 73, 141

Media Nations 55
Middle East 42, 43, 45–7, 83, 111, 112, 121–6, 128–33, 137, 141, 144, 145, 147
   Arabic language 13
   Arab uprisings 145

Davos incident   42
Gulf War   32
Hamas   42, 53, 121, 131
Iran   28, 42, 46, 89, 130, 131, 145
Mavi Marmara   42
Syrian uprising   132, 145
US occupation of Iraq   34
military   1, 3, 15, 17, 18, 24–6, 29–31, 33, 38, 39, 41–5, 60, 61, 71, 72, 80, 84, 93, 95, 104, 108, 113, 115, 116, 120, 140, 143, 145
modernity   27, 31, 56, 84, 86, 88, 92, 93
modernization   15, 17, 18, 22, 24, 37, 41, 85, 111, 142
Muslim identity   6, 10, 98, 100, 118, 137
    Muslimhood   19, 88, 94, 102, 103, 119, 132, 140
myths   12, 49, 58

narrative   14, 40, 46, 59, 65–8, 71, 74, 78, 81, 90, 94, 115, 124, 129, 139–42
nationalism studies   11, 138
    Anderson, Benedict   49, 54, 55, 70 (*see also* Imagined Communities)
    Billig, Micheal   54–6, 58, 70, 139
    Breuilly, John   49
    Gellner, Ernest   18, 49, 54
    Hobsbawm, Eric J.   49
    Mihelj, Sabina   55, 56, 92 (*see also* Media Nations)
    Renan, Ernest   17, 57
    Smith, Anthony D.   1, 11, 20, 37, 44, 49, 57
nationalist imagination   5
national security   30, 38, 122
national unity   10, 30, 50, 93, 109
National War of Independence   21
    anti-imperialism   16
    First World War   14, 16, 17, 20, 37, 51, 124
    Hakimiyet-i Milliye   16
    independence   16, 19, 27, 34, 36, 37, 68, 72, 84, 99, 102, 110, 111, 118, 123, 141, 142
    Irade-i Milliye   16
    Lausanne Treaty   20
    National Pact   16, 128
    nation-state building   12, 16
NATO   38, 44, 46, 47
new media   52

New Turkey   2–5, 7, 10, 32, 43, 45, 47, 59, 72, 78, 83, 100, 104, 113, 125, 132, 136, 138, 144, 146
    post-Kemalist nation-state discourse   5
9/11   6, 10, 38, 39, 41, 44, 45, 52, 72, 73, 132

Ottoman Empire   12, 13, 17, 19–21, 23, 24, 36, 43, 72, 99, 100, 121, 128, 130, *see also* Ottoman sultans
    Caliphate   14, 19, 23
    millet system   12, 15
    pan-Islamism   4, 15, 16
    Tanzimat   14
    Treaty of Sèvres   18, 20
    Young Turks   12, 15, 16
Ottoman heritage   11, 46, 130, 135
Ottomanism   4, 14–16, 46, 129, 140
Ottoman sultans   23
    Murat II   13
    Sultan Abdulhamid   13, 14, 84

pluralism   10, 27, 35, 64, 85, 97, 129, 146
    heteronomy   89, 103, 106
    homogeneity   22, 118
    lifestyles   2, 44, 131, 142, 143, 145
political polarization   3, 25, 85, 98, 147
power relations   4, 6, 10, 18, 51, 56, 61, 62, 65, 67, 71, 72, 75, 78, 86, 91, 92, 97, 110, 111, 120, 122, 127, 137, 139, 140
power struggle   3–7, 10, 12, 35, 45, 47, 48, 50, 57, 59, 66, 72, 74, 76, 78, 80, 85, 87, 98, 101, 104, 105, 108, 110, 114, 117, 119, 122, 123, 127, 132, 135–8, 140, 141, 145, 146, *see also* political polarization; power relations
    antagonisms   6, 10, 74, 100, 132, 139
    competing discourses   3, 63
    competing perspectives   6, 50
    presidential elections   77, 79, 80, 84, 143
    Republican meetings   77, 93, 96
    status quo   66, 68, 82, 91, 99, 103, 109, 142
    symbiotic relationships   5
pre-Islamic Turkish history   13
    Oguz legend   13

reconstruction   4, 47, 60, 64, 66, 72, 74, 77, 97, 100, 104, 109, 115, 119, 122, 124, 127
religious minorities   3, 8
  Armenian   12, 21, 31, 41, 105, 110
  Cyprus issue   22
  Greek   14, 21, 22, 97
  Jewish   12, 21, 31
  non-Muslim communities   101
rights-based citizenship   40
rights-based perspective   108

secularism   3, 10, 15, 19, 22–4, 27, 35, 46, 47, 78–80, 84–6, 88–90, 96, 98, 99, 110, 118, 119, 137, 140, 142, 146, *see also* laicism; Niyazi Berkes
  Republican elite   18, 21, 45, 47
  secularization   14, 22, 23, 29, 85
  secular nationalism   11, 27, 141
  secular/religious binary   27, 28
self and other relations   6, 61, 71
  self-perception   118
single-party period   24
  assimilationist policies   29
  Capital Tax Levy   21
  homogenization   20, 21, 118
  Second World War   37, 52
  Turkification   21, 28, 30, 31
soft power   42, 51, 132, 141, 145
Strategic Depth   43, 45, 128, 130

threat   21, 22, 25, 36, 38, 44, 45, 62, 88–90, 99, 105, 111, 118, 142
transformation   5, 10, 17, 18, 25, 32, 35, 38, 43, 62, 64, 67, 73, 75, 77, 87–90, 97–9, 102, 109, 111, 117, 119, 122, 123, 129, 132, 133, 136, 139, 141, 142, 144, 146
Turkish Army   94, 111, 145, *see also* military
  28 February   26, 39, 116
  15 July   2016   146
  1971 military coup   25
  1980 military coup   1, 25, 91, 144
  Balyoz   116
  Constitution of   1982   29
  Ergenekon   116, 145
  postmodern coup   26, 39
Turkish economy   31

Turkish foreign policy   4–6, 38, 39, 42, 45–8, 50, 73, 75, 78, 80, 84, 120, 121, 123, 124, 126–33, 137, 141, 142, 144
  axis shift   75, 78, 80, 84, 120–2, 124, 126, 127, 129, 133, 141, 142
  geopolitical vision   4, 43, 47
  neo-Ottomanism   45, 120, 130
  New Turkish foreign policy   6, 45, 123, 128, 137
  reimagined Ottoman imperial project   47, 73
  rhythmic diplomacy   43, 128
  strategic alignment   46
  Western alliance   6, 37
  Western orientation   42, 43, 78, 121, 127, 128, 132
  zero problems with neighbours   43, 131
Turkish identity   3, 10, 12, 14, 19, 20, 22, 29, 37, 48, 55, 65, 69, 77, 83, 111, 118, 123, 132, 135–7, 139, 143
Turkish nation-state identity   3–6, 19, 43, 50, 66, 73–5, 77, 83, 100, 101, 104, 105, 119, 120, 132, 135, 138, 140
Turkishness   5, 13, 16, 23, 30, 33, 50, 65, 74, 75, 77, 80, 139, 140
Turkish media   3, 5, 7, 22, 50, 64, 70, 71, 73, 75, 77, 83, 85, 92, 96, 100, 101, 105, 108, 109, 111, 113, 117, 118, 120, 127, 128, 130, 132, 133, 135, 137, 140, 141, 143
  censorship   69, 133, 147
  Turkish media discourse   5, 7, 83, 101, 117, 140
Turkish nationalism   3, 5, 6, 9, 11, 12, 15–18, 20, 21, 25, 28, 30, 31, 33–5, 48, 50, 66, 71, 73–5, 77, 90, 100, 105, 118, 119, 135, 136, 140, *see also* Turkish identity
  Turkish-Islamic Synthesis   25
  Turkism   15, 20, 24, 103
  ulusalcılık   12
Turkish political leaders
  Ataturk, Mustafa Kemal   9, 16–19, 21–3, 28, 37, 44, 72, 84, 88–90, 93, 94, 99, 110, 111, 123, 125, 141
  Bahceli, Devlet   109, 121
  Ciller, Tansu   26

Index

Davutoglu, Ahmet   4, 43, 45, 47, 73, 123, 128, 130, 131 (*see also* reimagined Ottoman imperial project; rhythmic diplomacy; *Strategic Depth*; zero problems with neighbours)
Demirel, Suleyman   26
Erbakan, Necmettin   1, 25, 26, 94, 116
Erdogan, Recep Tayyip   2–4, 33, 42, 47, 73, 94–6, 107, 108, 116, 120, 121, 124, 125, 129, 133, 144–6
Gul, Abdullah   69, 78–80, 84, 90, 92, 96, 121
Menderes, Adnan   24
Ozal, Turgut   1, 25, 26, 32, 45
Sezer, Ahmet Necdet   79, 89–91
Yilmaz, Mesut   26
Turkish political parties
  Democratic Turkey Party   97
  Democrat Party   24
  Justice and Development Party   3, 10, 24, 25, 33, 72 (*see also* AKP)
  Justice Party   24
  MHP   30, 98, 109, 113, 114, 115, 118, 121, 141 (*see also* ethnic nationalism)
  Motherland Party   25
  National Order Party   25
  National Vision   92
  Republican People's Party   17, 85
  True Path Party   26
  Welfare Party   25, 26
Turkish Republic   9, 17, 19, 20, 27, 29, 72, 83, 91, 101, 102, 121

Van Dijk, Teun   36, 105

Western civilization   30, 33, 43, 47
Westernization   14, 15, 27, 31, 37, 43, 44, 75, 85, 95, 101, 120, 137
Wodak, Ruth   42–3, 84

www.ingramcontent.com/pod-product-compliance
Lightning Source LLC
Chambersburg PA
CBHW061835300426
44115CB00013B/2394